CALLING Th   OR

CALLING THE SOUL BACK

Embodied Spirituality in Chicanx Narrative

CHRISTINA GARCIA LOPEZ

THE UNIVERSITY OF
ARIZONA PRESS

TUCSON

The University of Arizona Press
www.uapress.arizona.edu

ISBN-13: 978-0-8165-3775-4 (cloth)
ISBN-13: 978-0-8165-4258-1 (paper)

Cover design by Leigh McDonald
Cover art: *Lift Me Up* © 2008 Maya Gonzalez

Publication of this book is made possible in part by the proceeds of a permanent endowment
created with the assistance of a Challenge Grant from the National Endowment for the
Humanities, a federal agency.

Library of Congress Cataloging-in-Publication Data
Names: Garcia Lopez, Christina, author.
Title: Calling the soul back : embodied spirituality in Chicanx narrative / Christina Garcia Lopez.
Description: Tucson : The University of Arizona Press, 2019. | Includes bibliographical references and
    index.
Identifiers: LCCN 2018037378 | ISBN 9780816537754 (cloth : alk. paper)
Subjects: LCSH: Spirituality in literature. | American literature—Mexican American authors—
    History and criticism. | Mexican American literature (Spanish)—History and criticism.
Classification: LCC PS153.M4 L656 2018 | DDC 810.9/382—dc23 LC record available at
    https://lccn.loc.gov/2018037378

Printed in the United States of America
♾ This paper meets the requirements of ANSI/NISO Z39.48-1992 (Permanence of Paper).

For the struggling souls, trying to find their way back

For Joaquin, who lights my way

CONTENTS

ILLUSTRATIONS

PREFACE

This book emerged out of my study of Mexican American culture and history and my desire to understand the resilience that has kept these communities strong despite extensive violence suffered. What I discovered in Chicanx literature was the story of an enduring spiritual knowledge that is also resistant, in that it records, bears witness to, and counters destructive forces of coloniality and modernity. After writing my doctoral dissertation, which explored spirituality as a means of healing social traumas, I found that audiences best understood the concept when it was linked to tangible, embodied experience. Thus I constructed this book with the aim of conveying what is both abstract and concrete, and in order to introduce readers to a variety of genres and texts that deserve either more attention or a renewed perspective. Further, I endeavor to feature spiritual discourses that highlight relationships to nature and consciousness rather than to institutional spaces. While I was raised Catholic and still identify as such, I am not attempting a theological reading here but rather an analysis of interconnectivity writ large, centered in human and land bodies. I approach this analysis as one that is inherently linked to material reality and significantly implicated in the pursuit of social justice. I draw on my training in Mexican American studies, literary studies, and American studies as well as my experience as an instructor in those fields. Though this book attends to questions and problems relevant across a wide period of time, I view it as particularly attuned to the challenges of our current moment on a local, national, and global level. Additionally, while my focus is on Chicanx texts and contexts, I anticipate that readers from a broad variety of backgrounds and fields may find useful connections and points of contact within the pages of this book. Finally, because there remain important inroads to be made, I hope this work can meaningfully add to existing discourse and facilitate future scholarship in the areas I treat here.

ACKNOWLEDGMENTS

This project has been inspired by, nourished by, and developed over the years with a broad web of influences, mentors, and supporters. Though any flaws in the work are my responsibility alone, I owe great gratitude to those who encouraged me along the way. Firstly, the foundations for this book emerge out of my time as a graduate student at the University of Texas at Austin, where I was fortunate to work with the Center for Mexican American Studies, which has a long history of fostering scholars through the space it provides for intellectual, professional, and personal development. The diverse body of research and the remarkable array of scholars I came to know there will impact me for a lifetime. I offer special thanks to my doctoral adviser José E. Limón, who first welcomed me into the center, providing both space and employment, and who listened attentively to my chaotic ideas, discerning the scholarly project that was in my heart and mind. This project likely would not exist without the careful guidance and support he gave in those years, as I might not have believed it was possible. Of course, I am indebted as well to my co-adviser Cary Cordova, who helped me transition from graduate student to professor, supporting me through the process. Additionally, I thank each professor there who so graciously worked with me, both through CMAS and the Department of American Studies, offering their time and knowledge. An added benefit of my time at UT Austin was having the illustrious Nettie Lee Benson Latin American Collection at my fingertips; there were times it became my second home, and I have nostalgic memories of afternoons under the shade of its broad trees, where hungry squirrels would battle me for my lunch. The bountiful materials, exhibitions, and skilled librarians at the Benson are truly a treasure.

However, it is in my current academic home at the University of San Francisco that I wrote the contents of this book, with the assistance of invaluable institutional resources. In particular, the space and time to write has made all the difference. Thank you to the organizers of the Faculty of Color Writing Retreat, the Saturday and weekend writing retreats provided through the College of Arts and Sciences and CRASE, and the weekday writing teams in Kalmanovitz Hall. Coming together in community with fellow writers and pushing each other forward with encouragement (and snacks) alleviates the isolation and procrastination that can so often sabotage writing. Further, USF's admirable support for scholarly activity has permitted me the ability and mobility to consistently attend academic conferences central to my areas of research, such as the U.S. Latina/o Literary Theory & Criticism Conference, El Mundo Zurdo, and the Latina/o Studies Association Conference; these spaces were pivotal in pushing my work forward, giving me the opportunity to test the ideas in these chapters among fellow scholars in my fields. In addition, I am grateful to work for a university that gives me the freedom to create my own courses geared toward my areas of specialty; as a result, conversations with students about much of the literature in this book have spurred my own imagination and analysis.

Instrumental in drafting and revising this book were generous informal readers who willingly gave of their time and insight to offer me feedback at various stages of writing. This includes Dean Rader, Carol Batker, Brant Torres, Marisol Silva, Susy Zepeda, Angela Fillingim, Georgina Guzmán, Lydia CdeBaca, Brenda Beza, Jackie Smith-Francis, and Melanie Shelton, as well as others who offered thoughtful points and critiques along the way. Your feedback provided me with the fresh eyes and perspective needed to strengthen this work. And of course I am indebted to the official peer reviewers who facilitated this project's development through their helpful recommendations and suggestions. Most especially, I extend special gratitude to Kristen Buckles and Stacey Wujcik from the University of Arizona Press; working with you has been a pleasure at every step of the way. Your confidence and guidance are greatly appreciated. Additionally, I give special thanks to Ester Hernández, the Gloria Evangelina Anzaldúa Literary Trust, Lee & Low Books, and Irma Mayorga for permissions to include the images in this book.

Finally, thank you to my family. I am fortunate to be the child of a mother and father who not only believed in me from the beginning but taught me not to be afraid of hard work. My mother used to say, "You can always get up an hour earlier and go to bed an hour later," and I have taken that advice to heart. To Jenny, thank you for your devoted encouragement and for showing me what strength looks like; it was our conversations that inspired me to delve into the issue of embodiment, so I hope you will find something in this book for yourself. Jaime, thank you for the endless stream of warm meals made with love and for your enduring patience with my long hours; most of all, thank you for making me believe in myself. And to my son, Joaquin, your smile is my motivation and your hugs are my reprieve; you make everything possible.

CALLING THE SOUL BACK

Introduction

Approaching Narrative as Healing Work

Calling the Soul Back surveys literary expressions of spirituality as an embodied state of being and knowing—a state that deeply *involves* the body—in Chicanx narrative. For the purposes of this book, I approach *spirituality* as an active mode of being that consciously centers an epistemology of interconnectivity between elements of existence; I reserve the term *religion* to refer to organized, institutional practices often associated with spirituality. Through readings of pivotal writers such as Gloria Anzaldúa, Sandra Cisneros, and Rudolfo Anaya, alongside other key voices, I consider how Chicanx literary narrative creatively maps vital connections between mind, body, spirit, and soul; here, *spirit* suggests the animating force of interconnection between all forms of existence, whereas *soul* signifies the unique essence of a person, place, or thing. Thus I posit *spirituality* as encompassing the many ways in which conscious interconnectivity of spirit is lived out, inherently involving the body through which such integrated consciousness is expressed and experienced. Reading across narrative nonfiction, performative monologue, short fiction, fables, illustrated children's books, and a novel, I ask how these narratives draw on the embodied intersections of epistemology (which regards ways of knowing) and ontology (which regards ways of being) to shift readers' consciousness. In so doing, I also ask how reflective reading can change our ways of viewing the world and interacting within it; in other words, how can we read narratives of embodied spirituality as performing important political work?

Sometimes dismissed as inconsequential to lived, material conditions, spirituality refers not only to what we believe or know about the interconnectivity between beings across space and time, but also to the ways in which we sense, interpret, and respond to the world in which we live. Thus spirituality dramatically shapes our experience of and approach to concrete social conditions. In the narratives that I examine, spirituality matters because it affects not only *what* we think we are, but also *how* we are. Amid the present U.S. climate of political and social anxiety over an intensification of white supremacy and religious intolerance as well as large-scale threats to civil rights, women's rights, and environmental rights, rethinking relationality is critically important; I contend that this rethinking includes a spiritual context. To provide a tangible point of entry to a subject some scholars may regard with ambivalence, or even disregard entirely, I address spirituality in these narratives via the lens of the body, something we all share, and the actions, experiences, and felt sensations of the body. Thus I am concerned with a spirituality that integrates mind, body, spirit, and soul, variously expressed in this book as "mindbodysoul" or "mindbodyspirit."* For, as Anzaldúa wrote, "spirit and mind, soul and body, are one, and together they perceive a reality greater than the vision experienced in the ordinary world" ("Flights" 24). I have chosen works that encourage readers to reconsider expectations of what spirituality encompasses, as not all of these texts are overtly spiritual on their surface, yet all of them ask us to look beyond the veil of ordinary perception. As I argue, each of these narratives is deeply engaged in restorative work, healing the wound of spiritual trauma—a fragmentation rooted in colonization and the ongoing, systematic denial of ancestral and instinctual knowledge.

Curanderismo: A Healing System

Each work that I examine confronts the disconnection, isolation, and alienation that emerge from the imposition of binary modes of thought—for example, the

---

*See Gloria Anzaldúa's use of "bodymindsoul" in "Now Let Us Shift . . . Conocimiento . . . Inner Work, Public Acts," first published in *This Bridge We Call Home: Radical Visions for Transformation* (2002). Also, see the use of "bodymindspirit" by Irene Lara in the same collection, in the essay "Healing Sueños for Academia." In addition, "bodymindspirit" is used in *Fleshing the Spirit: Spirituality and Activism in Chicana, Latina, and Indigenous Women's Lives*, edited by Elisa Facio and Irene Lara (2014).

rationalist splitting of mind from body or humans from nature. The spiritual healing in these texts develops through a myriad of encounters (with land, memory, and other bodies) that enable reintegration and conscious connection. Working from this premise of a spirituality based on reciprocal balance and harmony, I draw on the frameworks of *curanderismo*, the traditional healing system that evolved out of the colonial process in Mexico and is commonly referenced in Chicanx literature and art. As Luis D. León explains, "The crux of *curanderismo* is formed in the religious matrix emergent in colonialism: it inscribes ancient Mexican rituals and idioms onto Catholic grammars and symbols. . . . Though based in Catholicism, *curanderismo* . . . narrates across conventional religious borders into creative and expansive social terrain. Further, it is a distinct persistence of pre-Columbian Mexican religious practice" (*La Llorona's Children* 130).

Due to the "religious matrix" León describes and the subsequent impact on the formation of a Mexican Catholicism and popular practices of curanderismo, the narratives I examine are contextualized by the commingling of seemingly competing systems of spirituality—namely, Indigenous systems and Christianity. The "Catholic grammars and symbols," such as references to God, La Virgen, saints, and the miraculous, exist alongside and overlapped with emphases on intimate, embodied relationships with earth's minerals, elements, animals, and landscapes. In these narratives, wind, earth, water, and fire take on significant meanings. For example, wind is depicted not as inanimate but as living and full of potential information, while water takes on a feminine, maternal power as a source of creation and destruction. Further, the expansive temporality signaled by these elements is linked to ancestral memory, and strict divisions between humans and nature are collapsed as earth and cosmos are perceived as sites of knowledge that involve the body.

As a set of specific practices, curanderismo can involve midwifery, herbal remedies, bonesetting, massage, divination, and, most relevant here, spiritual healing ceremonies (León, *La Llorona's Children* 129–30). In relation, I understand the fragmenting ruptures expressed in the narratives analyzed in this book through the lens of *susto* or soul-fright, a spiritual ailment in which the soul (or part of it) is frightened out of the body following trauma. Just as the *curandera* might use ritual (involving prayers, herbs, and waters, for example) to call the ruptured soul back into the body, I suggest that these writers use narrative to ritually "call the soul back" into a body variously conceived of as an individual body, an ancestral body, and/or a collective body. Further, these writers frequently return to the elements of the earth in order to remind readers what is elemental about ourselves and our ancestors.

I build on the work of Chicana scholars such as Laura E. Pérez, Irene Lara, and Theresa Delgadillo, who have laid important foundations for critical analysis of spirituality in literature, art, and culture. Indeed, I keep in mind Pérez's assertion that "conjuring and reimagining traditions of spiritual belief, traditions whose cultural differences have been used by discourses of civilization and modernization to justify subjugation and devaluation, are conscious acts of healing the cultural *susto*" (*Chicana Art* 21).[†] Following this line of thought, I situate Chicanx narrative as a productive site of spiritual reintegration and decolonization, particularly when it engages readers' embodied ways of knowing and being in the world in order to reclaim a holistic sense of self. These narratives are not isolated or independent from other cultural narratives of spirituality (Chicanx and other narratives are, in fact, deeply interconnected), but my emphasis on Chicanx narrative acknowledges a specific history and context of coloniality and cultural expression. I use the term *Chicanx* as an umbrella signifier to refer to these narratives and the larger body of work from which they emerge as a whole diverse entity that should not be reduced to an either/or binary. While I refer throughout this book to individual works, characters, and writers in accord with their gender-specific or nongendered contexts, I use the *x* in the title to reflect an array of positionalities, especially in terms of a broadly imagined community of readers that includes Chicana/o/x identities.

Story, Spirit, and Body

Based on the given contexts of integrated spirituality as well as trauma and healing, readers might ask what makes narrative in particular a productive site of study. Storytellers do their work with bold disregard for what is (and is not) considered legitimate in the institutional frameworks of rationality. Thus literary narrative has more frequently reflected the complexity of spiritual ways of knowing and being in communities of color than has scholarly discourse. In her essay "Spirit Matters," Demetria Martínez asserts that the writer's work is

---

[†]While I specifically cite Laura E. Pérez's book *Chicana Art: The Politics of Spiritual and Aesthetic Altarities* (2007), these ideas previously emerged in her 1998 essay "Spirit Glyphs: Reimagining Art and Artist in the Work of Chicana Tlamatinime," published in *MFS: Modern Fiction Studies*.

to "tell stories as we find them" and "to be faithful . . . to what our five senses tell us about the world around us" rather than qualifying stories with ideologies or doctrines: "The writer who cannot love the color gray, who cannot embrace a world that is anything but black and white, will not last long. Our creations will die for lack of compassion if we replace truth telling with moralizing" (54). The storyteller's obligation to be faithful to the senses and to remain loyal to the pulse of the story can translate into a resistance to the boundaries of institutional religion. While institutional religion, specifically Catholicism, signifies an important cultural context for the works I examine, these works are not centrally *about* institutional spaces or practices; more often they take place in unsanctioned natural spaces and convey a reaching past permissible knowledge in search of an expansive spiritual understanding. Moreover, these narratives position interconnectivity as a powerful source of knowledge, resistance, and transformation. As a result, the authors addressed often reflect a spirituality that is syncretic in nature, tracing connections between various systems including but not limited to curanderismo and the popular Catholicism that inflects it, as well as Indigenous and Yoruba cosmologies.

While written narrative can regard the life of the soul and the existence of spirit, it deals equally with bodies, precisely because of their absence. Narratives frequently require readers to draw on the reference point of the body to interpret stories grounded in sensate experience. Stated differently, it is because the body is not physically present that writers exercise various tools such as descriptive language to draw forth the reader's imagination and provide a tangible point of reference. For this reason, I emphasize the sensory body—the body that feels, hears, sees, tastes, and smells—for the ways in which it contributes to our sense of *knowing*, informing our experience and perception while creating a basis for the development of compassion and empathy. What are the textures felt, the magnitude of force, the quality of light and sound, the memories of taste, and the responses to smell? All of these elements and more must be described, and such descriptions move us closer into inquiry regarding lived experience, enabling readers to reconceptualize the bodies and lives of others, as well as their own. In their edited collection on the body in literature, David Hillman and Ulrika Maude propose, "Writing can forcefully return us to the body, or, perhaps better, return the body to us" (4). In other words, narrative can effectively counter the Cartesian split, bringing consciousness back into relation with the body. However, I also focus on the body because it plays a critical role in mediating our relationships and physical movements, which are informed by particularities such as gender, race, age, class, and sexuality. The body brings together our spiritual consciousness and material experiences in significant ways; thus, by centering on the body, my work demonstrates that what we might think of as intangible or ineffable can usefully be understood through corporality, albeit never completely.

Ultimately, I focus on narrative and its embodied sensibilities because narrative holds a particular power to engage readers' imaginations while also leaving room for the collaborative making of meaning. In my consideration of narratives across a range of genres, I emphasize how they imaginatively reflect and enact embodied spiritual reintegration for readers. To borrow Theresa Delgadillo's phrasing, these works are significant for their "participation in the creation of new forms of consciousness—a route toward new ways of thinking and being in the world" (*Spiritual Mestizaje* 2). While I examine a field of texts not exclusively authored by women, I take a Chicana feminist perspective and approach (emphasizing intersectionality and the dissolution of binaries) to build on the strong tradition of Chicana theorists, scholars, and writers who have been attentive to the spirit. Additionally, I draw on American studies, the capaciousness of which inspires me to delve more deeply into a range of works that includes not only traditional literary texts but also children's picture books, performative monologue, and an illustrated fable. Indeed, following my interest in understanding the social, cultural, and political contexts of these narratives alongside their more formal aesthetics, I turn not only to literary critics and Chicanx studies scholars, but also scholars in religious studies, feminist studies, sociology, environmental studies, philosophy, and Indigenous studies, alongside various other disciplines.

Specifically, the primary works at the center of this project are narratives of bodies in trauma, bodies engaged in ritual, grieving bodies, bodies immersed in (and part of) nature, and dreaming bodies. Throughout my inquiry into these works, I maintain curiosity about the role of narrative and its effect upon readers' lived experience. What can we, as readers, learn from these stories that might be applied to our own lives and our questions about being in the world? When examined deeply, what kinds of consciousness do these narratives emerge from and give shape to that can be usable, even transformative, as we seek healing from cultural fragmentation? Further, I ask how these narratives might alter our perceptions of reality, space, and time, as well as our embodied relationships to nature and our ancestors.

"Calling the Soul Back": A Conceptual Framework

While the issues I address and the interventions I seek to make are diverse, they are distilled in the phrase "calling the soul back," which carries its own instinctual resonance but should be situated within a particular trajectory of knowledge. In using this phrase, I refer to the restorative healing work of the narratives I analyze, as well as to culturally specific practices and knowledge forms rooted in curanderismo, as previously described. More specifically, curanderismo is a healing tradition based on pre-Columbian Indigenous medicine in intersection with African, Moorish, and European systems (Avila and Parker; León, *La Llorona's Children*; Gonzales). Though this book does not take curanderismo as its central subject, the tradition is a useful reference point for an inquiry into Chicanx embodied spirituality; this is due to the historical processes of colonialism that it emerges from and survives, as well as the ongoing communal healing it signifies. Further, curanderismo offers a particularly salient framework through which to consider a spirituality that deeply intersects with the material, highlighting the intertwined nature of humans and the natural world. As curandera and writer Elena Avila explains in *Woman Who Glows in the Dark*, co-authored with Joy Parker, "In curanderismo, there has never been a severing between the emotional, physical, mental, and spiritual totality that makes up a person. There is no separation between the nature of humans and their environment" (16–17). This sense of "spiritual totality" deeply informs the work I attempt here regarding an embodied spirituality that intersects with social contexts and natural environments. The emphasis on balance, integration, and relationality gestures toward a necessary decolonization of binary worldviews that split the self from the environment and the body from the soul, and which guide our everyday experiences in a capitalist society steeped in the residues of colonialism. Avila and Parker describe the significance of the principle of harmony in relation to well-being: "Curanderos believe that human beings— along with animals, plants, minerals, water, earth, air, and fire—are a part of the living earth system. Illness occurs when one does not live in harmony with all aspects of self and nature. Curanderos believe that it is not enough to heal the body. One must heal the wounded soul as well" (19). As I demonstrate in this study, narrative storytelling powerfully seeks to heal the "wounded soul" that has been split or fragmented by the colonization of epistemologies and ontologies that hold spiritual totality central; in this sense, it can serve as a decolonizing practice capable of dramatically altering the way we relate to each other and to our environments and social struggles.

As Jungian psychoanalyst Clarissa Pinkola Estés asserts in *Women Who Run with the Wolves* (1992), "stories are medicine," for they contain "remedies for repair or reclamation" and are "embedded with instructions which guide us about the complexities of life" (15). More specifically, numerous writers have found the reference point of curanderismo deeply relevant to a conversation about literature as curative work. In the classic essay "Poet as Curandera" (1993), Pat Mora articulates this connection: "Just as the curandera uses white magic, manipulates the symbols that are part of her patients' experience base to ease communication, the Chicana writer seeks to heal cultural wounds of historical neglect by providing opportunities to remember the past, to share and ease bitterness, to describe what has been viewed as unworthy of description, to cure by incantations and rhythms, by listening with her entire being and responding" (131).

Here the writer is conceptualized as healer, able to draw on intimate knowledge of the community, including its history and its wounds, and to powerfully acknowledge that which has been silenced, creating a space where suffering can be heard and shared and the self can be reclaimed. For those who carry in their bodies, minds, and spirits the visceral pain of knowing that their own story is "viewed as unworthy of description" or attention, such narrative spaces can be sacred, as listening and responding is central to the power of narrative. In *Women Singing in the Snow* (1995), Chicana literary critic Tey Diana Rebolledo elaborates on the role of the archetype of the curandera: "She listens carefully, thus understanding human as well as animal behavior. She uses her knowledge of group as well as individual psychology, a psychology embedded in ethnic beliefs and practices" (88). Thus the cultural specificity of the narrative—its familiarity—plays an important role in the healing potential of literature.

Chicano writer Rudolfo Anaya, author of the widely read novel *Bless Me, Ultima* (1972), has also made clear connections between the practices of writing and healing. In his 1999 essay "Shaman of Words," Anaya delves deeply into the spiritual context of writing: "The shaman of words can have many songs. Each poem or story or book becomes a song. Prayer and song are efficacious for healing. Books, too, have this power. Our stories use the pain and suffering of the characters in a transformative way" (57). Here Anaya describes storytelling as spiritual practice and the story itself as powerful medicine, clearing a path for transformation. Helena María Viramontes's more recent reflections on the practice of writing echo this sentiment: "I think it's like a prayer—there always has to be a consistency to commitment which then transforms into a meaningful practice. If there was no meaning, the motivation to practice (and practice here is essential) would sour any faith. Too, in order to connect with your subconscious, you really have to train it to go into a space of sacredness, because there is nothing more sacred then [*sic*] being in your own imagination" ("Faith" 260). Like Anaya, Viramontes situates writing as prayer and as a practice of faith, and further, she emphasizes the commitment the writer must demonstrate in order to enter and find new ways of being within what she terms the sacred space of the imagination. For it is the ability and willingness to enter into that space of creation and possibility that enables a pathway toward transformation for both writer and reader.

Specifically, "calling the soul back" refers to the ritual through which a curandera or curandero heals a patient suffering from susto (soul-fright or soul loss). This cure, called a *limpia* (spiritual cleansing), involves the ritual sweeping of the body (with an egg or herbs, for example) to absorb negative energy and ritually call the soul back into it. In *Red Medicine* (2012), Patrisia Gonzales describes pre-Columbian practices of healing soul sickness as being focused on "restor[ing] the *tonal* or tonalli, an irradiating vital force or internal sun" (202). Further, as she states, "susto was referred to as *nematili*, while calling the spirit back was termed *tonalzatzilia*" (202). Thus this practice has a long history, and while the concept may be unknown to some, Avila and Parker explain that the susto which a limpia treats is a condition commonly experienced though often unacknowledged: "Soul loss can happen at any time, as we live through the traumas and shocks of our lives, and experience the violation and denial of our nature. Even if you are a person to whom nothing very dramatic has ever happened, you are not exempt from soul loss. Every one of us has, at one time or another, lost a part of our soul because of the cultural values we have all been forced to embrace" (186). Beyond the major and often sudden traumas that befall us in our lives, what Avila and Parker describe here suggests, more generally, the wound of spiritual trauma in a society that systematically cuts its members off from ancestral and instinctual knowledge. Thus (as I discuss in chapter 1) the limpia as a restorative cure has been useful in thinking through the collective healing desired by those recognizing trauma in their families, communities, and nations.

Ultimately, "calling the soul back" gestures toward an active process of healing the wound of spiritual trauma by reclaiming an embodied state of relational knowing and being that has been displaced. For the soul is called not simply back, but back into the body, signaling a process of reintegration. Returning to Anaya's essay "Shaman of Words," he postulates that a "shattered" or fragmented essence can torture the flesh, indicating that problems of the spirit are felt deeply in the body: "The most potent sickness in our world today is soul sickness. Perhaps it has always been so. The essence is not integrated. It is shattered, searching here and there for focus. It strikes out in false directions, carrying the flesh with it, torturing the body. There is more need than ever for the medicine men and women who know about the soul, who know the shamanic journey to reintegrate the soul. The journey to the world of spirits. For me writing is such a journey" (61). Here Anaya calls on readers to become more conscious of the soul and the dangers its fragmentation poses to the entire self, including the body. For when the soul "strikes out in false directions," the flesh suffers consequences until the healing of reintegration can take place, something that does not occur once and for all but rather is conceived of as a journey.

There are various ways in which we might approach the concept of soul loss on a collective level. Significantly, Gloria Anzaldúa theorized what she termed *desconocimiento*, by which she indicated far more than general ignorance. She conceptualized this state as "the shadow side of 'seeing'" and further specified it as "an unwillingness to 'see' or [a state] of being forced not to look" due to "being overwhelmed by reality and not wanting to confront it" ("Bearing Witness" 31). This suggestion that the overwhelming aspects of our reality—whether political, cultural, or personal—can blind us or cause us to turn ourselves away from substantive knowing refers to a set of cultural values that collude against spiritual totality, manifesting a type of soul loss. Estés similarly theorizes what she terms the "overculture," or "the narrow range of stories" that build barricades "to protect the nailed shut and approved boxes of histories" and, in the process, "limit fresh ideas," "bind accountability," and "muffle diverse voices from reaching through . . . to add to the whole story" ("Foreword" xiii). This limiting of the range of stories through which we interpret experience is damaging as a result of the stories and people left out; yet at the same time, the cultural barricades created by such narrowing are strengthened by the human desire to belong to a collective narrative.

Elsewhere Estés describes the process through which such barricades are built, stating, "A modern person is often well and properly socialized in early life, but also in some ways deeply misled," in that such a person "is often wrongly encouraged, rewarded and even threatened into living a life that excludes an entire continent of knowledge—the life of the soul" ("Introduction" 7). Here it is made clear how we come to embrace the very cultural values that systematically blind us to a totality of knowledge that would include "the life of the soul"; through a series of alternating rewards and threats received throughout a lifetime of institutional encounters—in schools, churches, workplaces, and even in our homes—we learn the boundaries of permissible knowledge and, being thus disciplined, begin to participate in cutting ourselves off from "an entire continent of knowledge." This subjection to the collusion of forces that blind us to the many available ways of knowing speaks to precisely the desconocimiento Anzaldúa theorized. And it is this desconocimiento that must be overcome (seen through) in order to cultivate the expansive spiritual awareness, or *conocimiento*, that she argued could be a powerful tool of activism in our everyday lives: "Conocimiento pushes us into engaging the spirit in confronting our social sickness with new tools and practices whose goal is to effect a shift. *Spirit-in-the-world* becomes conscious, and *we* become conscious of spirit in the world" (Anzaldúa, "Let us be" 19). Thus expansive spiritual consciousness is posited as an activist objective which must be struggled toward with deliberate intention in order to overcome the boundaries imposed on knowledge and narrative.

Chicana feminist writer Sandra Cisneros identifies an awakening to and awareness of epistemological subjection when she writes, "It occurs to me there's a global conspiracy to keep me in the dark about certain simple truths" (*House* 299). Cisneros, who has written about the painful loss of each of her parents, expresses what it means to regain spiritual totality. For, as she describes, upon the loss of her father, she came to know him not as eternally absent but rather as a "spirit ally"—a presence who could be summoned from the other side to surround her and calm her. Wary of the anticipated reception of such a statement, she explains:

> I know this sounds like a lot of hokey new-age stuff, but really it's old age, so ancient and wonderful and filled with such wisdom that we have to relearn it because our miseducation has taught us to name it "superstition." I have had to rediscover the spirituality of my ancestors, because my own mother was a cynic. And so it came back to me a generation later, learned but not forgotten in some memory in my cells, in my DNA, in the palm of my hand that is made up of the same blood of my ancestors. (*House* 195)

Cisneros counters the anticipated dismissal of her ideas as disreputable "new-age stuff" with the assertion that far from being new, what she has learned through her father's passing is old. What she terms "miseducation" refers to that which displaces and discredits a previous (ancestral) knowledge; and yet, for Cisneros and the other authors discussed here, even such miseducation cannot erode the vitality of the knowledge that remains in the body. The ancestral memory she describes here is not simply of the mind but also embodied, and in this sense it cannot be forgotten; rather, it must have room made for it and be relearned, must be psychically recalled or called back. In this sense, then, I use the phrase "calling the soul back" to describe the reclaiming of what we already know, that which is already ours but which we have become alienated from and blinded to.

Spiritual Decolonization and Academic Spaces: A Rationale

As I argue, "calling the soul back" refers to a willful move toward a reintegration and transformation of consciousness that carries the potential to radically restructure how we experience and move through our lives. Importantly, this work can be carried out by scholars as well as the creative writers this book centrally addresses. Chicana scholar Irene Lara reflected in 2002 on the necessity of counteracting the "mind/body fragmentation" of academia, asserting: "I am indeed engaged in 'curandera work,' healing work. My tools are my words" ("Healing Sueños" 434). Calling our souls back is not only an act of resistance to desconocimiento but also an act to heal ourselves—in this case, through narrations and stories that become medicine. In academic terrains, such an emphasis on the concept of the soul can occupy a fraught space, for the institutions of the academy have typically insisted on a rational mind disconnected from matters of soul or spirit. My argument in this book is not in opposition to rationality and logic as useful methods of approach; rather, my argument is against positing these as our sole pathways to knowledge. More specifically, this argument is undergirded by the fact that the epistemological and ontological violence waged by drawing explicit boundaries around permissible knowledge is particularly salient for marginalized cultural communities who have experienced the ongoing devaluation of their knowledge forms.

Here I think of the student who arrives at the university only to learn that they—and by extension, their family and communities—are found lacking in the "appropriate" vocabulary, experience, and traditions; in such circumstances, it is easy to feel inadequate and even dispensable, perceived as a "blank slate" with little of value to bring to the intellectual table. In this age of diversity initiatives, questions about student retention often disregard the ways in which students can feel silenced by an institutional environment that was not built to acknowledge them or their communities as knowledge-holders. In my experience teaching courses that engage with religion and spirituality, oftentimes in classes made up predominantly of Latinx students, I sense a palpable hunger for a space in which critical inquiry regarding spiritual understandings and practices is permitted. Yet students often approach the subject with caution and hesitance (and sometimes nervous laughter), as they have already internalized the idea that spirituality is "just culture" rather than a complex knowledge system worthy of scholarly examination. This is particularly true when students internalize a harmful sense that marginalized cultures and experiences are less legitimate in institutional environments than dominant white cultural practices are.

I turn for a moment to my own experience as a doctoral student. Perhaps ironically, it was through my experience of academia—which hyperemphasized my mind and alienated me from the needs of body and spirit—that I truly came to understand the necessity of balancing and integrating all three. The feelings of bereftness wrought by neglecting those other essential parts of myself taught me a profound lesson that I might not have understood so well otherwise. The pressures of academia, pushing me into a difficult confrontation with myself and my beliefs, ultimately brought me into much closer relationship with spirit. Yet even as I integrated this consciousness into my daily life, it did not occur to me that it might become a legitimate feature of my scholarly work until a professor perceptively pointed out my persistent mentioning of spirituality and asked whether I was considering writing my dissertation on the subject. My surprised response was to immediately inquire, "Can I do that?" For although I had been reflecting on the issue of spirituality in my own life, it had not occurred to me that I could follow this line of interest in an intellectual manner. That I had prevented myself from considering this possibility even before asking reveals much about perceived messages regarding the disciplining of academic boundaries. I am grateful for the encouragement I received to pursue my scholarly interest in spirituality, both in my graduate work and in my current academic position. Yet it has also been clear to me that much work remains to be done in academia at large to create more consistent spaces in which critical scholarship on spirituality can be supported and fostered.

Spirituality has been and can be implemented within institutional spaces as a strategy for overcoming the challenges of those very spaces. I find Dolores Delgado Bernal's concept of "pedagogies of the home" useful, as she argues that "communications, practices, and learning that occur in the home and community" can be part of a "creative process that interrupts the transmission of 'official knowledge' and dominant ideologies" regarding gender, race, class, and sexual identity (113–14). Using the knowledge already in one's possession and recognizing one's own cultural and personal practices as a powerful source of resistance to repression can be key to negotiating the very environments that devalue those knowledge forms. I would suggest that treating spirituality as a "pedagogy of the home" means to treat it as "lived," which is to say that rather than being a fixed set of understandings or practices, spirituality is learned, interpreted, and even remade in relation to its practitioners and their changing conditions. For, as Delgado Bernal points out, pedagogies of the home do not necessarily remain static. Many find it necessary to approach spirituality as a "tapestry" that weaves together the teachings of family and community with one's own evolving personal consciousness; for example, while many Chicanas reject patriarchal elements of their "home religion," the spirituality they creatively construct for themselves often remains "connected to their commitment to their families and communities" (Delgado Bernal 126–27). This is an important distinction between institutional religion and the spirituality addressed in this project, as the works I examine treat spirituality as a creative process as well as a source of creativity.

The failure of Western epistemology to fully value or grasp forms of knowledge outside its own frameworks does not deplete the potential for these forms of knowledge to be leveraged as tools of empowerment and decolonization. Walter Mignolo describes what he terms "the spiritual option," or the move toward "decolonizing religion to liberate spirituality," as "opening up horizons of life that have been kept hostage (that is, colonized) by modernity, capitalism, and the belief in the superiority of Western civilization" (62). In this sense, working toward spiritual awareness is one way to seek beyond the boundaries and limiting frameworks that have been imposed by coloniality's regimes of knowledge and being. Mignolo further states, "That land goes hand-in-hand with spirituality should be the starting point of the spiritual option" (64). Indeed, each of the works discussed in this book expresses this connection between spiritual consciousness and land or the natural environment. Further, I would argue that even if several of these narratives are not overtly "political" in theme, the work they are doing to describe, illustrate, and inspire a radical shift in consciousness—away from the binaries that split and fragment—makes them both healing works and decolonial ones.

In *Decolonizing Methodologies: Research and Indigenous Peoples* (1999), Linda Tuhiwai Smith confronts the relationship between European imperialism, colonialism, and the process and meanings of "research" as defined by Western discourse. Arguing from an Indigenous perspective, she repositions research as "a significant site of struggle between the interests and ways of knowing of the West and the interests and ways of resisting of the Other" (2). Indeed, when research is situated this way, as an ongoing site of struggle over meaning, the importance of actively countering official, permissible forms of knowledge becomes clear. With specific reference to Indigenous spiritualities, Smith argues that spiritual concepts "are critical sites of resistance for indigenous peoples," stating:

> The arguments of different indigenous peoples based on spiritual relationships to the universe, to the landscape and to stones, rocks, insects and other things, seen and unseen, have been difficult arguments for Western systems of knowledge to deal with or accept. These arguments give a partial indication of the [. . .] alternative ways of coming to know, and of being, which still endure within the indigenous world. [. . .] The values, attitudes, concepts and language embedded in beliefs about spirituality represent, in many cases, the clearest contrast [. . .] between indigenous peoples and the West. It is one of the few parts of ourselves which the West cannot decipher, cannot understand and cannot control . . . yet. (74)

Here Smith puts forth a powerful claim about the epistemological and ontological difference marked by Indigenous spiritual concepts, a difference that cannot be fully deciphered, contained, or controlled within the framework of Western discourse. It is this difference and the paradigm shift it necessitates that manifest a potential force of resistance. The alternative ways of knowing and being that Smith references with respect to the "indigenous world," such as relationships to land, space, and time, are powerfully relevant to the Chicanx narratives I examine in this book. Indeed, the subjectivities these writers express in their works are bound up with implications about the remembering of land-based knowledges and spiritual relationships.

However, I approach these connections with the acknowledgment that a long shadow is cast by the appropriation of indigeneity in the nation-building projects of early twentieth-century Mexico and, later, the cultural nationalist projects of the Chicano Movement during the century's second half. Lourdes Alberto writes, "Through the construction of indigeneity as linked to the land, Chicano *indigenism*, similar to Mexican *indigenismo*, subsumed indigenous people (historic and contemporary) into a national figure" that "required the assimilation of Indian difference" (116). Despite the marked distinction between these two movements with regard to purpose and sociopolitical context (the Chicano Movement focused on resistance to cultural, social, and economic domination in the United States), the imperative to avoid subsuming indigeneity for the purposes of Chicanx identity formation is nevertheless crucial. On the matter of Chicana literary indigenism—namely, the use of myth and reenvisioning of Mesoamerican goddesses—Sheila Marie Contreras writes, "Chicana feminists have used the motifs of indigenist nationalism to . . . erod[e] the cultural authority of patriarchy" (105). However, Contreras also warns that, due to "the refocusing of Chicana/o critical discourse upon the figure of the Indigenous woman," there may occur the problematic rhetorical suggestion that "Chicana lived experience becomes the culmination of Indigenous history" (132). I review this background to emphasize the challenges of decolonization and, more broadly, the deep gashes and complex knots created by "centuries of violent becoming, of spatial practices centered on the domination, incorporation, exclusion, and control of the indigenous peoples, including indigenous Mexicans" (Saldaña-Portillo 231).

Given these challenges, it is still necessary to examine the threads of connection where they exist between Indigenous and Chicanx contexts, as these connections remain a persistent presence in the narratives precisely because they are a persistent presence in the consciousness from which those narratives emerge. As Cotera and Saldaña-Portillo write, "While Chicana/o connections to indigeneity have been attenuated by a Mexican national project that sought to recover the 'Indian' as a symbolic structure, rather than a lived reality, those connections, however submerged, do exist" (553). Thus, while the knotted history requires scholarly caution and at some points presents serious difficulty, it would be impossible to conduct a study of spirituality in Chicanx narrative without tracing these threads of connection. Indeed, returning to the concept of spiritual decolonization, there are meaningful connections between Linda Tuhiwai Smith's articulation of the challenge that Indigenous spiritual discourses pose to Western knowledge systems and Clarissa Pinkola Estés's discussion of overculture; for, as Estés argues, the narrow range of stories permitted by the overculture function "to protect the nailed shut and approved boxes of histories" ("Foreword" xiii). When we engage in research as a site of struggle over meaning, there is the potential to reveal and pry open the protection of officially sanctioned histories and narratives—a protection that contributes to the desconocimiento theorized by Anzaldúa just as it negates the value of spiritual ways of knowing and being in academia.

Highlighting this issue in the edited volume *Fleshing the Spirit: Spirituality and Activism in Chicana, Latina, and Indigenous Women's Lives* (2014), Elisa Facio and Irene Lara powerfully address a commitment to "decolonizing the academy that largely devalues or misunderstands spirituality, both as a serious academic topic and as an integral aspect of being alive" (Lara and Facio 3). Indeed, misunderstandings about spirituality have often obscured or flattened its complexities, social dimensions, and potentialities toward social justice. Far from treating spirituality as pure abstraction or as irrelevant to serious inquiry, Lara and Facio assert that "spirituality often plays a decolonizing role in creating meaning, inspiring action, and supporting healing and justice in our communities" (3). Likewise, the present study takes as its basis the acknowledgment that spirituality merits study not only as an important form of cultural practice, but as a central source of survival, sustenance, and the negotiation of material struggles related to ongoing damages caused by colonization and structural oppression. I seek to make meaning from the ways in which Chicanx narratives frequently invoke spiritual relationships to landscapes "seen and unseen" (to borrow Linda Tuhiwai Smith's words). It is in this context that I bring together writers who have grappled with the knowledge forms that come from their communities, often revising, questioning, and creatively improvising upon them, but always acknowledging them as viable sources of information.

Further, *Calling the Soul Back* approaches Chicanx literary criticism through an interdisciplinary lens that centers on the intersections between embodied spirituality and women of color feminisms. When I first read *Massacre of the Dreamers* years ago, I was struck by Ana Castillo's statement that, in her study of women's social struggles, she "tied in the spirituality that seems intrinsic to most women's sense of being" (1). This acknowledgment of spirituality as frequently integral to feminist, activist consciousness seemed revolutionary then and still does today; over twenty years after her book's publication, the nuanced ways in which Castillo articulated a whole self that is spiritual, erotic, and politically conscious still resonates as both radical and transformative. Similarly, in Gloria Anzaldúa's *Borderlands / La Frontera: The New Mestiza* (1987) I encountered a world of ideas that seemed to inherently challenge the official knowledge that academia rewards. Most remarkable was the discovery that the activism that Anzaldúa is so well known for is inextricable from spirituality, though this aspect was once less frequently discussed. Not only is spirituality central to her theoretical premise, but she was firmly cognizant of the intellectual risks she took in this path. In her archives at the Nettie Lee Benson library at the University of Texas at Austin, I viewed video footage of one of Anzaldúa's presentations, in which she boldly acknowledges the systemic challenges to centering culturally specific and spiritually informed ways of being and knowing in her work:

> The kinds of . . . theories that I talk about come from my culture, come from my cultural experience, my visual experience, my spiritual experience, my personal life. And . . . somehow or other . . . we are taught that the ideas, the theories that we should learn about should come from . . . people in authority, so if you're a queer of color and you happen to be a woman, like myself, and come from an underclass or working class . . . , the kinds of knowledges, the kinds of ideas, the kinds of concepts that people like myself produce are not validated by society. ("Feminist Knowledge")

Her insistence on taking seriously the devalued knowledge forms that emerge from the intersections of her own experience continues to be instrumental in the development of scholarship that resists such disavowal. These critical feminist approaches have focused intently on social transformation and fundamentally challenged the centers and margins of scholarly thought.

M. Jacqui Alexander speaks eloquently about the stakes of such scholarship when she asserts in *Pedagogies of Crossing* (2005), "Taking the Sacred seriously would propel us to take the lives of primarily working-class women and men seriously" (328). Indeed, scholars and writers focused on the histories, experiences, and cultural expressions of communities of color that have been largely working-class have a responsibility to acknowledge the knowledge forms of those communities, including the spiritual. Countering the dismissal of these epistemological systems as inherently inadequate or invalid, Alexander writes, "The knowledge derived from faith and belief systems is not uninformed epiphenomena, lapses outside the bounds of rationality to be properly corrected with rationality" (327). Rather than narrowly perceiving such belief systems as a lack, we must inquire about the kinds of knowledge and ways of being that they emerge from and in turn produce. Indeed, Alexander emphasizes the ontological aspects of faith systems, expressed through the everyday actions of "spiritual work," which "inheres the lived capacity to initiate and sustain communication between spiritual forces and human consciousness, to align the inner self, the behavioral self and the invisible" (328). In my view, this positioning of spirituality as a "lived capacity" for communication and alignment productively undergirds scholarly inquiry that rejects the discourse of "superstition" and takes seriously the implications of spiritual practices and worldviews.

Charting the Path: Existing Research

A solid body of research taking up this inquiry already exists across a variety of fields and continues to grow. In addition to the scholars and writers I have already mentioned, a broad array of works has contributed to its development, including though in no way limited to those I discuss here. Ada María Isasi-Díaz and Yolanda Tarango provided an early emphasis on the intersections between gender, ethnicity, and theological perspectives with their book *Hispanic Women, Prophetic Voice in the Church: Toward a Hispanic Women's Liberation Theology* (1988). Historical studies such as Ramón Gutiérrez's *When Jesus Came, the Corn Mothers Went Away: Marriage, Sexuality, and Power in New Mexico, 1500–1846* (1991) established important frameworks for understanding the contexts and consequences of colonization, while Jeanette Rodríguez's *Our Lady of Guadalupe: Faith and Empowerment Among Mexican-American Women* (1994) emphasized the critical role of La Virgen de Guadalupe as a figure of strength in contemporary women's lives. Taking a more theoretical approach, Kay Turner's *Beautiful Necessity: The Art and Meaning of Women's Altars* (1999) situated women's construction and maintenance of home altars as spiritual work enabling pathways to communication, reciprocity, and balance.

At the beginning of the new millennium, works such as *A Reader in Latina Feminist Theology: Religion and Justice* (2002), edited by María Pilar Aquino, Daisy L. Machado, and Jeanette Rodríguez, represented a growing community of Latina theologians taking an explicitly feminist perspective. Meanwhile, Lara Medina presented a valuable historical case study focused on a feminist organization and its political activism within the Church with *Las Hermanas: Chicana/Latina Religious-Political Activism in the U.S. Catholic Church* (2004). Bringing together the fields of borderlands studies and religious studies, Luis D. León introduced vital new perspectives on the cultural functions and meanings of religion in *La Llorona's Children: Religion, Life, and Death in the U.S.-Mexican Borderlands* (2004). And from a pedagogical perspective, Linda L. Barnes and Inés Talamantez brought together a variety of scholars offering approaches to course development relevant to issues of religion, healing, and the body in *Teaching Religion and Healing* (2006).

During the time that I initiated my own research relevant to this project, several books were published that signaled promising new developments in establishing spirituality as a recognized area of scholarship within the context of Chicanx and Latinx studies. Laura E. Pérez's *Chicana Art: The Politics of Spiritual and Aesthetic Altarities* (2007) reflects on a rich tradition of spiritual inquiry within Chicana arts and literature, including visual and performance arts. In positioning the Chicana artists and writers in her study as engaged in healing work, Pérez makes explicit the politics of spirituality. As she states, "It is perhaps more precisely a politics of the will to remember: to maintain in one's consciousness, to recall, and to (re)integrate a spiritual worldview about the interconnectedness of life, even if it is fragmented, circulating, as its pieces have, through colonial and neocolonial relations" (23). While the present work focuses more centrally on written narrative, that same politics is at stake in the works I examine, in the particular ways in which they exercise a "will to remember" and recall a more integrated consciousness capable of resisting the fragmentation that is caused by colonization and its ongoing effects. Another work that encouraged my early stages of research was the multidisciplinary anthology *Mexican American Religions: Spirituality, Activism, and Culture* (2008), edited by Gastón Espinosa and Mario T. García. Bringing together essays on the "critical intersection between Mexican American religions and literature, art, politics, and pop culture," Espinosa and García hoped to "spur on a new generation of scholars to explore the dynamic relationship between religion and Mexican American culture and society in the twenty-first century" (12). Together, these works signal a concerted effort to acknowledge a spirituality that could be engaged in activism and cultural transformation.

In terms of book-length studies dedicated specifically to Chicanx/Latinx narrative as a site for the unfolding and expression of the sacred, there have been few. In *Profane & Sacred: Latino/a American Writers Reveal the Interplay of the Secular and the Religious* (2008), Bridget Kevane asserts that the "persistent and strong religious and spiritual discourse in the works of most Latino and Latina authors" has often "remained marginalized from the theoretical and critical discussion of Latino literature" (2). Kevane's analysis, focused on narrative fiction, emphasizes how authors "engage in theological debates and how the religious discourse present in their work contributes to cultural renewal in their communities" (2). Significantly, Theresa Delgadillo's *Spiritual Mestizaje: Religion, Gender, Race, and Nation in Contemporary Chicana Narrative* (2011) followed soon after with a specific emphasis on Chicana narrative. Delgadillo offers an in-depth examination of Gloria Anzaldúa's theory of spiritual mestizaje, which she describes as "the transformative renewal of one's relationship to the sacred through a radical and sustained multimodal and self-reflexive critique of oppression in all its manifestations and a creative and engaged participating in shaping life that honors the sacred" (Delgadillo, *Spiritual Mestizaje* 1). Situating spiritual mestizaje in relation to fictional and documentary Chicana narratives, she examines both literature and film for their "participation in the creation of new forms of consciousness" (2). These works perform critical work in establishing a basis for the development of a discourse focused on the interplay between Chicanx/Latinx spirituality and narrative. As I expand on that foundation in this project, I read Chicanx narratives across a variety of genres, applying a feminist consciousness to texts that are not exclusively feminist in theme and a spiritual consciousness to texts not always immediately recognizable as religious or spiritual ones.

An emphasis on the relationship between Chicana feminism and spirituality with a particular focus on the Virgen de Guadalupe is demonstrated in publications such as Clarissa Pinkola Estés's *Untie the Strong Woman: Blessed Mother's Immaculate Love for the Wild Soul* (2011). Estés, a scholar, psychoanalyst, and poet, describes her intent and her multilayered approach when she states, "For all souls, these enclosed stories, prayers, and images I've written . . . are meant to be windows blasted through the thick concrete walls that some cultures have built around and over her living presence to sequester her, to 'disappear her' via only appearances duly 'pre-approved' allowing her to only say previously vetted words" (4). Such resistance to "pre-approved" images and narratives about La Virgen asserts a feminist resistance to the disciplining of spiritual knowledge. Clara Román-Odio traces a tradition of such resistance via iconographies of the Virgen de Guadalupe from 1975 to 2010 in *Sacred Iconographies in Chicana Cultural Production* (2013). Specifically, Román-Odio's study "analyzes the emancipated selves that Chicanas produce at the juncture of transnational capitalism, colonial expansion, and globalization and tracks their strategies for empowerment through feminist coalitions, literature, and art" (1). When these works are taken together, it is clear that spiritual discourses such as those revolving around the Virgen de Guadalupe continue to be closely associated with the imperatives of social justice and feminism. In a much broader context, regarding popular sainthood and saintlike figures, Desirée Martín's *Borderlands Saints: Secular Sanctity in Chicano/a and Mexican Culture* (2014) examines the cultural and spiritual contexts around Teresa Urrea, Pancho Villa, César Chávez, Subcomandante Marcos, and La Santa Muerte. Most significant to the project I exercise in this book, Martín posits that spiritual practice itself can be conceived of as a kind of narrative and that narrative practice may be conceived of as spiritual.

Focusing on Mesoamerican-based Indigenous medicine, knowledge, and ritual, Patrisia Gonzales's *Red Medicine: Traditional Indigenous Rites of Birthing and Healing* (2012) has been invaluable for its emphasis on relationships between body, spirit, and land. Gonzales's deep attention to the details of ancestral healing traditions, including curanderismo, provides a necessary basis from which to approach many of the thematic contexts I examine in this book, such as temporality, memory, and story. Her treatment of dreaming as a form of intelligence and her engagement with the issues of soul loss and purification rites enable a rich understanding of conceptual frameworks often overlooked in academic scholarship. In tandem, the anthology *Fleshing the Spirit: Spirituality and Activism in Chicana, Latina, and Indigenous Women's Lives* (2014) provides continued context for thinking through spirituality as a source of academic scholarship and activism. Bringing together scholars, activists, healers and others to analyze the political and intellectual contexts of spirituality in Chicana, Latina, and Indigenous women's lives, editors Facio and Lara posit spirituality as action. As they state, "Spirituality is something we do; it is part of creating culture and the production of meaning" (Lara and Facio 11). Further, they highlight the decolonizing impulse of the project, which "resists dominant western thought that would have us split our bodies, our flesh and bones and cells, from our spirits— the invisible, yet felt aspect of our beings that is part of our life force—as if they were separate or opposite" (11). The diverse range of voices and perspectives in this anthology provides a model and vision for the many directions in which future scholarship can and should develop. Indeed, while I focus on analysis of literary narrative rather than my own spiritual journey, I situate the present study on precisely the premise established by *Fleshing the Spirit*, a healing mode of resistance to the violent split between body, mind, and spirit.

More recently, Christina Holmes's *Ecological Borderlands: Body, Nature, and Spirit in Chicana Feminism* (2016) opens up space for critical discourse on

Chicana approaches to ecofeminism through arts and activism. Specifically, Holmes argues that "much of the environmental scholarship in Chicana/o studies is situated within an environmental justice framework that uses a social science orientation to document and respond to ecological injustices, yet silences remain around the ecological themes in cultural production" (8). In drawing attention to those ecological themes in creative cultural production such as literature and the arts, Holmes encourages us to consider how these themes generate "new ways to think about human-nature relations" (52). Importantly, Holmes attends to the intersections between ecological themes, embodiment, and spirituality, in ways immediately relevant to the present project and the narratives I analyze. In this and many of the other works I have covered here, there is a strong emphasis on a process of spiritual decolonization that does not refer to a return to the past but rather to a reintegration of what has been fragmented and ruptured.

Calling the Soul Back builds on the impressive body of scholarship addressed here, with a specific focus on embodied spiritualities in Chicanx literary narratives and the epistemological and ontological meanings that can be mediated through them. In so doing, I draw on numerous works that, while not necessarily specific to Chicanx or U.S. Latinx contexts, contribute to a deep analysis. For example, I look to sociological approaches to religion such as Meredith McGuire's *Lived Religion: Faith and Practice in Everyday Life* (2008), which engages deeply with the relationship between spirituality and the body, acknowledging its lived aspects and practices; more precisely, McGuire emphasizes "why bodies matter for both individual and collective spirituality" (100). Further, philosophical works such as Mark Johnson's *The Meaning of the Body: Aesthetics of Human Understanding* (2007) provide tangible contexts in which to situate issues including embodiment and phenomenology. Works of literary theory such as Laura E. Tanner's *Lost Bodies: Inhabiting the Borders of Life and Death* (2006) and Sharon Patricia Holland's *Raising the Dead: Readings of Death and (Black) Subjectivity* (2000) offer useful models for applying a discourse of the body to literature, and they also incorporate valuable theoretical perspectives regarding discourse on death, which is inevitably an element of any study on spirituality. And works such as Jane Bennett's *The Enchantment of Modern Life: Attachments, Crossings, and Ethics* (2001), which combines political theory, philosophy, and literary studies, provide important models for thinking through relationships between humans and the nonhuman world in modern times, as well as critical discourse on the role of nature. Though this book's sources are not limited to those I explicitly name in this introduction, these provide a snapshot of the interdisciplinarity this project undertakes.

Chapter Overviews

In devising this project, I aimed to read across a variety of genres representing both traditional forms, such as the novel, and those seldom acknowledged in literary scholarship, such as picture books. Part of what made this work compelling was the opportunity to reflect on numerous texts that have not yet received substantial treatment, including those by figures who are just beginning to receive scholarly coverage as well as newer offerings by more frequently discussed writers. Finally, I also hope to provide a fresh perspective on some classic work as a contribution to existing conversations. Throughout these analyses, I am concerned with questions of consciousness and how it is shaped through embodied encounters with physical environments as well as the mysteries that exist beyond those environments—the seen and the unseen. But further, I am interested in how these processes, which in some ways are too expansive to be fully put into words, can simultaneously be expressed so effectively through narrative.

Chapter 1, "The Body in Trauma: Healing a Collective Susto," reflects on the body as a site of trauma and healing within the context of national politics. Gloria Anzaldúa's essay "Let us be the healing of the wound: The Coyolxauhqui imperative—la sombra y el sueño" (2002) situates the national trauma of 9/11 within the culturally specific framework of susto; more specifically, she relates susto to her own embodied responses to visual media images of bodies in crisis leaping from buildings. Utilizing the language of the limpia, she imagines the waters of the ocean offering spiritual cleansing, with drummers lined along the beach calling souls back into their bodies. Anzaldúa situates her personal experience of trauma and healing within a collective spiritual context and centers visuality in significant ways. I read this essay alongside the 2004 monologue "Panza Brujería," part of Virginia Grise and Irma Mayorga's *The Panza Monologues*, which treats the body, and more specifically the *panza*, as a powerful source of knowing rather than a site of shame. This particular monologue, which emphasizes the "collective *panza*" in the context of the George W. Bush era, draws on the language of curanderismo and *brujería*, as the speaker calls both for a "national *limpia*" (aided by a rock passed over the body) and a leveraging of collective *ojo* (evil eye) exercised through the "third eye" of the panza. I argue that in these works cultural and ancestral knowledge of spiritual practices is brought to bear upon national traumas interpreted through the lens of susto; the body is situated as a site of suffering but also a source of healing and knowledge, particularly in its interaction with elements of nature.

Chapter 2, "The Ritual Body: Feminism and Spiritual Inheritance," moves away from national politics and turns toward interpersonal domestic rituals, arguing for the body as a site of feminist knowledge and spiritual inheritance. Helena María Viramontes's seminal short story "The Moths" (1985) serves as a valuable entry point for understanding ritual in the context of the home and as a potential site for countering patriarchal trauma. The embodied labors of the home, in both the garden and the kitchen, bring a young girl and her ailing *abuela* together in sacred community through a sensory interaction that encourages deep awareness. The transformation from girl—subjected to the patriarchal dominance of father and Church—to "priestess" is completed through the loving enactment of a caretaking ritual, that of washing the dead. Through both embodied ritual actions and the girl's careful attention to the body of her grandmother, time and space are altered to produce a sacred awareness; this chapter argues that through shared sensory experience and the production of ritual time-space, the logics of patriarchy are displaced by an inherited ancestral feminist knowledge, resulting in a radical transformation of consciousness.

Chapter 3, "The Grieving Body: Radical Reorientation," examines the transformation of temporality and spatiality through the embodied experience of grief. Rudolfo Anaya's novella *The Old Man's Love Story* (2013) and Sandra Cisneros's illustrated narrative *Have You Seen Marie?* (2012) fuse fable with personal experience to give shape to the ineffable—the disorientation and potential reorientation of self that is experienced amid the loss of a loved one. This chapter examines how Cisneros and Anaya narrate grief as an ongoing series of encounters with a world sensed and experienced in new ways, and describe their characters' search for the lost body of the loved one. I argue that in these narratives this disorientation drives the characters to reckon with their positionality in and relationships with the universe, including the spirit world and the natural environment. While Anaya's old man searches tirelessly for ways to reunite with his wife, so cherished that he revels in a world of memories and continuously converses with her spirit, Cisneros's protagonist searches for a friend's lost cat only to confront the much deeper sense of loss she carries after the death of her mother. In both of these narratives the protagonists are styled as reflections of the authors themselves, and the absent body of the loved one creates a crisis of self that cannot be assuaged by memory alone; rather, loss sends these characters into transformational confrontations with the worlds around them.

Chapter 4, "The Body Rooted and Flowing: Toward a Decolonized Spirituality," examines representations of embodied relationships to nature with an analysis of two bilingual children's books written and illustrated by Maya Christina Gonzalez. Both *I Know the River Loves Me / Yo sé que el río me ama* (2009) and *Call Me Tree / Llámame árbol* (2014) depict children encountering themselves in and forming relationships to the natural world in ways that directly counter the division between human and nonhuman. These works emerge out of the author's experience as a queer woman and represent the ability to find kinship with and community in nature. Indeed, Gonzalez approaches her visual images and written text with an affirmative framework emphasizing an epistemology of belonging; further, she depicts the characters' bodies as deeply engaged in a process of ontological becoming, with one narrator drawn purposefully "gender-free." Thus this chapter posits children's literature, and Gonzalez's work in particular, as a critical site of cultural intervention, offering foundations for a decolonized ontology via broadly accessible illustrated narrative. Reading children's books as being situated within the scope of literary narrative, I build on the foundation developed by scholars of children's literature such as Isabel Millán, Cristina Herrera, Larissa M. Mercado-López, and Elena Avilés.

Chapter 5, "The Dreaming Body: Resituating Time, Space, and Knowledge," examines the embodied state of dreaming as a site of knowing and transformational consciousness. This chapter analyzes the discourse of dream work in Luis Alberto Urrea's *The Hummingbird's Daughter* (2005) and, to a lesser extent, its sequel *Queen of America* (2011). In these historical novels based on the life of Teresa Urrea, the Mexican healer and popular saint exiled to the United States by Porfirio Díaz, dreaming and soul flight are depicted not as metaphor but as meaningful cultural practices. Thus this chapter considers the politics of dreaming, as well as dreaming as a site of ancestral knowledge; specifically, I focus on the relationship of tutelage between Teresa and Huila, the curandera who mentors her. The "dream time" they each experience suggests mysteries of the body, both in terms of the body that dreams and the body in dreams—for example, the body in flight. I argue that dreams in this narrative provide alternate conceptions of time and space that initiate an encounter with the sacred.

Finally, in the epilogue, I situate the implications of these ideas beyond academia, in the broader contemporary political and social context. When we are emboldened to understand our bodies and relationships outside the limited framework of rational logic, what becomes possible, and how does it alter our potentialities in a material sense? How can we draw on spiritual and ancestral knowledge to address current national and political traumas, particularly after the 2016 presidential election? Can domestic rituals transform the ways in which we encounter persistent patriarchal structures today? How does the altered knowledge precipitated by (personal and political) grief pertain to potentialities for social change? Can resituating our relationships with nature change our ways of approaching political, social, and environmental justice movements such as the protest against the Dakota Access Pipeline (DAPL)? When we understand our dreams as epistemological resources, can they inform our political empowerment? Thus I consider the implications of a spirituality that incites radical transformation of the ways we perceive the world and act in it, and I place special emphasis on the roles our bodies play in enacting that process.

Healing the Split, Awakening Consciousness

This book approaches spirituality as broadly encompassing the innumerable ways in which a consciousness of interconnectivity existing between all things is acknowledged, engaged with, and expressed. Rather than conceiving of spirituality as an abstraction existing solely in an unreachable beyond, this book considers it as something that is inherited, possessed, and passed on in specifically embodied ways. Further, in mapping narrative articulations of embodied spirituality within a Chicanx context, I posit narrative as one form through which writers and readers attempt to call back the soul—one's unique immaterial essence—into union with the body to restore an integrated consciousness. By counteracting the wounding fragmentation that cuts away instinctual, embodied, and spiritual ways of knowing, Chicanx narrative performs a labor that shifts epistemological and ontological frameworks to heal the binary split that emerged out of colonization and persists today. In the texts I address, spirituality is positioned as a decolonial praxis through which readers have the opportunity to reimagine their worlds and give them new shape, countering the boundaries of permissible knowledge. Addressing the intellectual significance of these discourses as well as their social and political stakes, this book contributes to the development of contemporary scholarship in a variety of fields, including Latinx and Chicanx studies and ethnic studies more broadly, literary and narrative studies, American studies, studies in religion and spirituality, and women's and gender studies. Most significantly, by focusing on the body's role in spirituality, I seek to provide usable, tangible entry points to what is regarded as ineffable and to situate spirituality as existing not only "out there" but also right here, in the lived, everyday experiences of our communities.

As I turn now to the readings that make up the focus of this book, I offer a brief note regarding my own positionality as a reader. I, like many others, approach narrative as part of my own ongoing search for meaning—an encounter with truth—in the sense that it is an opportunity for deep contemplation and the suspension of the experience of living on the surface of things. I view reading as a chance to feel deeply and to encounter the underground terrains of my own existence as well as that of others. As I see it, reading offers an opportunity to learn from the human flow of experience. Much of what I have learned about compassion and my connection with others, as well as the importance of being present and of listening, comes from reading narrative. On one hand, as I encounter sensory language in literature, I become more attuned to my own senses and more capable of listening to the way my body speaks to me. But further, because reading enables me to experience the worlds and feelings of others and to live within those worlds temporarily, I learn to recognize my connection to something far greater than myself. Ultimately, reading lays the groundwork for reflective action in daily life because it awakens me; it changes the way I move through the world and engage with it, encouraging me to be more deliberately aware of the ways in which I connect to those around me (both in a present sense and an ancestral one), the environment I exist within, and the universe at large.

The Body in Trauma

Healing a Collective Susto

For the Chicana writers and artists addressed in this chapter, creative production has been a method of confronting political, psychological, and spiritual alienation. Drawing on intimate lived experience, cultural and ancestral knowledge, and the very facts of their bodies, their works displace the centers and margins of national discourse. Their salient political critique is intertwined with a decolonial mode of thinking and being, invoking the healing work of restoring balance in their communities. I understand this Chicana creative production as a ritual through which to propel the self across time and space into emergent possibilities that are not new but rather unveiled. In the healing consciousness invoked by these artists, we stand not in isolation but always in relation to a broad constellation of bodies, voices, and experiences. I begin with Gloria Anzaldúa's essay "Let us be the healing of the wound: The Coyolxauhqui imperative—la sombra y el sueño" (2002) and move into an examination of narrative monologue with Virginia Grise and Irma Mayorga's published script (2014) and recorded performance (2008) of "Panza Brujería," as each engages with embodied traumas of the George W. Bush era. Incorporating culturally specific spiritual discourses of curanderismo and, in the latter case, brujería, these works interpret shared trauma through the lens of susto, each advocating a collective limpia and the development of inner sight. As these narratives bear witness to a collective trauma, they situate the body as both a permeable site of suffering and a source of healing interconnection. Further, this chapter examines these artists' treatment of a bodily knowledge activated by sensory interactions with natural elements and landscapes, with which they communicate a reinvestment in the sacred that transcends the boundaries of the nation.

As common discourses in Chicanx literature and art, the knowledge systems of curanderismo and brujería place the integration of mindbodyspirit at their center and represent durable, living forms of counterknowledge, even as Western culture casts them as superstition. In the works examined in this chapter, curanderismo and brujería offer a framework through which to resituate consciousness; more specifically, the spiritual malady of susto provides culturally relevant vocabulary with which to articulate a shared experience of trauma and alienation in contemporary life. In this work I draw on Laura E. Pérez, who links the concept of "cultural *susto*" to the "unbridled capitalist and imperialist visions of reality" that Chicana cultural workers "attempt to interrupt" (*Chicana Art* 21, 23). Rather than evoking cultural nostalgia or a failure to deal with material conditions, Pérez argues that the invocation of spiritual discourses pushes toward "an essential sense of personal wholeness, communal interdependence, and purpose in the social, global, and cosmic web" (22–23). In this, she expresses the strategic and political value of invoking the very belief systems Western rationalism has delegitimized; moreover, her words acknowledge a framework for susto that extends beyond the individual soul/body, expressing the need for a broader healing that collectively connects us to a cosmic awareness. Following these points, I argue that the restorative work of "Let us be the healing of the wound" and "Panza Brujería" begins with bearing witness to trauma that is at once personal and shared, rooted in the national crises of the George W. Bush era. Yet, through their spiritual discourses, these narratives evoke awareness of the body as a mediator of healing interconnectivity that is global, even cosmic in nature.

Anzaldúa, Mayorga, and Grise confront the assumptions and limits of dominant cultural frameworks by recasting the challenges of the political moment in their own conceptual terms and worldview. Further, a central element of the worldview these works establish is the integrated relationship between body, spirit, and land. For example, Anzaldúa uses her essay to recall the susto of the World Trade Center attacks on September 11, 2001, and speak out against the responses of the George W. Bush administration as she intermittently narrates a ritual walk along the ocean's edge. Meanwhile, "Panza Brujería" incorporates ritual use of *piedra alumbre* (alum stone), known for its healing properties, as an element of performance in a monologue that directly challenges the perceived corruption of *políticos*. Situated alongside these political critiques, the embodied sensory relations proposed in each work between a permeable human body and natural elements emphasize a restoration of balance in response to fragmentation. Relevant to this discussion, Christina Holmes writes about *performative intersubjectivity* in Chicana feminist creative work and activism, which she describes as "a mode of disrupting/re-creating the self through practices that actively stage [a] relationality" that occurs "between selves, landscapes, and spirit" (10). This concept of performative intersubjectivity is valuable in application to the main works examined here, as it provides a framework for understanding the disruptive quality of an aesthetically activated perception of self that extends beyond the individual. Such disruption is generative rather than destructive or nostalgic, inviting readers and audience members to reimagine their embodied relationships to the universe outside of the ruptures of Western binaries that split the self from land and spirit.

As I will show, narrative engagement with the ways in which the body senses, experiences, and interacts with external natural bodies is deeply connected to a desire for political and social transformation. In its call for healing, Anzaldúa's essay asks us to imagine a politics in which we can come to grips with our collective shadow, cleansing ourselves of the fear and spiritual alienation associated with 9/11, and rediscover our interconnections beyond national paradigms. Meanwhile, Grise and Mayorga ask us to imagine our bodies as invested with ancestral agency in order to confront and transform a corrupted political system. In the process, both texts incorporate the concept of susto, an illness of the mindbodyspirit, to describe the consequences of national traumas, politics, and rhetorics. In correlation, each text prescribes the ceremonial ritual of spiritual cleansing known as limpia as a decolonial healing mechanism that requires and reinforces intersubjectivity. In her work on Mexican traditional medicine (MTM) and Indigenous knowledge (IK), Patrisia Gonzales explains, "Limpias and susto reflect a web of inter-relationships" in that they "operate through transference of energy" (204). In other words, the epistemological worldview that conceives of susto and its ritual cure (limpia) is predicated upon intersubjectivity, in that it recognizes a flow and transference of energy that can cause illness as well as healing. Specifically, the narratives I examine in this chapter respond to a negative transference of energies mediated through the body during the George W. Bush years (e.g., the trauma of 9/11, political alienation and fatigue) by turning to the restorative energies of ocean and mineral. I emphasize that these narrative acts of healing are embodied ones, for, returning to Holmes, intersubjectivity is not only a state of consciousness but also an ongoing "process that is both material and forged through the relay of affect that regulates connections between bodies" (14). This relay of affective energies applies not only to the limpia invoked in these narratives but also to the strategic performance of *mal ojo* ("evil eye") in "Panza Brujería." In these texts, an intersubjective awareness of energy transference between bodies empowers the narrator to be an agent of healing in her community.

Importantly, the speaker in each work is situated as both patient *and* healer (whether curandera and/or *bruja*), revealing her experience of pain as a conduit to disrupting the split sense of self produced by the binaries of ongoing coloniality. Further, each speaker becomes a seer who encourages readers and audience members to develop their own sense of inner sight or third eye, an instinctual knowing that can see through the illusions created by life under capitalist imperialism. Thus these texts perform important political work in that they invite us to imagine a reality in which we are empowered by our own spirits, bodies, and relationships to the land, so that we might heal ourselves and each other from the wounds caused by fragmenting conditions. Indeed, the social and political moments narrated in these texts are ones of crisis and fatigue, situating the narrative as a creative platform for replenishing energies necessary for personal and social transformation: "Orienting ourselves to the divine may draw us together, refresh us after the exhaustions of resistance, and stage practices of intersubjective collectivity as a response to the social fragmentation produced by empire" (Holmes 19). Anzaldúa, Grise, and Mayorga activate the narrative space as a sacred terrain; the role of storyteller is enacted in its fullest sense—that of being a dispenser of medicine, one who conjures visions and sensations to be used as information to guide one's path through material conditions that blunt the soul and weaken the body. Thus these works allow us to remember the recuperative power we inherit from those who have come before, and in the process we are reminded how to move through social and political conditions that inspire division, fear, and hate. By reframing the concept of self, these works empower readers and audiences to resituate political engagement; thus, while the context of the works in this chapter is the events of the George W. Bush era, the lessons they impart continue to be relevant to the contemporary political landscape, such that, by looking back, we might begin to look forward.

Recalling Rupture in "Let us be the healing of the wound"

"Let us be the healing of the wound: The Coyolxauhqui imperative—la sombra y el sueño" was originally written for and published in a collection of *testimonios* responding to the events and aftermath of September 11, 2001, edited by Claire Joysmith and Clara Lomas (Keating, "Appendix 5" 191). *One Wound for Another / Una herida por otra: Testimonios de Latin@s in the U.S. Through Cyberspace (11 de septiembre de 2001–11 de marzo de 2002)* was published in 2005, placing Anzaldúa's essay alongside contributions from writers such as Elena Poniatowska, Ruth Behar, Norma Elia Cantú, Inés Hernández-Ávila, and Aurora Levins Morales. The essay's roots in this collection reflect Anzaldúa's lifelong participation in a community of writers, artists, and activists who have spoken out on challenging yet timely issues of social and political concern. When the essay was subsequently included in *The Gloria Anzaldúa Reader* (2009) as part of her later writings, this inclusion signaled the significance of the essay within her larger body of established work. That significance was strongly affirmed when "Let us be the healing of the wound" was published as the prologue to *Light in the Dark / Luz en lo oscuro: Rewriting Identity, Spirituality, Reality*, a book of essays written by Anzaldúa and edited by AnaLouise Keating, in 2015. As Keating relates, Anzaldúa, prior to her passing in 2004, planned to use the essay as the project's prologue because it included so many of the central concepts conveyed by the work as a whole ("Appendix 5" 192). With this brief account of the essay's publication trajectory, I hope to illustrate its role as a culminating work in Anzaldúa's wide and influential body of writing.

The opening words of Anzaldúa's essay are "The day the towers fell," invoking a historical point in time that, for many, is as much a part of personal as collective memory. Instantly, most readers know which towers and which day she is alluding to without it needing to be specified; further, the informal language she uses imbues the text with a deliberate sense of intimacy, as if one is hearing a story told by a friend. Continuing, Anzaldúa recalls her response to that day's tragedy: "The day the towers fell, me sentí como Coyolxauhqui, la luna. Algo me agarró y me sacudió, frightening la sombra (soul) out of my body. I fell in pieces into that pitch-black brooding place" ("Let us be" 9). This initial statement articulates her experience as a susto, a wounded state of shock that grabbed her, shook her, and frightened her soul out of her body. Susto is typically understood as a spiritual illness associated with a series of symptoms, the result of the soul or parts of the soul being frightened from the body. Rooted in Mesoamerican contexts, belief in susto continues to exist in many Latinx communities today. Luis D. León explains: "Dating back to pre-Columbian Mesoamerica, susto is ubiquitous throughout the Latino Americas (including North America). From the earliest Nahuatl rendition, loss of soul or susto was associated with the loss of *tonalli*" ("Borderlands Bodies" 302). According to Davíd Carrasco, *tonalli* refers to the "spiritual force sent by the Aztec god Ometeotl, the sun, and fire into the human body, giving it character, intelligence and will" (170). Anzaldúa was well versed in Nahuatl thought and the Nahuatl worldview, but on the more general level on which many readers would understand her reference to susto, it conveys the significant relationship between body and spirit, and a "loss of vital forces that keep the body in balance" (León, "Borderlands Bodies" 302). Thus it is through this familiar cultural-spiritual lens that Anzaldúa expresses the complexity of her felt experience following the towers' collapse.

Significantly, Anzaldúa depicts this loss of balance as a fragmentation, situating her personal experience in the context of the Aztec myth of Coyolxauhqui, a frequent figure in her work. Goddess of the moon and daughter of the earth goddess Coatlicue, Coyolxauhqui is said to have been dismembered by her brother Huitzilopochtli, the war god, who threw her head into the sky (Keating, "Glossary" 320). Thus, when she writes that "me sentí como Coyolxauhqui, la luna" (I felt like Coyolxauhqui, the moon), Anzaldúa expresses her own sense of being torn apart and falling "in pieces" ("Let us be" 9), an understanding she later applies to the nation as well, describing the country as "torn apart . . . internally" (15). Just as Coyolxauhqui's bodily fragmentation occurs at the hands of the god of war, this fragmentation of the personal and national psyche correlates to acts of violence, those that took place on September 11, 2001, and the retaliatory acts in their aftermath. Theresa Delgadillo argues that through attention to pre-Columbian figures, Anzaldúa "addresses the way that politics and gender interact with religious and mythological narratives and symbols" (*Spiritual Mestizaje* 24). In the case of 9/11, the myth and symbol of Coyolxauhqui, dismembered by a war-driven impulse, signals the social and political rupture caused by the event. Yet, as indicated by her concept of the Coyolxauhqui imperative, Anzaldúa also uses this myth and symbol of rupture to point toward the potential for healing reconstruction outside the paradigms of patriarchy; for it is through her dismemberment that Coyolxauhqui comes to embody and reflect the wholeness of the moon. Thus, for Anzaldúa, the personal and collective fragmentation experienced in response to 9/11 and its political fallout is characterized by both painful rupture and the potential for radical transformation. Additionally, her statement that she "felt like Coyolxauhqui" reveals that her personal reaction to 9/11 is rendered not only through a spiritual epistemology but also a spiritual ontology, or what Keating refers to as Anzaldúa's onto-epistemology (Keating, "Editor's Introduction" xxiii). In opening her essay with this evocation of Coyolxauhqui, Anzaldúa emphasizes a conceptual understanding of the historical moment through a spiritual system of knowledge and myth as well as a felt sense of being in the world based on that worldview.

Etched on the Mind's Eye . . . *Todos Caímos*

Importantly, Anzaldúa's incorporation of the moon goddess Coyolxauhqui more specifically articulates, in this essay, the fragmentation caused by witnessing televised images of violent destruction. She reflects, "Each violent image of the towers collapsing, transmitted live all over the world then repeated a thousand times on TV, sucked the breath out of me, each image etched on my mind's eye" (Anzaldúa, "Let us be" 9). Here she describes a susto triggered by televised images of the World Trade Center towers collapsing, underlining the power of witness and the primacy of image. The relationship Anzaldúa draws between the visual images of 9/11 and her experience of susto prompts inquiry into the meaning and consequences of visual experience. Even through the mediation of television, the shock of those images as they are repeatedly played back yields for her a spiritual and embodied trauma, attesting to their psychological intensity and consequent impact on the mindbodyspirit. Writer Joy Harjo articulates how witnessing atrocity can function as a type of participation: "Of course, seeing is a kind of participating. You are present at the moment. And what you've seen and taken in is dangerous—to the mind, body, soul, and spirit—and can infect everyone, not just in the present moment but through all time" (Harjo and Winder, "Becoming" 9). This concept of visual participation helps clarify how horrified yet captivated viewers who watched helplessly from the relative safety of their homes, schools, and workplaces on September 11 were not "safe" from the resonating, lingering impacts of those images, which even now continue to have repercussions on the collective consciousness. For Anzaldúa, these images took the breath and soul from her body as they inscribed themselves on her inner consciousness.

Of course, Gloria Anzaldúa herself conceived of the image as primary in the human imagination. In her 1987 work *Borderlands / La Frontera: The New Mestiza*, she wrote: "Images are more direct, more immediate than words, and closer to the unconscious. Picture language precedes thinking in words; the metaphorical mind precedes analytical consciousness" (91). This perspective is consistent across her body of work, as she frequently emphasizes in her writings the role of the image in the activity of the imagination. Further, she often sketched images related to her conceptual ideas and used those images as tools in spoken presentations to discuss and teach her theories (Keating, "Gallery of Images" 217). Many of these sketches and recorded presentations are held in her archive in the Benson Latin American Collection at the University of Texas at Austin; for the archival visitor poring over these materials, the interplay between her visual imagery and theoretical, creative work is tangibly evident. Given the immense value that she personally placed on the conceptual and psychological power of visual experience, we can more meaningfully understand the susto she describes as related to the images from 9/11, which were jarring in their violent and repeated nature. To draw on Harjo's concept of visual participation, intense presence of attention in witnessing the televised footage of the bombings could result in one's taking in or absorbing conscious and unconscious meanings of that violence; within the logic of mindbodysoul integration, such a shock to the mind might indeed dislodge the soul (or parts of it) from the body.

Importantly, Anzaldúa describes the soul's fragmentation from the body as itself an embodied experience, continuing: "Wounded, I fell into shock, cold and clammy. The moment fragmented me, dissociating me from myself. Arresting every vital organ in me, it would not release me" ("Let us be" 9). In this case, "the moment" of witness is a visceral entity or force acting upon her body, whose normal temperature and functioning are "arrested." Her reference specifically to a felt sense of disruption of her inner organs communicates an experience that is not only psychologically "wounding" but distressing in an embodied sense as well. Interestingly, she uses the psychological term "dissociated," suggesting a link between the concept of susto, which she invokes at the essay's opening, and post-traumatic stress. Clinician Bessel van der Kolk, a specialist in post-traumatic stress, explains that trauma can cause people to lose their sense of self and "feel separated from their bodies," adding that "the self can be detached from the body and live a phantom existence of its own" (101–2). Bringing these discourses together, one might correlate this loss of one's sense of self to loss of soul or, more specifically, to the loss of tonalli, that vital energy residing in the head that provides character yet can escape from the body. Anzaldúa frequently drew connections between distinct areas of thought, such as in this case, where she traces connections between Western psychology, Mesoamerican concepts, and popular spiritual beliefs. While she does not equate these concepts with one another, her writing makes use of various epistemological systems in the process of making meaning and the pursuit of understanding.

As the essay progresses into its second paragraph, Anzaldúa reflects not only on her visceral response to images of the towers collapsing, but also on images of victims whose names she cannot know but whose bodies register an unfathomable connection to her own: "Bodies on fire, bodies falling through the sky, bodies pummeled and crushed by stone and steel; los cuerpos trapped and suffocating became our bodies. As we watched we too fell, todos caímos" ("Let us be" 9). Here she begins with a repetitive, punctuated structure that catalogues "bodies" in various states of extreme suffering, conveying the psyche's struggle to comprehend overwhelming forces of violence. For it is the incomprehensibility of such images that reduces the person in pain to a body in pain, as the viewer must grope for understanding. As Tim Gauthier explains in *9/11 Fiction, Empathy, and Otherness*, public responses to these images were varied, "mak[ing] apparent the tension between . . . the realization that this can actually happen to a human being (including myself) and the refusal to believe that this can actually happen to a human being (especially myself)" (48). Anzaldúa's essay emphasizes the experience of an empathetic viewer for whom the witnessed body becomes not a distanced body but a proximate one; thus, in the act of witnessing pain that cannot be measured or comprehended, she undergoes her own psychological rupture and descent through the lens of her own body. In addition, she uses the plural form—in the assertions that their bodies "became our bodies," "we too fell," and "todos caímos"—thus situating her experience within a larger collective experience and acknowledging the trauma as shared.

The embodied empathetic experience she describes in response to witnessing mediated images of death reflects a significant discourse in 9/11 studies. In *9/11 and the Visual Culture of Disaster*, Thomas Stubblefield explains that images of falling bodies would become "a primary nodal point around which the memory and experience of the disaster would materialize," thus requiring us to consider their "intense, unruly affective charge" (58–59). This affective charge has been the subject of thoughtful scholarship regarding the contemporary role of mediated images in shaping public consciousness. Alongside recognition of the rhetorical and often nationalist appropriation of such images, Laura E. Tanner argues for the value and importance of "embodied perception as a critical frame for understanding 9/11" ("Holding On" 59). For, as Tanner states, we must account for "the increasingly complex ways we experience embodied subjectivity, as well as public life, through the mediation of screens" (59) and, in general, the expanded ways in which "we experience connections through the body and space" (61). Indeed, Anzaldúa's intimate reflection on her own experience highlights the potentiality for embodied relationships even across the mediated barriers of televised space. Highlighting the way in which the body functions as a central category of understanding and experiencing, theologian M. Shawn Copeland asserts, "The body incarnates . . . what is 'the most immediate and proximate object of our experience' and mediates our engagement with others, with the world, with the Other" (7). In "Let us be the healing of the wound," Anzaldúa articulates her body—and our bodies—as mediating an engagement with the falling, trapped, and suffocating bodies witnessed via screen images, an encounter both painful and fragmenting.

The trauma of this experience is reinforced as she describes herself falling into a "pitch-black brooding place" (Anzaldúa, "Let us be" 9). This psychological descent is aptly illustrated in an early sketch included in her archive in the Benson Latin American Collection, entitled "Woman Falling" (figure 1). Labeled "28 enero 89" (January 28, 1989), this image long predates 2001 but deeply evokes the torment of the internalized fall within oneself. Drawn in what appears to be marker of a reddish-brown color, the image is a simple outline of an amorphous body with downcast head; while the sketch is mostly unfilled, the center of the head contains scribbles that, when viewed in contrast with the white space of the body's interior, evoke the mental chaos of a person lost to themselves and the world. The title "Woman Falling," written directly below the sketch, further elucidates the idea of mental chaos as both a psychological and physical descent into the kind of "pitch-black brooding place" she describes in "Let us be the healing of the wound." Her expressed inability to detach or emerge from "the victims and survivors [of 9/11] and their pain" ("Let us be" 9) portrays how connection to the pain of others in a gripping moment of rupture can yield a state of trauma.

FIGURE 1 Gloria E. Anzaldúa, "Woman Falling," from sketchbook, 1987–1990, box 149.3, Gloria Evangelina Anzaldúa Papers. © The Gloria Evangelina Anzaldúa Literary Trust. May not be duplicated without permission from the Trust.

Speaking Through the Chasm of Grief

Importantly, however, Anzaldúa draws on spiritual epistemology and language, situating her personal experience as one of susto: "In the weeks following éste tremendo arrebato, susto trussed me in its numbing sheath. Suspended in limbo in that in-between space, nepantla, I wandered through my days on autopilot" ("Let us be" 9). Here she uses the word "arrebato" to signify how the moment snatched her soul away, suspending her in a state of shock that enveloped or locked her in its "sheath," numbing her feeling. On the one hand, she evokes this state of numbness through the term "autopilot," which denotes a lack of decision-making and willful action. This connects meaningfully to van der Kolk's description of people who experience trauma as being stuck in a state of "suppressing inner chaos, at the expense of spontaneous involvement in their life" (53). Yet, significantly, Anzaldúa also uses the Catholic term "limbo" to describe the experience of inhabiting a liminal space that is neither here nor there, neither heaven nor hell; she further connects this idea to the Nahuatl concept of *nepantla*, which she frequently invokes in her work to express the in-between spaces of existence and identity. In Anzaldúa's conception, these spaces can be both painful and productive in the insight they generate for those who occupy and move through them. However, the above passage specifically emphasizes the alienation of being suspended and unable to move in numbness and inaction. Further, she emphasizes feeling cut off from the events and people in her own life, writing, "This wounding opened like a gash and widened until a deep chasm separated me from those around me" (Anzaldúa, "Let us be" 9). The likening of her state of shock to a physical "gash" and a "deep chasm" artic- ulates a felt sense of distance created between herself and the outside world. Perhaps ironically, it is empathetic, embodied connection to the pain of others that causes her social isolation in the weeks following 9/11. For taking in the violence of those images results in "numbness, anger, and disillusionment," all feelings that she refers to as "desconocimientos," as they cut her off from con- scious awareness (10).

In the struggle to cast off this desconocimiento, she tries to speak through her wounds, allowing the pain to arise and making meaning from it that con- nects her to others, even while "clawed by the talons of grief" (Anzaldúa, "Let us be" 10). The very nature of trauma inhibits this process of articulation and yet precisely requires it. For, as van der Kolk asserts, "while trauma keeps us dumbfounded, the path out of it is paved with words, carefully assembled, piece by piece until the whole story can be revealed" (234). That gradual struggle to bring together the pieces of a story that feels unspeakable and perhaps unrep- resentable is precisely what Anzaldúa strives to achieve; as a writer focused on the spiritual imperative of collective healing, she writes not only to heal herself but to inspire readers toward a path of wholeness. Thus, it is from the space of nepantla that Anzaldúa connects her personal struggle to a larger collective struggle when she asserts, "We are a nation in trauma" ("Let us be" 10). Inter- estingly, while she refers to her own experience in the specific cultural context of susto, a condition situated within the framework of a disrupted integration of mindbodyspirit, she describes the post-9/11 nation as experiencing trauma. This distinction between terms suggests the significant epistemological differ- ence between her own formulation of spiritual consciousness and the script of a national consciousness that fails to acknowledge such principles of inte- gration. In this sense, the statement "We are a nation in trauma" can be read both as a compassionate recognition of collective struggle and as a more crit- ical engagement with the necessity of reevaluating and reconsidering national paradigms. For example, she writes, "Besides dealing with my own personal shadow, I must contend with the collective shadow in the psyches of my culture and nation—we always inherit the past problems of family, community, and nation" (10). Reflecting here on the shadow of desconocimiento, those feelings and ideas that blind us to more expansive awareness (conocimiento), she articulates how one's personal story deeply intertwines with that of culture and nation. From the chasm of pain and grief that disassociates her from daily life, she describes an effort to gradually reemerge into conscious awareness and reflective action.

Importantly, Anzaldúa articulates this effort toward conocimiento as one that involves an embodied process of sensory awareness: "I take my sorrow for a walk along the bay near my home in Santa Cruz. With the surf pounding in my ears and the wind's forlorn howl, it feels like even the sea is grieving. I struggle to talk from the wound's gash, make sense of the deaths and destruction" ("Let us be" 10). Here, taking her sorrow "for a walk" articulates the embodiment of this palpable emotion that lives in her body. Her sensory alertness to the sounds of the ocean and the wind and to the messages they convey enables her to begin to process and speak the trauma that has numbed her. This is relevant to what van der Kolk describes as "befriend[ing] the sensations in [one's] body"—in other words, noticing and describing one's embodied feelings (102). For in the passage above she not only notices the external sounds and motion around her, but also recognizes how these stimuli register in her body; she feels the sea's grief through the pounding of the surf and the howling of the wind in her ears. This attunement to her environment allows her to begin an internal process of questioning that leads more specifically to spiritual inquiry: "I continue walking along the sea trying to figure out what good, if any, can come from death and destruction. Death and destruction do shock us out of [the] familiar. . . . They expose our innermost fears, forcing us to interrogate our souls" (Anzaldúa, "Let us be" 16). In this passage, she uses the plural form "us" to indicate that the discernment she actively seeks is focused not only on personal reintegration but also on collective healing. Further, the healing she seeks cannot be limited to the individual or the psychological; rather, it has at its center a spiritual evaluation and an awareness that acknowledge interconnectivity. As she observes other peoples' shadows gliding over hers on the beach, the intertwined nature of a shared struggle can be read on the landscape (16). Moreover, she interprets this process of inquiry enabled by her embodied, sensory awareness as itself a healing consciousness and conocimiento that connects her to others (17–19).

Intersubjectivity and Disidentification

In intimately recounting to readers her personal experience of September 11 and its aftermath, Anzaldúa reflects an awareness that she cannot disentangle her story from a larger narrative of "family, community, and nation" ("Let us be" 10). However, this entanglement does not mean that she cannot engage in critique or, as Leela Fernandes writes, "disidentify from [a] hegemonic sense of American identity" (34). Indeed, Anzaldúa's self-narration of personal trauma develops into a detailed confrontation with the larger global conditions of inequality that existed before 9/11 and followed after. As she recounts personal and collective complicity in global systems of structural violence, racism, and consumption, she asserts the imperative to speak out against these forces. In her political critique of the war-centered response of the George W. Bush administration to the events of September 11, she considers a large range of topics ranging from Afghan women and refugees to globalization and the historical use of the military for economic and imperial interests. Additionally, she includes various statistical figures, recording congressional votes, the numbers of the dead both in the United States and around the world, the number of workers who lost jobs and insurance as a result of 9/11, and the disproportionate percentage of resources consumed by U.S. Americans. In providing a direct and elaborate response to the circumstances surrounding the U.S. response to September 11, she asserts, "If I object to my government's act of war I cannot remain silent. To do so is to be complicitous. But sadly we are all accomplices" (Anzaldúa, "Let us be" 10). This passage makes it clear that the imperative to transform the violence she has witnessed into a more expansive consciousness as well as reflective action is rooted in the felt sense that she is implicated in what she has seen, not simply morally but spiritually. This engaged response highlights what Fernandes describes as the "spiritual responsibility" of witnessing (84), when a person who is transformed by what she has seen thereafter "assume[s] a sense of responsibility for what she has witnessed" (90–91). This closely relates to Anzaldúa's conception of spiritual activism, which brings together our conscious interconnectivity with tangible acts toward social justice. The intensive political critique Anzaldúa constructs in "Let us be the healing of the wound" signifies a call for collective confrontation, examination, and transformation of social conditions based on a spiritual obligation toward humanity rather than nation.

Anzaldúa emphasizes the cultivation of compassionate awareness as a global spiritual project that includes the nation but is not defined by it. Bemoaning retributive, war-driven responses to tragedy and us-versus-them paradigms of identity, she writes: "It's unfortunate that we get our national identity and narrative from [those] who refuse to recognize that conflict is not resolved through war. They refuse el conocimiento (spiritual knowledge) that we're connected by invisible fibers to everyone on the planet and that each person's actions affect the rest of the world" (Anzaldúa, "Let us be" 15). It is this spiritual awareness of the human threads of interconnection that grounds her use of personal narrative and political critique to rewrite the social narrative, pushing past a national paradigm to a planetary one. Rather than dividing us, Anzaldúa asserts, shared trauma bears the potential to transform us into a state of greater wholeness if it moves us to enact a consciousness based on intersubjectivity: "A calamity of the magnitude of 9/11 can compel us to think not in terms of 'my' country or 'your' nation but 'our' planet" (20). Here she negotiates the fragmenting disorientation of collective trauma, signified by Coyolxauhqui, through a shift toward a planetary consciousness of interconnection, enacted through testimony and social critique. Through the narrative act of remembering and accounting for violence, she models the Coyolxauhqui imperative, a process of creatively and continuously re-membering the dismembered parts of ourselves and our societies into new constructions. Thus her essay evokes the desire to utilize fragmenting, divisive experiences to draw closer to others. Toward the essay's end, she returns to the reparation of the mindbodyspirit relationship as enabled by an environmental intersubjectivity. The reader rejoins her as she walks along the beach, reflecting, "I listen to waves impact the shore, waves originating from beyond the far edge of the sea, perhaps caused by a storm in a distant corner of the earth" (21). By listening to the ocean and attuning her sensibilities to its life and motion, she conceives an understanding of how actions ripple and create change, even across great distances. Like the distant storm, human actions—whether good or ill—travel to the shore, substantiating the imperative to act consciously.

More specifically, she returns in the last paragraph of the essay to the imperative of healing the collective susto. I read the scene of her meditative walk along the beach through the lens of a limpia, an embodied ritual healing, with Anzaldúa figuratively transitioning from patient to curandera. Indeed, in his reading of her children's book *Prietita and the Ghost Woman* (1995), George Hartley situates Anzaldúa's work as "a form of curanderismo," in that "she consciously applies the concepts and practices of the curandera to the social ills of colonialism that she hopes to help heal" ("Curandera" 141). Given her political critique of U.S. military acts as tied to imperialism and neocolonialism (Anzaldúa, "Let us be" 12), I would argue that the healing she formulates in this text functions in a similar way, culminating in the cleansing practice of limpia. As Luis D. León writes, "susto is cured by administering a limpia [cleansing] while calling the soul back to the body" ("Borderlands Bodies" 302). The details of the ritual can vary, and different tools may be used—such as eggs, plants, smoke, lemons, or alum rock—to sweep the body, in combination with petitions or prayers.

Thus, in reading the following narration in the context of the practice of limpia, I draw on Holmes's concept of performative intersubjectivity, which refers to "practices that actively stage relationality . . . between selves, land-scapes, and spirit" (Holmes 10). Further, in staging such relationality, Anzaldúa invokes an intersubjective awareness specifically focused on collective healing. She writes: "Down on the beach, drummers serenade Yemayá, ocean mother. I'd like to think they're beating the drums of peace, calling our souls back into our bodies. We are the song that sings us. . . . I watch the grey pelicans rise up, up. As day swallows itself la luna rises, rises, guiding me home—she is my third eye. Her light is my medicine" ("Let us be" 22). The ritual beating of drums signifies a transition from the "drums of war" referenced earlier in the essay (11) to "drums of peace." Significantly, Anzaldúa uses the drumming to link a plurality of spiritual meanings, as she draws together the medicinal powers of the waters via Yemayá, Yoruba goddess of the ocean, and the rising guiding "light" of Coyolxauhqui, the moon of Mesoamerican mythology. As the drummers honor the Yoruba ocean mother, Anzaldúa imagines their drums "calling our souls back into our bodies," invoking the reintegration of mindbodyspirit through the tradition of limpia. Patrisia Gonzales writes, "Numerous Indigenous peoples in Mexico and their relations in the United States practice variations of the ceremonial limpia called *levantando la sombra*, or raising the shadow / calling the spirit back [from the place of traumatic occurrence]" (206). Anzaldúa spe-cifically emphasizes the collective body and psyche, with the plural forms "us" and "our" placed alongside her personal reflection. As "our souls" are called back into "our bodies," she asserts that "we are the song that sings us," suggesting that we create ourselves through our acts, including creative acts. Thus collective healing requires our presence, participation, and willingness to be transformed. As she notices the pelicans flying higher into the sky, the sun's cyclical setting, and the moon rising into the night, she expresses how external awareness—an attention to one's environment—can cultivate inner awareness, balance, and harmony. Thus, the "third eye" of the moon refers to an inner awareness that aids us in "seeing" past the blinding fears and ignorance of desconocimiento and into a larger potentiality for conocimiento, expansive spiritual awareness.

Signed as a letter would be, with her name and the date, February 2002, Anzaldúa closes her essay with the phrase "Contigo en la lucha." This assertion concisely reflects the theme of collective effort always woven into her writings, simultaneously bent on social and personal transformation. What did it mean for Anzaldúa to be with us in the struggle? As I have tried to show, it meant offering up her own testimony as well as a mirror for critical self-reflection, both personally and collectively. In bearing witness to violence as well as the embodied practices of attunement to her environment, she demonstrates how the wounds of trauma might become an opening toward a healing reconstruction marked by planetary, spiritual consciousness of the invisible threads that bind us. These themes of collective transformation through witness, the body, and environmental attunement are reflected as well in the next work I will turn to examine, addressing the use of monologue as a medium for personal, social, and political empowerment.

Tending to the Altar: Body, Spirit, and Story in *The Panza Monologues*

In the foreword to the second printed edition of *The Panza Monologues*, Tiffany Ana López describes the work as "a declaration of its authors' commitment to forging Chicana discourse about embodiment and epistemology" (xvi). As I discuss here, that discourse is forged through both performance and the printed script. Directed by Irma Mayorga and performed by Virginia Grise, both of whom collaborated as playwrights, *The Panza Monologues* is a play presented as a series of monologues crafted from Grise's and Mayorga's individually written pieces as well as contributions by Bárbara Renaud González, Petra Mata, and María Salazar (Grise and Mayorga xxviii). Each monologue centers the *panza* (belly, midsection) as a site of information, creation, and story, emphasizing a body knowledge that resists the twin forces of shame and silence. This focus on the panza casts the production as coming from a specifically Latina cultural context, which Irma Mayorga addresses as intrinsic to the project's purpose: "We, of course, were both familiar with [Eve] Ensler's solo performance success with *The Vagina Monologues*, but unlike Ensler's wider ethnographic reach, we wanted our work to be culturally specific. We didn't want to look outward for our stories but rather inward, to the *historia* held on the tongues of San Antonio Chicanas—something we believed was not in the public sphere" (Grise and Mayorga 15). Thus, while *The Panza Monologues*, like its predecessor *The Vagina Monologues*, centers on women's bodies and embodied experiences, it uses a Chicana feminist lens to bring a regionally and culturally specific story into wider public discourse. Interestingly, while *The Panza Monologues* is based on the regional context of San Antonio, Texas, the play made its world premiere in Austin, Texas, in 2004. In that same year, ALLGO and Evelyn Street Press published its script; four years later, in 2008, the play was filmed for DVD in Los Angeles (at Plaza de la Raza), and in 2014 a second edition of the script was published by University of Texas Press.

In that edition, Mayorga and Grise explain the important distinction between the printed script and the play itself: "The script of a play is not the play. Technically, a play exists only when it is played out in performance, when it is *playing*—on bodies, in space, in a visual, visceral conversation with an audience" (Grise and Mayorga xxviii). This articulation of performance as an active *doing* that "plays" or works on (and through) the performers and audience situates theater as an activation of knowledge and lived experience carried in the body. Playwright Cherríe Moraga writes, "Experience first generated through the body returns to the body in the flesh of the staged performance. . . . Theater requires the body to make testimony and requires other bodies to bear witness to it" ("Irrevocable Promise" 34–35). Because *The Panza Monologues* is a play both about and of the body, this concept of performance is instrumental, as it describes how the *doing* of the play returns experience to the flesh in a form of witnessed testimony. Given these critical imperatives of the play itself, publication of the script was initiated in response to frequent requests for a printed version, which has enabled the play to be taught, broadly circulated, and even performed in classrooms and small local venues. The existence of the DVD version aids in that broad circulation, bringing the experience of theater to the classroom, living room, or community center. Mayorga explains: "We wanted our DVD's viewer to be positioned as an audience member. . . . We hoped viewers could feel as if 'they were there'—in community, watching, hearing, and participating in the vibrant response of the audience, and watching Virginia respond to them. . . . We hoped that somehow a DVD experience would capture the stimulating energy of *a play* in performance, not supplement or erase it" (Grise and Mayorga 30). In this way, the DVD becomes a resource with which to highlight the intersubjectivity of theatrical experience, reminding viewers who may have previously only read the script that plays position us as creative participants in community. In the reading that follows, I focus on the script from the second edition and the recorded DVD performance, reading both as narrative forms for the storytelling work they do and the specific strategies they enact. However, I do so with the strong acknowledgment that these forms do not replace the living play itself, for they cannot account for factors such as the variability and flux of performance in real time.

As with plays in general, the stage setting holds a key function, providing a visual language for the audience and a material environment with which the performer interacts. Thus, from an analytical stance, the stage setting of *The Panza Monologues* can be read for the information it conveys about the cultural and political grounding of the play; each item on the stage reflects an intentional crafting of meaning and action. In Mayorga's explanation of her role as director, the significance of the stage becomes evident: "As a director, you are shaping the schematics of all the events on the stage, from atmospheric moods to bodies" (Grise and Mayorga 19). This shaping of schematics includes the actual objects on stage, which significantly contribute to the tone of the play, and the movement of bodies. Seated upstage left are Los Flacasos, the four sharply dressed musicians (including both women and men) who provide live musical accompaniment for the play and thus significantly contribute to its tone. On the stage itself is featured a lovingly decorated altar, placed upstage in the center. The stage directions in the script note, "*Decorations and meaningful* obsequios *have been placed on the altar, including electric candles, pictures of the playwrights as young girls in various outfits that show their bare panzas, family photographs,*" and various props to be used in the play (Grise and Mayorga 39). These carefully chosen objects indicate the altar, and subsequently the stage itself, as a sacred space where memory can be invoked and honored. The candles provide light to illuminate images of the playwrights baring their panzas, signaling that this is a space for the body to be honored rather than shamed. Further, these images are placed alongside family photographs, indicating that the stories to be shared recognize the larger intergenerational story of which they are a part.

Importantly, because the props of performance are integrated with these personal objects, Grise, as solo performer, must return to the altar repeatedly throughout the play, taking the props from it and placing them back on it. Thus, as T. Jackie Cuevas explains, the altar functions to provide the performance with a sense of intimacy, but it also meaningfully situates Grise "both as caretaker of the altar and as cultural storyteller, such as might perform informally at a Chicana/o familial or community gathering" (2). In other words, the setting of the altar not only signals the play's cultural context and the stage's role as a site of memory, but also invests the performer with a sense of authority as storyteller, keeper of culture, and tender of memory. Stage directions note that the altar also holds "piles of books by women of color feminist writers such as Cherríe Moraga, Gloria Anzaldúa, June Jordan, Audre Lorde, and Sharon Bridgforth . . . as well as plays that serve as inspiration" (Grise and Mayorga 39). In one sense, the inclusion of these works on the altar places these writers in an intimate, familial, and loving context; simultaneously, their inclusion casts a political context of women of color feminism over the sacred, familial, and cultural space of the altar, the memory it invokes, and the play itself. A student of Moraga, Irma Mayorga explains how the development of her own "*concientización* (political awakening) as a woman of color artist" enabled her to recognize the politics that were already part of her family's story—the "political ideas and radical ways of thinking that had already been planted in me, learned through my mother's own counterhegemonic . . . actions" (Grise and Mayorga 154). In this way, placing the personal and family photographs alongside women of color feminist works intertwines the intimate and the political, providing a key context for the play. But further, the altar, representative of religious and spiritual practices in both the home and the community, places these personal and political elements in the context of the sacred. Interpreting the altar as "an homage in the tradition of el día de los muertos," Cuevas writes that its presence on stage signals "a recognition of panzas past and a celebration of living" (2–3). In this sense, the altar brings together the memory of the departed—honored family members and feminist icons now passed into the next world—with the fleshed, embodied practices of the living, who undertake performative actions as a ritual of remembering and accessing their knowledge and power. The audience also partakes in this ritual of remembering, one that may empower them to reflect on the strength of their own bodies, stories, and political consciousness.

Political Context of "Panza Brujería"

The script of "Panza Brujería" is included in the second edition of *The Panza Monologues* with a prefatory passage explaining that while the printed script reflects the 2008 DVD performance, the narrative that opens and contextualizes the monologue changed with each live performance (Grise and Mayorga 83). Performances variously addressed a range of figures and issues, including "George W. Bush; former Attorney General Alberto Gonzales; the Iraq War and war in general; SB 1070, HR 4437, and other unjust immigration laws; and the presidential candidates of both the 2004 and 2008 elections" (83). This prefatory note highlights the difference between the stable document of the text and the shifting contours of performances situated within particular political moments. Further, the note acknowledges that each performance was a response to the specific political anxieties that performers and audiences were experiencing. However, for the purposes of this chapter, I will be analyzing the script and corresponding DVD performance of "Panza Brujería," for even if they are not the living play itself, the narrative work they do is still powerful, as they invoke the meanings, knowledge, and ancestral memory held in the body. Further, they also function as cultural artifacts of a particular historical point in time, offering a markedly Chicana/Tejana perspective on national discourse.

Dressed simply in black pants and a black tank top, with simple jewelry—hoop earrings, bracelets, and a ring—Grise performs barefoot. Throughout the entire monologue she is accompanied by the upbeat tempo of Los Flacasos, who provide a Latin funk sound with a clave, tambourine, bass, and twelve-string guitar with a wah pedal. This tempo and style give the piece an energetic tone, whereas it might otherwise carry a more somber mood. Like Anzaldúa's recounting of her experience witnessing the towers burning on 9/11, this four-minute monologue begins with a testimony of witnessing a political moment—the 2004 election of George W. Bush for a second term. As narrator, Grise recalls the experience of living through his governorship in Texas as well as both presidential campaigns (in 2000 and 2004), appealing to her audience's memory as well: "I was living in Austin, Texas, when George W. Bush was governor, and we all knew what to expect when he announced he was running for president. And we watched as he stole the elections in Florida, and I, like you, I'm sure, watched for hours and hours and hours into the next day as he became our president for a second time" (Grise and Mayorga 83). In this introductory narrative, Grise attests to an individual experience situated within a collective one, drawing on both the personal "I" and the collective "we." Rooting this memory in a particular place and time, she establishes her authority as a speaker by referencing her residence in Texas's capital city during Bush's tenure as governor. Yet she also appeals to the audience, asking them to engage in a shared moment of remembering by reminding them of the "stolen" 2000 election and the national controversy regarding Florida, which potentially induces audience members to recall where they were in 2000. Groans from the audience make it clear that they are indeed engaging in their own acts of remembering. When she moves into her discourse on the 2004 election, Grise establishes a commonality between her election-night experience and that of her audience members, using the phrase "I, like you, I'm sure" to verify not only her own claim to experience but also a claim to collectivity. In the recorded performance, as she describes the prolonged anticipation of awaiting election results, she turns her body into a clock, using her left arm as the hour hand, moving it down one position with each repetition of the word "hour." In this way, she uses her body to mark the passage of time, suggesting her experience of that election night as an embodied memory.

As she grabs a stool and sets it up, she recounts that "half the nation had voted for a man who had lied, cheated, and murdered," marking each of these last three verbs with a pause for emphasis (Grise and Mayorga 83). Here she invokes the same kinds of scathing critiques of Bush's presidency that Anzaldúa offers in her own essay but delivers her lines from a later point in time; thus she demonstrates her frustration that, despite his perceived corruption, Bush was granted a second term. Next she takes a bowl from the altar behind her and rests it on the stool, explaining, "In the South, 60 percent of Latinos voted for him" (83), at which point mournful groans can again be heard from the audience on the DVD recording. As she delivers these lines, she takes a small flag from inside the bowl and unfurls it, waving it with a twirl before placing it in the bowl right side up. Then, invoking the concept of the panza for the first time in the monologue and placing her hand on her own panza, she asserts, "And we are going to feel the repercussions of that presidency in our *panzas* for generations to come, and it's gonna take a lot more than the *promise* of change to make it all better" (83). Here, as the audience applauds, she turns the flag upside down and places it back inside the bowl. This small, simple gesture renders a complex narrative of its own, reflecting what Leela Fernandes refers to as disidentification from nationalism (Fernandes 34). Referring to the frequent display of flags after 9/11 as "a form of identification in response to high levels of anxiety and insecurity," Fernandes interprets flag-waving (and other similar actions) as "based on the mistaken notion that security can be grounded in an external, material form of identification" (28). Thus, by turning the flag on its head, Grise performs a disidentification that expresses alienation from the belief that nationalism offers security for herself or her larger communities. Further, the phrase "that presidency" both refers to Bush's presidency and marks the temporal period from which she performs the monologue, recorded in 2008, the year of Barack Obama's first presidential campaign. As she refers to the "promise of change," this phrase easily conjures images of posters with Barack Obama's face printed in red, white, and blue above the word "CHANGE." Thus the monologue more broadly enacts a disidentification from national discourse and political promises that do not fully acknowledge the ways political repercussions are felt, experienced, and carried in the body, not just for a moment but for generations, until active healing is established.

Performing a "National *Limpia*"

As Grise places the flag upside down in the bowl, she takes out a piece of piedra alumbre, or alum stone, and raises it in the air as she announces, "I think what we really need is a collective healing, a national *limpia. Hay que curar el susto*" (Grise and Mayorga 83). By placing "I think" at the beginning of this line, the narrator enacts the subject position of the curandera, offering a diagnosis and establishing herself as a potential agent of healing and a holder of knowledge. Simultaneously, she identifies herself as a patient, part of the collective "we" that requires healing. Patrisia Gonzales writes of the concept of becoming "Curandera de yo misma," or "Curandera of myself," one who is able to transmit the power to heal themselves, recalling, "I remember asking a ceremonial leader once for a limpia, and she responded that she could give me one or she could teach me how to do my own. Like a lot of women, I did not think I had the right or permission to do one, for that was the domain of elders" (20). In a similar sense, the monologue enacts a powerful sense of agency, demonstrating that we must each identify our own actions for healing our communities and ourselves and resist the overwhelming sense of powerlessness that emerges from political alienation, exploitation, and subjugation. Rather than waiting for permission to act, Grise takes an active subject position, becoming a curandera of herself and the community that is her audience. Ana Castillo writes, "An individual who does not sense herself as helpless to circumstances is more apt to contribute positively to her environment than one who resigns to it with apathy" (170). Indeed, in this monologue, the narrator positions herself as an active figure who senses her own power over her circumstances and her ability to draw on cultural and ancestral knowledge to offer healing.

Additionally, she shifts the dominant narrative from accepted political terms by invoking not only the idea of a "collective healing" but more specifically a "national *limpia*." As many U.S. Americans are unlikely to be familiar with the ritual or even the term *limpia*, its use signals the intentional centering of a specific cultural knowledge marginalized by the rhetoric of the nation. This centering of marginalized knowledge is reinforced as she proceeds to use the piedra alumbre to perform a limpia to cure the collective susto. As described in stage directions, "*She passes over her body with the rock, both arms, both thighs, both legs, her* panza—*giving herself a* limpia. *Then shakes the rock at the audience sitting on the left, in the center, and on the right, to 'clean' them as well*" (Grise and Mayorga 84). Here the use of the rock to execute the limpia brings us back to Christina Holmes's discussion of performative intersubjectivity, for the performance presumes a permeability between the bodies of the performer, the rock, and the audience. As she sweeps the rock over the various parts of her body, the audience is able to witness Chicana agency, but they also witness a breaking down of the barriers between bodies. As Patrisia Gonzales explains, "The human body interacts with, impacts, and transmits energy with the natural world and constructs the sacred landscape and ceremonial ecology" (86). Thus this ceremony of limpia is predicated upon the implied interaction and transmission of energies, or spirit, between the rock and human bodies, ones that in this case belong to Grise and her audience. In this way, even as Grise's extravagant performance of the limpia purposefully rouses laughter from the audience, she enacts an epistemological resistance to Western paradigms of thought, subsequently opening up new avenues of possibility, imagination, and healing for our minds, bodies, and spirits. Thus the use of the rock as a purifying technology invests the performance not with some nostalgic idea of magic but rather with an understanding of the natural world, of which humans are a part, as a powerful medium of healing for the mindbodyspirit.

Of course, implicit in the need for a national limpia is the preliminary assumption that susto exists. Importantly, the discussion of susto in reference to the nation compels us to think about the nation as body, and more specifically as a body suffering in ways that require spiritual resolution or attention to interconnectivity. Here I find relevant Moraga's assertion that through stage performances "the violation of the collective body is re-membered" ("Irrevocable Promise" 39). In the specific context of "Panza Brujería," the violation of the collective body can refer simultaneously to specific communities—here,

communities of color—and to the national body. In either case, the monologue draws on the playwrights' (and in some cases the audience's) culturally
specific knowledge of curanderismo and the cleansing ritual of limpia to rid
the collective body of susto and thereby heal or "re-member" it. As Grise
performs the limpia, she states, "We have to get rid of this fear, and this pain
and this *coraje* that we feel in our *panzas*" (Grise and Mayorga 84). Here the
collective pronouns "we" and "our" indicate a shared experience, but further,
the emphasis on the panza indicates a specifically embodied suffering; not
only do we feel fear, pain, and anger, but we carry it in our bodies as illness.
In her essay "Spirit Journey," Elisa Facio describes her own story of susto and
her physical inability to go on carrying "the frustration, rage, and anger that
consumed my body for so many years" (66). If a similar embodied concept
of susto is applied to the national context in "Panza Brujería," we may arrive
at the interpretation of the national body as consumed by the fear, pain, and
anger it can no longer carry.

Of course, the monologue more tangibly demonstrates this shared suffering
as it functions in the individual body. This is clearly articulated a bit further on,
when Grise explains to the audience with performative physicality, "You see, I
feel heartache in my *panza*. Comes from the side like a sucker punch, the kinds
you throw when people ain't lookin. Causes me to bend over. Grab my *panza*.
Anger flush. Cheeks red. Heartbeat fast. When the shit's bad I feel it here. Right
here in my *panza*, not my heart. I feel deep within me" (Grise and Mayorga 84).
This portion of the monologue acutely emphasizes the way in which national
politics affects our embodied states; the deeply felt pain described comes not
from person-to-person encounters but from existing daily in a social world
in which political messages, decisions, and actions register as violence. Thus
the "sucker punch" is not simply an idea of intellectual disenchantment but a
physical sensation in response to external events. Neither can it be reduced to a
pain of the heart—an emotional pain—for it is a pain that registers throughout
one's entire body, radiating outward from the panza, from one's center, the guts.
The pain is made worse by the fact that "people aint' lookin," which is to say
that the national politics that causes these embodied responses—for example,
the rhetoric of criminalization and policies negatively and disproportionately
targeting marginalized communities—is often executed without general public
notice or large-scale protest. In this sense, both the individual and the collective
body (including the national body) require a cure that acknowledges embodied

suffering as well as the potential for embodied healing. Thus, through the performance of limpia, which itself is rooted in a mindbodyspirit framework, the audience is able to witness the body as, to borrow Facio's words, "a site of physical and political resistance" (70).

However, "Panza Brujería" makes it clear that healing is not achieved all at once or easily, for, after cleansing her body and the audience with piedra alumbre, the narrator cautions us, "We may have to do it more than once" (Grise and Mayorga 84). As she delivers this line, *"she takes out a lighter from the bowl and 'lights' the rock, lets it catch fire for a brief time"* (84). This action reminds us that the illness that was in our bodies has not disappeared but rather has been absorbed by the rock, which itself must be purified by fire. This reminder of the transference of illness from our bodies to the rock reaffirms the permeability between various types of bodies as well as the care that must be taken with the sickness that we carry, even when it cannot be seen. Whereas many people might be more familiar with the use of an egg for the cleansing ceremony of the limpia, which is typically accompanied by the reading of the egg after it is cracked open, Patrisia Gonzales provides a contextual framework that aids in understanding the role of piedra alumbre in this monologue: "Some limpias entail fire ceremonies, in which susto is cleansed with the *piedra alumbre*, a candle, or a piece of copal, which is later burned and examined and read to determine the cause or success of the treatment. . . . This practice expresses a pre-Columbian continuity in that a person's body was swept with a rock or mineral, which was then burned and read. . . . This ritual role was named *tlapoalitzli* in Nahuatl" (Gonzales 206). Though Grise does not "read" the piedra alumbre in this monologue, the burning of the rock enacts the aspect of the "fire ceremony" that Gonzales references here and gestures toward threads of continuity with pre-Columbian epistemologies. While the monologue makes no specific note of Nahuatl practices or the Nahuatl language, the visual language of the performance interjects an identifiably non-Western knowledge base into U.S. national discourse. The value of this is that it shifts the audience's reference point and opens up new potentialities for addressing the pain, fear, and anger described in the previous scene. As Suzanne Bost writes, "It is the juggling of different kinds of knowledge that most provocatively pushes at the limits of identity, of the flesh, and of our ideas" (29). Thus, in the context of this monologue, the performance of the fire ceremony—and the limpia more broadly—can meaningfully push at the boundaries of our thought as well as our assumptions about bodies, spirit, and nation.

Old-School Brujería

As the rock burns, Grise transitions from the limpia to the practice of *mal ojo*—or, as it is popularly referred to in English, "evil eye"—linking the two as forms of ancestral knowledge. In common usage in Latinx communities, *mal ojo* can refer to physical symptoms arising from being looked upon with envy or simply "excessive admiration, usually of those too weak to absorb it," such as babies (Torres, *Healing with Herbs* 14). In other words, despite the name, it does not always refer to illness derived from evil intent, but it does refer to the power of the gaze. However, in this monologue, mal ojo is positioned specifically within the context of brujería and, more specifically, the practice of intentionally channeling the power of looking to curse another person with an *hechizo*, or spell. This also relates to the belief within curanderismo that "persons can cause physical and emotional illnesses in others by use of personal power or with the help of noncorporeal beings" (Castillo 155). While a curandera would likely focus on curing that illness rather than causing it, this monologue invokes the practices of brujería in ways that raise a line of significant inquiry regarding women's political power as connected to spiritual, embodied, and ancestral knowledge.

Grise begins, "In times like these, I think it's important that we look to the teachings of our ancestors" (Grise and Mayorga 84). The reference to "times like these" seems to suggest a time of political exasperation in which there is strong need for social transformation. In such times, Grise affirms, we must look to a different kind of knowledge, one that has been passed on to us by those who came before us, not necessarily in books, but through oral tradition and, most significantly, through the body. For, as she states, "my grandmother taught me that as a people we have enough power inside of us that we could curse somebody just by the way we looked at them" (84). What is key here is the acknowledgment of her grandmother's teachings as not just worthy of remembrance but also useful as political tools. For, as the monologue relates it, this knowledge is about the power that we carry within ourselves, which connects us to all of life and the universe; thus, when we remember abuela's wisdom, we are remembering our own power, which is of course an embodied power. Stage directions note that Grise "*points at someone in the audience, giving them the evil eye*" (84). This action models a demonstration of power rather than an intent to do harm to audience members; indeed, in the DVD performance, Grise performs this act with a playfully menacing look that draws laughter from the audience (no doubt partly related to the perception of evil eye as superstition).

Importantly, Grise declares a desire to "put our collective energies together to give George W. Bush and all other evil *políticos ojo*" (Grise and Mayorga 84). The emphasis on "collective energies" must be addressed for the complexity of its meaning. The notion that energy running through our bodies, even as we stand still, can be leveled for a collective purpose signals the populace (and more specifically a marginalized populace) as agents invested with power. Significantly, the implied power is leveraged through the material body and can be exercised through intention; thus, in this case, to stare is *not* to do nothing, but rather to "see" with intention. In an essay on the relationship of spirituality to the politics of solidarity and transformation, Inés Hernández-Ávila writes, "We are seers, we have seen the depths of degradation, and lived to tell of it, and in the telling, we release la carga energética = the energetic charge of the violation" (535). In this sense, to bear witness to injustice means to see it as well as to tell the tale; and in that process, the negative energy incurred might be in part released, moving the "seer" toward healing. In this monologue, the energetic charge of violation is released not only through speaking but through returning the gaze, which suggests the power of staring boldly and without apology at politicians whose actions irresponsibly cause damage to one's community, and of demanding political accountability.

When Grise asks the audience, "Can you imagine the power?" (Grise and Mayorga 84), she encourages us to imagine the collective agency we hold within ourselves as we confront the political realities of our own moment, opening new pathways of possibility. It is this power that the monologue refers to as "Panza Brujería"; more specifically, the performer issues a possessive claim, specifying it as "my . . . *Panza Brujería*" (84). It is worth pausing to consider the meaning of laying possessive claim to the term *brujería*, especially as it is commonly understood as referring to practices that engage negative forces. The term *bruja*, which denotes a practitioner of brujería, is often associated with a feminine figure inspiring great fear because of the sexual and potentially destructive power that she wields. Irene Lara explains that part of the fear associated with this figure is due to (1) her "symboliz[ation] of power outside of patriarchy's control that potentially challenges a status quo" and (2) her status as "a racialized cultural figure" who is "associated with 'superstitious' and 'primitive' Indian and African beliefs and practices" ("Bruja Positionalities" 12). Thus when Grise, as narrator of this monologue, lays claim to brujería, we must understand the resistance that this gesture signals toward the patriarchal framework of George W. Bush–era politics.

Further, by embracing a system of knowledge that is racially inscribed, she rejects the presumption of her own marginalization. Indeed, Lara argues for "the development of a Bruja positionality within Chicana/Latina studies that includes developing our own bruja-like epistemologies in the re-membering, revising, and constructing of knowledge as well as participation in other forms of social change" ("Bruja Positionalities" 13). Thus, in their role as the playwrights of this monologue, Grise and Mayorga devise a positive and empowering conception of brujería that answers such a call, particularly in the context of social change and epistemology. "Panza Brujería" develops a bruja positionality that works from the body, and more specifically from the panza. In her performance, Grise asserts, "So when I send that shit back out into the universe. When I gots to do some of that old school *brujería*. You know, the shit our grandmothers used to do. I throw'em *ojo* from the *panza*" (Grise and Mayorga 85). If the panza is the site where she feels pain burrow deep within, it is also the site from which she "sees" and bears testimony, transforming pain into power that can be sent back into the world. In this sense, then, the panza becomes a place of and medium for transformation, and a possible starting point from which to initiate change in the external world.

Keeping the Third Eye Open

Grise's invocation of ojo as old school brujería is exercised with a difference, in that it is delivered from the "third eye" of the panza—the belly button. Thus, placing her hands in a triangle over her panza, she playfully warns the audience, "That's why you gots to keep the belly button clean. You don't need no *mugre* up in there cloudin up your vision, half blind. Keep the third eye open, *mugrosa*, cuz sometimes you gots to give *ojo* to protect yourself" (Grise and Mayorga 85). In the DVD performance, the audience, invoked here as "mugrosa," or dirty, laughs loudly at this admonishment to keep their belly buttons clean; yet the comic aspect of these lines does not detract from the deep significance expressed. That the body can "see" and know and protect only if it is prepared to do so deserves close examination. Protecting oneself by seeing with the panza suggests another form of body knowledge. The "third eye" is generally associated not with visual sight but a deeper kind of knowing or seeing, and with an ability to see through externalities. Anzaldúa refers to the third eye as "the reptilian eye looking inward and outward simultaneously" ("Now Let Us Shift" 120).

This concept of a living, conscious awareness that sees in multiple directions is linked specifically to the belly button in this monologue, evoking the body's deep interconnection with spirit and healing.

This connection is brought into focus when we consider Patrisia Gonzales's explanation of the significance of the belly button in Mexican Indigenous practice: "The ombligo is the seat and regulator of the spirit. The belly button is also the physical site of numerous medicinal practices" (144). For, as Gonzales also states, "the ombligo connects to—and is—the center of the world" (142). Grise's warning to keep the belly button clean thus takes on another level of meaning given that it is through the belly button that the body connects to the cosmos. In this way, the body not only connects us to other bodies across space and time but is itself a center or axis of sorts; our bodies are thus marked as sacred geographies. Here we might turn to Davíd Carrasco's writing on Mesoamerican religions, in which he states, "The most pervasive type of sacred space where elaborate ceremonies were carried out was the human body. The human body was considered a potent receptacle of cosmological forces, a living, moving center of the world" (66–67). In this portion of the monologue, the ceremony is the work of throwing ojo from the panza—the center of oneself—and more specifically from the third eye of the belly button: the center of the world. In this way, "Panza Brujería" performs the body as ceremonial space. More generally, keeping the inner, outward-looking third eye open and clean suggests keeping it prepared for illumination, able to "see" past the desconocimientos produced and circulated through the political discourse that shapes public consciousness.

Next, Grise performatively illustrates the embodied ritual of throwing ojo from the panza, as she explains: "When I give *ojo*, I reach my right hand over to my back. Fingers open. Palm touchin skin. I send the energy from the bottom of the spine through the body & out from the depths of my *panza*, full moon belly" (Grise and Mayorga 85). On the DVD, as she demonstrates the act of forcefully projecting power from the body, Grise turns her body sideways so that the audience can observe the physicality, process, and method. As she puts her right hand behind her on the small of her back, she enacts "palm touchin skin"; this encourages one to reflect on skin as a carrier and transmitter of ancestral memory, in the very evidence it presents of the past. The flesh of her hand, combined with her intention, directs the power from the base of her spine through the "depths" of her panza, from where it is purposefully released. Her rearticulation of her panza as a "full moon belly" connotes the power of Coyolxauhqui; this allusion suggests her own embodiment of a specifically feminine agency that can illuminate the darkness, providing a path toward healing reconstruction. This demonstration of feminine, embodied agency reaffirms Lara's commentary on brujas as holding power outside of the patriarchal system. Through the performative enactment of her own body's power, she utilizes the pain, fear, and anger manifested deep within her, releasing it outward in a new form. Hernández-Ávila asks, once we have learned to identify and take control of the pain of violation (ancient, colonial, and ongoing) that we hold within ourselves and witness in each other "by releasing it through our tongues / hands / pens / creative forces / work, through our loving, why do we have to hold on to it?" (534). In "Panza Brujería," the narrator names and speaks the pain she feels deep within as a result of external forces—a political climate that disregards her voice, needs, and reality, as well as those of her communities. Further, she uses her body to answer the question that Hernández-Ávila poses, demonstrating a transformation of that violation's energetic force and a determination to redirect it outward and enact change in the world.

In Grise's performance of "Panza Brujería," we can conceive of the body as a site not only of ceremony but also of ancestral memory. As she dramatically enacts her method of throwing ojo from her panza, she vocalizes the way this power moves through her body as well as its ancestral lineage. She explains to the audience, "The *ojo* of the *panza* shoots the energy through my left palm facing away, and I unleash from the depths of my *tripas* all the fury of my grandmother, María de Jesús Yee Cortez, *curandera* life healer with broken heart" (Grise and Mayorga 85). In the DVD performance, she stands sideways and uses her left arm (in view of the audience) to demonstrate unleashing the energy. Placing that hand on her panza, she stands with feet firmly planted and her right palm still placed upon her back; she then extends her left arm outward and upward with each part of her grandmother's name, pushing the energy out, bending and curving her body back, head tilted upward. The audience can visualize the invisible energy released through her palm from the depths of her *tripas* or guts, a place of instinct and knowing (i.e., "I know it in my gut").

Importantly, as she expels the violation from her body, it is with "all the fury" of her grandmother, whose curing knowledge and "broken heart" continue to live within her. The suggestion that we can draw on our own pain, frustration, and anger as well as that of our ancestors to heal ourselves signals an embodied ancestral memory. In "Epílogo: Xicana Mind, Beginner Mind," Cherríe Moraga relates what she has learned from elders in ceremony: "That our actions in this life can heal our ancestors on the other side, that this corporeal knowing

FIGURE 2 "Panza Brujería" performed by Virginia Grise. From *The Panza Monologues* world premiere produced by ALLGO, Austin, Texas, 2004. Photograph by Irma Mayorga.

does not hold us, that we can remember histories and futures through and in spite of the body we wear. And my relatives are with me before and after my coming" (198). Grise's performance of mal ojo significantly reflects these lessons, for as we witness her embodied and willful expulsion of trauma, we might imagine that she is acting not only for herself but also for her abuela, who is no longer held strictly by "corporeal knowing" but whose wisdom and experience can nonetheless be felt in and through the body. "Panza Brujería" suggests a consciousness that is not insular but rather conjoins various sites in space and time, felt within the body though not held by it. In her prose "autogeography," included in the second edition of *The Panza Monologues*, Grise pieces together the places and stories of her ancestry, explaining that her grandfather was a Cantonese immigrant to Mexico, where he married her grandmother and worked selling fruits and vegetables in the market (Grise and Mayorga 131). Their daughter, Emma Lesi Yee Cortez, married a white soldier from Indiana and moved with him to the United States, where Grise was born on a Georgia military base; returning to those market streets of Mexico as an adult, Grise would "searc[h] for [her] dead ancestors" (133–34). Significantly, in "Panza Brujería," her ancestry is located, felt, and accessed through the nexus of her body, functioning as a powerful resource and source of strength.

In her final lines, Grise turns her body forward to the audience and warns, with great bravado in her gestures and tone, "So don't fuck with us. Me and my ancestors. Me, my ancestors, my *ojo*, my *panza*. Don't fuck with us, a'ight" (Grise and Mayorga 85). In this statement, many are contained within her body, such that she becomes an "us" that includes her ancestors as well as the formidable power invested in her body—and more specifically her panza. After the initial sucker punch she describes earlier in the monologue, she draws on an energetic knowing that allows her to confront external powers with her own embodied, ancestral power. Her exclamation "Don't fuck with us" suggests precisely the kind of "awesome deliberate coraje" that Inés Hernández-Ávila describes as manifesting wherever "grief has turned into creative rage" (534). This *coraje*, which can variously refer to courage, guts, and anger, signals the alignment of the speaker with her own embodied sense of ancestral knowledge and agency.

Conclusion

In this monologue, as in Anzaldúa's essay, the expressed ability to heal the susto of the George W. Bush era reinforces both an individual and collective power to incite change and resist political complacency as well as complicity. Both works have at their center a Chicana subject position that draws deeply on ancestral practices and knowledge forms located in the body and concerned with spirit. Each work narratively invokes the culturally grounded practice of limpia as a cure for the susto of living in a starkly fragmented society, ruptured not only by the events of September 11, 2001, but also by the nationalist discourses that followed thereafter. Indeed, contemporary Chicanx readers might easily insert their own experience of living during the Trump administration into an interpretation of these texts, which offer meaningful approaches to us still. Invoking the return of the spirit through the limpia, these works disidentify from dominant nationalist discourses and suggest a healing that functions by placing the individual in relation to others, demonstrating a power that is not isolated but shared. In addition, Grise and Mayorga include in "Panza Brujería" the practice of throwing ojo, extending the consideration of healing to the ways we can use the coraje we hold in our individual and collective bodies to create political accountability and transformative change. Thus, both texts not only offer a significant rendering of a particular historical moment in the United States but also continue to hold political resonance for a broad community of Chicanx readers. In the next chapter, I change focus and consider how embodied ritual functions in a more intimate and domestic context, between a young girl and her abuela, opening the way to ancestral knowledge.

The Ritual Body

Feminism and Spiritual Inheritance

n "Toward an Epistemology of a Brown Body," Cindy Cruz argues that "our production of knowledge begins in the bodies of our mothers and grandmothers" (61). This chapter takes as its premise this assertion of the body as a central site of ancestral knowledge and focuses on the embodied spiritual labor of ritual transformation in Helena María Viramontes's short story "The Moths." This celebrated story, first published in 1985 in a collection bearing the same title (*The Moths and Other Stories*), has been a staple in college classrooms and the subject of thoughtful literary criticism. More than three decades after its original publication, this six-page story continues to hold considerable value for practitioners of Chicana feminist studies and, as I will discuss, offers particular insight regarding the role of Chicana/Latina spiritual inquiry in art and everyday life. As discussed in the previous chapter, the link between embodied ritual and spiritual epistemologies has been a vital part of Chicana creative expression and performance. Whereas chapter 1 emphasized this link in works with overtly political contexts, addressing questions of nationalism and globalization, I turn here to the intimate, interpersonal, and domestic contexts of Viramontes's now-classic story "The Moths." In my reading of this story, I highlight its representation of embodied spirituality enacted between a young

An earlier version of this chapter was first published as "With the Sacredness of a Priest: The Body as Ritual Site of Feminist Knowledge in Viramontes' 'The Moths,'" in *MELUS*, vol. 43, no. 4, Winter 2018.

girl and her abuela and of the inheritance of ancestral knowledge through ritual labor. With her caretaking actions, the girl ushers her abuela into the next stage of existence, culminating in the washing of her body; she confronts the embattled life of the spirit that is both her own and her grandmother's, as well as her role in an ongoing ancestral story of women that includes her mother.

The rituals lovingly enacted by Viramontes's fourteen-year-old female protagonist in the home of her abuela do not simply demonstrate gendered, domestic labor; rather, the story's scenes acknowledge a spiritual labor of inheritance that effectively restructures space and time, resulting in a transformation of consciousness. The protagonist's emergence into self-knowledge, as Viramontes presents it, is inherently connected to the realization and actualization of interconnectivity with others. Specifically, I argue that Viramontes utilizes sensory elements of interaction with lived bodies and their mappings to create a textual experience that centers the body as a site of knowledge and connects the reader, like the protagonist, to a sacred epistemology. In particular, it is the ritual attention to the body that delivers the protagonist, and potentially the reader, into a self-knowledge capable of unhinging the logics of patriarchal space. To clarify, my reading links the story's attention to Chicana feminist ways of knowing to its carefully crafted scenes of embodied ritual, emphasizing the implied spiritual dimensions. I interpret the protagonist's discovery of self-knowledge in "The Moths" as being intrinsically linked to the processual development of sensory awareness of interconnection with others both living and dead. Crossing into such conscious awareness signifies (1) a departure from an understanding of the self as disconnected and alone, and (2) an inheritance, or gift, reciprocally rendered through attentive, intentional bodily engagement. In this story, the body is not simply a shell or vehicle; it is a place and source of knowing upon which experience is inscribed and through which ancestral interconnection is made legible and tangible.

Viramontes describes her writing practice as aimed toward more than "just an aesthetic experience" in that she prioritizes reader/writer engagement and perceives the challenges of that engagement as allowing her to "open up other veiled realities" ("Faith" 254). In my analysis, I attempt to demonstrate how. Firstly, I focus on Viramontes's emphasis on alternative sacred spaces as feminist sites of embodied ritual and knowledge production. For these are the spaces—the garden, the kitchen, the rooms of her abuela's home—where the narrator experiences bonding activity and escapes the patriarchal control of her own house, commanded by her father's rule, and the Church, figuring as an extension of that rule. Participation in collaborative ritual alongside her abuela—gardening and cooking—prepares her to transition into a caretaking role that figures as the central focus of the second part of this chapter. I treat the scenes of ritual care for her abuela, first in illness and then in death, as representations of embodied acts of reciprocity and a form of critical witness. Central to my examination as a whole is the way in which Viramontes's use of sensory language communicates an embodied experience that is epistemologically transformative. This is perhaps most clear in the narrator's final caretaking actions, which culminate in a poignant washing of the body when her abuela passes into death. Thus in the last part of this chapter I focus on the protagonist's creation of a new ritual, and her positioning as "priestess" presiding over what I interpret as ritual time-space. For through embodied actions that alter typical understandings of space and time, she becomes the recipient of a sacred knowledge of intersubjectivity uniting her with her grandmother and mother.

In this reading, then, I take seriously Cruz's assertion that "our production of knowledge begins in the bodies of our mothers and grandmothers" (61), for the story's transformative power is ultimately achieved through the protagonist's reflective engagement with the body of her abuela. The development of the young protagonist from a subject position of emotional isolation, inadequacy, and restriction into the subject position of "priestess" narratively expresses an inheritance of knowledge and agency, or a crossing over into a larger sacred story of women whose bodies, like compasses, gesture toward hidden pasts and possible futures. The ultimate depiction of the protagonist as "priestess" in her ritual care for her grandmother's deceased body represents the kind of "crossing" that M. Jacqui Alexander has theorized as a space of "convergence and endless possibility" (8). That space of convergence and crossing is a space where, as Alexander posits, "we put down and discard the unnecessary in order to pick up that which is necessary" (8). That which is *necessary* in Viramontes's narrative, that which the protagonist yearns for, is an interconnection capable of displacing the deep loneliness of life and what she describes as "the misery of feeling half born" (Viramontes, *Moths* 32). As she learns to trust in her abuela's knowledge and ability to comfort, heal, and protect, she increasingly trusts in her own hands' ability to reciprocate these gifts; importantly, she learns that her subjectivity is embedded in a larger trajectory of women with shared struggles and gifts.

The narrative ultimately plots the process of learning that, in actively laboring to embrace, love, and honor those who nurture our growth, we may increasingly embrace and accept the significance of our own role in a larger, shared story. Juan D. Mah y Busch suggests that the liberatory potential of Viramontes's story comes from "its possible relationship to learning" (150) an epistemology that connects the protagonist's loving action to the "transformation of social relations" (156). Indeed, in six short pages, the story functions as a succinct yet complex narrative, demonstrating a usable consciousness capable of transforming readers' ways of being in the world. This process of learning relates to not only those who are living, but also those who have passed and yet remain a part of our community. In examining this story, I thus situate literature as an important site of inquiry regarding Chicana spiritualities. As Bridget Kevane argues in *Profane & Sacred: Latino/a American Writers Reveal the Interplay of the Secular and the Religious* (2008), "There is a persistent and strong religious and spiritual discourse in the works of most Latino and Latina authors that cannot be dismissed" (2). Yet, as she pointed out at that time, "until recently, theological, religious, or spiritual readings of Latino literature remained marginalized from the theoretical and critical discussion of Latino literature" (2). Thus I read this Chicana story with attention to the ways in which its narrative reflects a broader consciousness about the existence of a sacred story. The contribution I endeavor to make here is a consideration of how Chicana feminist narrative reflects a spiritual epistemology rooted in the body and its rituals, as I meditate on the relationship between embodied ritual action and inherited feminist knowledge.

Consequently, before moving further into analysis, I briefly discuss the working relationship between ritual, spirituality, and feminism that my reading is premised on. Theologian Barbara J. McClure defines ritual as "forms of communication about oneself and about an enduring reality of life" (734). She explains that although ritual is deeply connected to daily life, it departs from ordinary routine in that it "increases our awareness of a kind of ontological inter-relatedness and interdependence of all persons" (736). In McClure's view, and significantly for my argument, the quotidian becomes ritual "when understood as embedded within, participating in, and helping create a larger and communal reality, connecting the practitioner to a longer historical narrative" (735) in which we are reminded that "we are loved and that we can love" (736). While the protagonist's actions in "The Moths" may not be immediately evident as ritualistic, I find McClure's concept of ritual powerfully relevant to the story's underlying meanings.

The willingness to take ritual and its epistemological meanings seriously has specific implications for feminism, for, as Alexander argues, "Spirit knowing" has long been utilized by women around the world "as the mechanism of making the world intelligible" (15). In other words, the feminist project of discovering how to live in and transform our social worlds requires a discernment that, for many women, is interlinked with spiritual epistemologies and ontologies. For such women, "making the world intelligible" requires a deep sense of knowing how one stands within, and in relation to, the world. And yet, as Alexander adds, "because experience has been understood in purely secular terms, and because the secular has been divested of the Sacred and the spiritual divested of the political, this way of knowing is not generally believed to have the capacity to instruct feminism in the United States" (15). In this critique of a secularized feminism and depoliticized spirituality, Alexander draws attention to how feminism's parameters, aims, and methods are defined within narrow confines that discount the ways in which feminism is lived and enacted by a large proportion of women in the world.

The kind of "Spirit knowing" I am interested in here, in connection to feminism, is a specifically embodied one. To understand the ways in which women of color *know*, we must be attentive to their bodies, including the multigenerational experiences those bodies undergo, hold, and respond to. The body is a repository, producer, and receiver of information, enabling us to understand more cogently what seems illegible. Sharon Stockton observes that the Latina body is always inscribed with meaning that bears the weight of patriarchy's legacy but can be contested and remade: "In order to redefine the identity thus constructed for her, then, the Chicana/Latina must reclaim control over the content of the 'messages' her body sends, thus reconstructing . . . the possibilities open to female subjectivity" (212). Reading against prescribed bodily narratives reinterprets the meanings and markings of the Chicana/Latina body, reconstructing the possibilities of a corresponding subjectivity and potentially altering Chicana/Latina experience. Centering the body in feminist inquiry, Gloria Anzaldúa wrote, "My feminism is grounded not on incorporeal abstraction but on corporeal realities. The material body is center, and central. The body is the ground of thought. The body is a text" (Anzaldúa, "Gestures" 5). If the body is the site from which knowledge and action grow, it is imperative for literary scholars to consider narrative representation of the Chicana body, including its ritual actions.

Alternative Sacred Spaces: Nourishment, Connection, and Embodied Sensation

For readers approaching Viramontes's work, close attention to the various implications of the real and symbolic spaces she presents is key to interpreting the narrative. As her characters inhabit and navigate shifting social and psychological environments, temporalities are often blurred, creating what Margarita T. Barceló describes as "intricate tapestries of space-time" in Viramontes's fiction (124). Thus, in this analysis of "The Moths," I alternatingly and at times simultaneously emphasize spatiality, temporality, and the highly sensory language she consistently employs. Additionally, I interpret the narrative as one centered on the struggle to relocate a lost connection and to remember the spiritual source of our collectivity. As I discuss here, the narrator's gravitation toward, and prioritization of, experiences that highlight embodied sensation and interconnection places the body at the center of social engagement and epistemological becoming. The particular spaces in which those experiences emerge (or fail to do so) are important to understanding the story's lessons about a developing feminist knowledge.

Early in the narrative, the young narrator describes her grandmother's home as "cradled within" and "shielded by" chayote vines, denoting it as a space of protection, a reprieve and sanctuary from the everyday forms of patriarchy battled at home and in the Catholic Church (Viramontes, *Moths* 28–29). This marks the home of her abuela, Mama Luna, in stark contrast to her fraught homelife, in which she feels like an outsider, unable or unwilling to fulfill the gendered expectations dictated to her by, for example, her father: "[Apá] would pound his hands on the table, rocking the sugar dish or spilling a cup of coffee and scream that if I didn't go to Mass every Sunday to save my goddamn sinning soul, then I had no reason to go out of the house, period. Punto final" (29). The consequences of her resistance to her father's aggressive authority and threats of isolation increase as her mother receives his ire "for her lousy ways of bringing up daughters, being disrespectful and unbelieving" (29). This conflict culminates in resentment on the part of her sisters, who threaten to "kick the holy shit out of [her]" for her "selfish" behavior and the collective suffering it supposedly causes (29); this dynamic demonstrates the way in which patriarchy forcibly implicates women as both subjects and objects of its violence. The narrator's deep sense of helplessness is expressed as she describes her feelings of being "angry and just so tired of the quarrels and beatings and unanswered prayers" (30). Here the domestic conflict emerging from the frustrations of patriarchal domination is linked to "unanswered prayers," or the perceived failure of prescribed religious ritual. This failure of prayer concisely expresses the extent of the narrator's trauma, for if ritual is about conscious interconnection, then failed ritual (in this case, prayer) signals a longed-for connection ultimately denied.

Furtively escaping to abuela's house instead of Mass, the narrator describes the contentment she derives from planting heliotropes and cilantro, *hierbabuena*, avocados, and chayotes in Hills Brothers coffee cans. She describes the processual labor she performs in her grandmother's garden, puncturing holes in the cans, filling them with mud, packing the mud, and then making a hole for the roots which "would burst out of the rusted coffee cans and search for a place to connect" (Viramontes, *Moths* 28). Like those roots seeking connection, bursting forth from their space of confinement and requiring the nourishment of water (symbolic of birth, the flow of life, and transformation), the narrator describes her own sensation of feeling "safe and guarded and not alone" under the watchful eye of her abuela, who makes her feel "like God was supposed to make you feel" (28). This language suggests firstly that God, as defined by the context of the patriarchal, institutional Church, does not fulfill the promise of protection and unity that she seeks, and, secondly, that she is instead discovering the nourishment of God in the quiet communion of her labors alongside her abuela. Indeed, Mama Luna's very name indicates her divine healing power, as it references the feminine aspect of the moon, whose light counters the darkness of night. Her name further alludes to that figure common in Chicana feminist discourse, Coyolxauhqui, the goddess of Aztec mythology whose brother, the god of war, decapitated her and threw her head into the sky, where it became the moon. The sacred story of this mythology counters the Christian narrative of the Catholic Church, just as Mama Luna's garden and home figure as an alternative sacred space that counters the institutional space of the church.*

Like the garden, her grandmother's kitchen functions in the narrative as a space of connection and freedom for the protagonist. Gabriella Gutiérrez y Muhs argues the importance of such spaces in Chicana literature, and in Viramontes's work in particular: "The kitchen as a space for cooking, a symbol of oppression in mainstream feminist theory, is oftentimes identified as a space of accomplishment and empowerment for Chicanas. . . . The kitchen allows for creativity, nurturing, and experimentation, as well as empowerment and balance" (13). Indeed, as the protagonist learns to garden and cook alongside her abuela, she learns to be a creative spiritual force, capable of transforming her inner and outer worlds. The knowledge that passes from grandmother to

---

*Bridget Kevane asserts that the search for alternative sacred spaces is a common theme in Latinx narrative: "Many characters, trapped by their oppressive surroundings, patriarchal systems, exploitation of genders, and struggles against all of these earthly systems, are forced to seek alternative sacred spaces" (7).

granddaughter not only displaces patriarchal religious authority but also figures as a transformative inheritance. This is particularly evident in a flashback
scene of her abuela's kitchen, a memory revisited from the institutional space
of the church. As she sits in a chapel across from the local market where she
will purchase goods to care for the abuela her mother has revealed is dying, she
experiences the place as empty of connection, offering only high ceilings, cool
marble, and "frozen statues with blank eyes" that make her feel alone (Viramontes, *Moths* 29). As she sits in a space that the narrative clearly associates with
the patriarchal domination of her father, who would "grab [her] arm and dig his
nails into [her] to make sure [she] understood the importance of catechism,"
her mind wanders to her grandmother's kitchen, the place she would escape to
under the guise of attending Mass (29). Here the protagonist takes on a role
frequently assumed by characters in Latinx narratives who, as Bridget Kevane
describes it, reject the "symbolic boundaries of their faith—the geographical
space of the church or synagogue" and instead "search for answers outside fixed
sacred spaces" (7). However, it is not only the space itself that is important, but
also the embodied ritual labor that takes place in such spaces.

As she regards the cold emptiness of the chapel, the girl recalls the process-
oriented labor of her abuela's kitchen—pounding chiles in a *molcajete*, peeling
the chiles as they burn her eyes and fill the air with their toasted scent, crushing
and twisting the tomato, garlic, and peppers amid fresh-cut roses (Viramontes,
Moths 29–30). Implied in the sensory memory of the kitchen is the significance
of experiential labor that places her in relationship to and connection with her
abuela.[†] For the fourteen-year-old narrator poised on the edge of adolescence,
her kitchen ritual of preparing chile for hot menudo is collaborative, overseen
by her abuela, who "lifted the burnt chiles from the fire and sprinkled water on
them until the skins began to separate," finally placing them in front of the girl
to peel and grind (29). From the space of the chapel, she recalls the "gagging
scent" of those toasting chiles, figurative of her resentment toward her father's
command to attend Mass and the guilt she feels toward her mother, who would
consequently receive her father's retribution (29). The transformation of the
chiles denotes her inner transformation as well, as indicated in her memory:

[†] Audre Lorde's classic biomythography *Zami: A New Spelling of My Name* (1982) figures as
an immediate comparison. Published within three years of Viramontes's story, Lorde's queer,
feminist life narrative presents a deep connection to her Afro-Caribbean heritage and, like
"The Moths," contributed significantly to the women of color literary canon; both draw on
mortar-and-pestle imagery to evoke the body as a critical site of feminist knowledge.

"I . . . began to crush and crush and twist and crush the heart out of the tomato, the clove of garlic, the stupid chiles that made me cry, crushed them until they turned into liquid under my bull hand. With a wooden spoon, I scraped hard to destroy the guilt, and my tears were gone" (30). As she works the molcajete, she also works her frustration, sadness, and guilt, crushing the "heart" of it all until her tears disappear. The kitchen ritual thus becomes a remedy, fostered by the accompaniment and alternative space her abuela provides. The rhythm and warmth of her grandmother's kitchen, much like the safety and protection of her garden, engenders a creative, collaborative performance; for it is through mutual work that her father's condemnation of her "Goddamn sinning soul" (29) is displaced. The embodied action of grinding enables her not only to resist the guilt incited by her father and the Catholic Church, but also to transform it into something else.

For example, the "bull hand" she uses to grind the chiles is the same hand that "just couldn't do the girl things [her sisters] could do," such as crocheting and embroidery, a perceived failure that earns her shame (Viramontes, *Moths* 27). These are the hands that elsewhere in the story "han[g] helplessly by [her] side," signifying her sense of uselessness (30). Thus her ritual collaboration with her grandmother is one of active resistance, healing, and pleasure: "Abuelita touched my hand and pointed to the bowl of menudo that steamed in front of me. I spooned some chile into the menudo and rolled a corn tortilla thin with the palms of my hands. As I ate, a fine Sunday breeze entered the kitchen and a rose petal calmly feathered down to the table" (30). The grandmother's touch here gestures toward the matriarchal body itself as an alternative sacred space and source of wisdom, effectively displacing the patriarchal authority of the institutional Church. Through the ritual performed under her grandmother's touch and guidance, the "gagging scent" of the kitchen has given way to the pleasure of consuming their creation amid a satisfying breeze; the rose petal floating and settling in front of her signals a fineness and beauty that she has achieved despite her "bull hands." Her sense of her body as helpless or inadequate is transformed through this processual labor that teaches her not what her hands cannot do, but rather the creative acts of which they are capable. As Sonia Saldívar-Hull observes, her abuela's house functions as a sanctuary space (132) in which her "bull hands" can be transformed into "healing hands" (134–35) because it is situated away from the logics of patriarchy that pit her father and sisters against her. I would add that this collaborative ritual with her abuela opens up a space in which alternative knowledge can arise; the lesson derived is one that places value on the creative act, signaling the assumption of agency and the acknowledgment of oneself as invested with the authority to construct ritual. This cooperative work prepares her to create her own sacred ritual of caretaking as *despedida*, a farewell to honor her grandmother's passage into death.

Caretaking as Embodied Reciprocity and Ritual Witnessing: Returning the Gift

In the very first lines of "The Moths," Viramontes's narrator explains, "I was fourteen years old when Abuelita requested my help" (27). As we come to learn, unlike the collaborative work in the garden and kitchen described above, "this was a different kind of help" because "Abuelita was dying" (28). Her ritual labor as a caretaker in her abuela's home will not be collaborative work but, instead, an act of service, and more specifically an act of reciprocity. For it is in reciprocation for the home remedies given over a lifetime that the young girl readily accepts her grandmother's request for aid and, in doing so, inherits her role as healer. She recalls her abuela "placing, removing and replacing potato slices on the temples of [her] forehead" to treat scarlet fever, and the mixture of dried moth wings and Vicks that Mama Luna rubbed into her swollen hands, "shaping them back to size," giving her the intense sensation of "bones melting" (28). She recalls these gifts of healing from a powerful woman whose remedies she once questioned but eventually came to trust. She reasons that "it seemed only fair" that her hands, which her grandmother had once healed, would in turn "[find] use in rubbing her caving body with alcohol and marijuana, rubbing her arms and legs, turning her face to the window so that she could watch the Bird of Paradise blooming or smell the scent of clove in the air" (28). These physical acts of caretaking, in addition to toweling her grandmother's face and holding her hand for hours on end, represent a reciprocity in which she returns the gifts not only of healing and comfort but also of olfactory, tactile, and visual sensation. If we consider such sensation as being essential to the ways in which we experience and intuit our environment, then we also understand that the narrator is assisting her abuela, on an epistemological level, to know the world even as she passes out of it.

Such knowing is inherently connected to the spiritual. We might take as an example the protagonist's seemingly simple, loving act of turning her grandmother's face to better view the flowers blooming outside her window. Rather than mere observation or aesthetic appreciation, the ability to witness that blooming suggests broader implications about one's relationship with and connection to the universe. For "you could see her gray eye beaming out the window, staring hard as if to remember everything" (Viramontes, *Moths* 28–29). This effort to remember "everything" signals the process of reflection and the passage her grandmother is preparing for. As described by Anzaldúa, spirituality can be conceived of as a pursuit of balance with one's environment: "A human yearning and an essential human need to witness the flow of life and the patterns . . . manifested in life, the spiritual is a deep sense of belonging and participation in life" ("Flights" 39). Thus I would argue that as the girl enables her abuela to witness the blooming transformation of the bird-of-paradise, she also enables her sensory participation in the flow of life. Through the girl's touch and caretaking, her grandmother is better able to experience sensory perception of the world as well as her transforming relationship to it.

To shed more light on the meanings of such embodied reciprocity, I briefly turn to Patricia J. Williams's 1988 essay "On Being the Object of Property," in which she shares her own intimate story of ritual caretaking:

> Two years ago, my godmother Marjorie suffered a massive stroke. As she lay dying, I would come to the hospital to give her her meals. My feeding her who had so often fed me became a complex ritual of mirroring and self-assembly. The physical act of holding the spoon to her lips was not only a rite of nurture and of sacrifice, it was the return of a gift. It was a quiet bowing to the passage of time and the doubling back of all things. The quiet woman who listened to my woes about work and school required now that I bend my head down close to her and listen for mouthed word fragments, sentence crumbs. I bent down to give meaning to her silence, her wandering search for words. (17)

As expressed here, the reciprocity of caretaking's ritual labor is linked to the development of subjectivity as well as entrance into a different temporality. To feed one who has fed you, to nourish them, with a willingness to listen for what perhaps cannot be said enables what Williams describes above as a "ritual of mirroring and self-assembly." To give back what has been received leads us to know and make ourselves in relation to the other. Further, it is the embodiment of the giving—the holding of the spoon and the patient bending of the head to listen—that allows the giver not only to sense "the passage of time" but to honor and enter into it. The "doubling back of all things" seems to acknowledge the sacred, even mysterious, ebb and flow of energies between people and bodies across time. This is likewise evident as Viramontes's protagonist inherits her abuela's role as caretaker, honoring her transition into death. In this work, she learns that to "return the gift" means to acknowledge a link to others via a remembered past and an imagined future.

Near the end of "The Moths," the narrator recalls preparing a can of soup for her abuela as the setting sun figuratively signals the arrival of her death, "finally sink[ing] into the realization that it cannot with all its power to heal or burn, exist forever" (Viramontes, *Moths* 31). While the metaphor of the sun as abuela renders a lyrical beauty, the messiness and reality of death is not skirted. The girl vividly describes the circumstances in which she discovers her grandmother's passing: "The room smelled of Pine Sol and vomit, and Abuelita had defecated the remains of her cancerous stomach" (31). Here death is viscerally invoked through the reader's sense of smell. The strong chemical scent of Pine Sol, associated with hospitals for its disinfectant properties, does not cancel out the presence of sickness but rather suggests even more powerfully the stench of defecation and vomit. Readers' likely aversion to the implication of this stench is rooted in an aversion to confronting death. And yet Viramontes's protagonist directly confronts this messiness with decisive action, as she sets to caring for her grandmother's body.

Viramontes writes: "From the cabinet I got a tin basin, filled it with lukewarm water, and carried it carefully to the room. I went to the linen closet and took out some modest bleached white towels. With the sacredness of a priest preparing his vestments, I unfolded the towels one by one on my shoulders" (*Moths* 31). Though previous elements of the story clearly illustrate the protagonist's resistance to institutional religion, and more specifically the Catholic Church, this scene suggests that in this moment she views herself as a priestess in her own right. She prepares to initiate a sacred rite for which her previous collaboration and service has readied her. The protagonist discerns the moment as preparation for what is not simply an obligatory act of cleansing but also a ritual act that encompasses the sacred, in that it connects her to a larger narrative beyond her own, and beyond that which can be known. Further, the intentionality in the girl's careful unfolding of the bleached white towels, which she will use to wash her grandmother, suggests her awareness of the act as ritual. McClure describes rituals as "deeply relational" (736), in that they "bring us to the present, bind us together, and embed our experiences within a larger sacred story" (737). That larger sacred story is evident as the young girl reflects,

"Although endings are inevitable, they are necessary for rebirths" (Viramontes, *Moths* 31). Thus she is acutely aware of her active participation in the cycle of life and death through her ritual labor; not only has she become the priestess, but one day she too will be the setting sun. Her self-perceived authority to administer these rites indicates the development of the protagonist's subjectivity. Her once unsure and inadequate hands now confidently set to work without any external direction. Sharon Stockton argues that "as 'priest,' the narrator clearly usurps the male prerogative of interpretation and of redemption, and by so doing she replaces the role of her father and of the Catholic Church" (215). This usurpation is indeed important, and even more critical to my reading is the modeling of spiritual authorship this scene offers to readers as a key element of a developed Chicana subjectivity.

Further, Viramontes writes the washing of the body as a markedly physical, embodied ritual labor, distinct from general domestic labor. Alexander argues, "Spiritual work is different from the category of domestic labor . . . although the spiritual workplace is usually constituted as home" (15). Labor in the domestic space is elevated to spiritual work when it enables the manifestation of a deeper form of knowing and perception that emerges through the body and links one to a broader field of existence. It is through spiritual work that "sacred knowledge comes to be inscribed in the daily lives of women" and "made manifest through flesh" (Alexander 14–15). Thus, while Viramontes's narrator prepares her "vestments" in the domestic space of her grandmother's home, her labor reaches spiritual heights in that her ritual cleansing of the body/flesh is rooted in and engenders a sacred discernment. As the story progresses, we witness the narrator's efforts to read the text of her grandmother's body in a way that more fully marks its (formerly) lived condition as well as its mystery. Thus, as priestess, the girl will draw on her own evolved subjectivity to ritually wash her beloved abuela's body and interpret its signs, honoring the story that it tells as well as the secrets that it keeps.

In the following passage, the narrator describes the ritual, intentional process by which she bears witness to and cares for her grandmother's body: "I removed the sheets and blankets from her bed and peeled off her thick flannel nightgown. I toweled her puzzled face, stretching out the wrinkles, removing the coils of her neck, toweled her shoulders and breasts. Then I changed the water. I returned to towel the creases of her stretch-marked stomach, her sporadic vaginal hairs, and her sagging thighs. I removed the lint from between her toes and noticed a mapped birthmark on the fold of her buttock. The scars on her back . . .

made me realize how little I really knew of Abuelita" (Viramontes, *Moths* 31). This process of removing her grandmother's clothing in order to methodically cleanse the various parts of her body becomes ritual through intentional reflection upon each moment.‡ That reflection is revealed as the girl reads her abuela's body; for example, she does not only towel her grandmother's face, but reads that face as "puzzled." Further, she attentively turns to the hidden places of the body—the coils of the neck, the creases of the stomach, and the spaces between the toes. In this attentiveness, she notices the secrets this body holds: the birthmark on abuela's buttock that "maps" her birth, the stretch-marked stomach that speaks of childbearing, the vaginal hairs that have become sporadic, marking the passage of time. In the narrator's act of cleansing her grandmother's body, she becomes witness to the narrative arc of her grandmother's life: its beginning (birthmark), its middle (stretch marks), and its gradual move toward an end (only sporadic vaginal hairs).

Gloria Anzaldúa reflects on the mapping of bodies as territory and text, situating the body as a site that is written upon and, to some extent, can be read. She writes: "Our bodies are geographies of selves made up of diverse, bordering, and overlapping 'countries'. . . . Like a map with colored web lines of rivers, highways, lakes, towns, and other landscape features en donde pasan y cruzan las cosas, we are 'marked'. . . . Life's whip makes welts and thin silver scars on our backs" ("Geographies" 69). Reading this statement next to Viramontes's scene of ritual cleansing, it becomes clear that the scene is also one of ritual witness to her grandmother's life. Her wrinkled skin, sagging thighs, and the folds of her buttocks draw "highways" of lines between the "rivers" and "towns" of her existence. The body as landscape tells a story about *las cosas que han pasado y cruzado*—a story marking temporalities and geographies that in their passing have left an imprint. As Saldívar-Hull observes, "The old woman's body maps new cartographies for the young Chicana narrator" who is witness to that body (136). The witnessed body in this story is a source of knowledge as well as mystery, a text only partially revealed, suggesting realities while holding secrets back. For the girl, the scars on her abuela's back indicate a life larger and more complex than previously imagined, causing her to reflect on her grandmother's life beyond known parameters. What were the truths hidden in those scars? Or, to draw on Anzaldúa's words, what had "life's whip" meant for her? What silent

---

‡Barbara J. McClure discusses intentionality as central to ritual: "Rituals differ from routines in that they embody a kind of intentionality. Rituals are about intentional reflection on the moment" (738).

sufferings was her body carrying, from other times and places, through to her last breath? What were the words never spoken that sought to make themselves legible on her body as text?

By engaging in the struggle to assign meaning to her grandmother's body, Viramontes's narrator wrestles with the meanings and possibilities of her own subjectivity, as the act of reading the body makes her part of its story. She also acknowledges that her abuela possessed in life what sociologist Meredith B. McGuire terms a "'lived' body": "The 'lived' body is our vehicle for perceiving and interpreting our world. As material reality, human bodies also vividly experience the material conditions of social existence. Society inscribes itself upon the concrete bodies of its members" ("Religion and the Body" 284). Through her caring engagement with her grandmother's body, the girl not only bears witness to the marks of her lived experience but also engages in an "embodied practice" linking her spiritually to her grandmother. McGuire soundly argues that "embodied practices . . . link our materiality as humans and our spirituality" ("Why Bodies Matter" 15), strengthening "our sense of connection with our spiritual community" (3). Indeed, Viramontes describes the girl's grandmother as her central source of spiritual community, who wordlessly made her feel "safe and guarded and not alone" (*Moths* 28). Furthermore, embodied care for and witness to her grandmother's body, comprehended as a reflective process of action and reciprocity, links her not only to the spiritual community of her grandmother but to a larger historical community of women.

To Dream the Craft of a New Compass: Ritually Restructuring Space and Time

"The Moths" not only emphasizes the importance of bearing witness to the lived body, but further emphasizes the ritual use of our bodies to enact a transformative consciousness that makes us more aware of our ancestral interconnectivity. An intrinsic link is drawn between a spiritual labor that necessarily invokes community and the feminist project of generating transformative selfknowledge. More specifically, that link makes possible a historical consciousness that empowers the self to transform the future. In her work on rituals and embodiment, Jaita Talukdar asserts, "Women's bodies are not merely loci of frustrations with circumscribed lives but also tools with which women circumvent or subvert forces of subordination into meaningful engagements with the self" (142). Such subversion is revealed in the story as the girl proceeds with the ritual cleansing, carrying her grandmother's lifeless body to the bathtub; for as she engages in that labor, she engages with her own embodied perceptions of space and time: "She was not as heavy as I thought and when I carried her in my arms, her body fell into a V. And yet my legs were tired, shaky, and I felt as if the distance between the bedroom and bathroom was miles and years away" (Viramontes, *Moths* 31). The visual imagery of the elderly woman's body hanging in the shaky arms of the fourteen-year-old girl complements the temporal and spatial disorientation implied when the bathroom is described as seeming "miles and years away." This disorientation speaks not just to the difficulty of carrying the body, which the girl asserts is not as heavy as she supposed, but also to the way in which this active, embodied ritual of compassion literally transforms her sense of the world. The short distance she must travel becomes both physically and temporally far.

This altered sense of spatiality and temporality, experienced through embodied ritual work, incites an alteration of consciousness, an opening up of new epistemological possibilities regarding the perception of existence. As McGuire writes, "Our material bodies come to be linked with spirituality through social senses and through the ritual restructuring of our sense of space and time" ("Why Bodies Matter" 15). Because embodied ritual alters our spatial and temporal experience, it allows an increased ability to perceive our bodies and their connections to others in new ways, as well as to perceive spiritual interconnectivity. In this story, "ritual restructuring" of the girl's sense of space and time permits the further development of a feminist epistemology and ontology. As Jean Franco argues, this story "evokes a womantime that precedes clocktime," for "it is through the maternal line that [the women in *The Moths*] encounter not only the lost place but the lost past" and achieve "the recovery of ancestral memory" (xviii). I would apply this concept of "womantime" to this scene in particular, as it describes an experience of embodied consciousness that transcends the limitations of the current moment, making us aware that we are linked to others in our maternal line across a spectrum of time and place. Carrying her grandmother's body across the room and into the bath, the protagonist transports herself across temporal and spatial boundaries of consciousness, manifesting the inherited knowledge that we are connected to one another even beyond death. Indeed, this knowledge is the recovered ancestral memory the story evokes. Remarkably, such recovery requires an unhinging and disorientation of accepted norms of time and space, for it is through temporal and spatial disorientation that the world can be restructured and reimagined. Entering into such consciousness becomes a sacred crossing, the kind that M. Jacqui Alexander theorizes as "that imaginary from which we dream the craft of a new compass" (8). For when we reconceive the positionality of our existence and the nature of our relations, new paths and directions open up. We might imagine the "new compass" of possibilities engendered as the girl picks up her grandmother's body and puts down the felt sense of being fundamentally alone in the world.

At the story's end, the girl recalls gently, slowly entering a tub of hot water with her abuela's body, using careful movements to keep from burning her grandmother's skin (Viramontes, *Moths* 32). Though her abuela has passed, the girl's protective caution and loving speech acknowledge her as still precious and deserving of care: "There, there, Abuelita, I said, cradling her, smoothing her as we descended, I heard you" (32). Whereas earlier in the story it is Mama Luna's house that is cradled by chayote vines, marking her home as a space of protection (28–29), now the girl, cradling her grandmother's body, becomes her own source of nurturing and protection. In her assurances to her abuelita that she has been heard even when she cannot speak, the girl recognizes an essential need that she herself shares; and indeed that mutuality is emphasized as they descend into the water together. This scene, marked by physical and emotional acknowledgment, speaks to the crossing from one world and its attendant epistemologies into a new one, as symbolized by the waters of the tub, which suggest rebirth via the process of ritual. This interpretation is further reinforced when the narrator explains her longing to "return to the waters of the womb with her [grandmother]" (32). That desire for a shared rebirth is also marked by the release and expression of suffering and anguish, represented in two ways: (1) through the gray moths suddenly released from the grandmother's soul, exiting through her mouth and "fluttering to light"; and (2) through the tears the girl cries, forming "circles and circles of sadness and relief" (32).

Firstly, the narrator interprets the moths exiting her grandmother's mouth and ascending toward the light as moths that "lay within the soul and slowly eat the spirit up" (Viramontes, *Moths* 32). This interpretive knowledge, indicated as having been passed on from her abuela (32), is not based on rational epistemology but rather asserts the "heightened consciousness or awareness" that Gloria Anzaldúa described as conocimiento ("Flights" 40). For this last phase of ritual cleansing in waters figurative of the womb is marked by an expunging of shared trauma from the spirit and body of both characters; the moths, released from her grandmother's soul through her mouth, reflect the embodied relationship to spirit. In her analysis, Saldívar-Hull describes this final image as a "feminist counter-Pietà" for its depiction of a subversive consciousness and its suggestion of "alternative possibilities for Chicanas" (137–38). I would add that when we read this story today, a reclaimed spirituality functions as an important part of that subversive consciousness for all that it signifies regarding the potential power of acknowledged ontological and epistemological interconnectivity.

Just as moths fluttering to light are expressive of released suffering, so are the circles in the water created by the girl's tears. Here the circles, a common motif in Viramontes's writing, refer not only to the "sadness and relief" of the narrator but also to a larger historical trajectory of patriarchal and colonial domination. The seemingly unending circles, indicated by the repetition in her expression of "circles and circles," reflect the cyclical violence in which her own suffering is situated alongside that of her mother and grandmother. Thus this cleansing ritual deeply recognizes redemption and liberation as being linked to an acknowledgment of shared suffering, while previously in the story her suffering isolates her from others. For example, when earlier in the narrative she encounters her mother crying over the abuela's impending death, she looks into her mother's eyes, which are "filled with sorrow," but can feel only her own anger at the domestic conflicts caused by her father's patriarchal domination and at her mother's perceived complicity (Viramontes, *Moths* 30). Unable to physically or emotionally comfort her mother, she isolates them both, leaving to sit and ask herself with "words like rosary prayers: when do you stop giving when do you start giving when do you. . . ." (30; ellipsis in original). This prayerlike inquiry into the nature of giving denotes her own hesitancy to fully give, based on the hurt she has experienced. Yet, through her intensely embodied engagement with her abuela's death and her efforts to honor her in that death through a ritualized cleansing, she engages with her own emotions in a way that allows her to give fully and without hesitation. The deep sadness that she feels for her abuela allows her to open herself up to her personal sorrow as well as that of her mother; this opening of the self is its own kind of relief and rebirth, denoted by the bath's womb-like waters.

The narrator's desire for sustained spiritual connection is clear as she reflects, "Dying is lonely and I wanted to go to where the moths were, stay with her" (Viramontes, *Moths* 32). Here, dying is lonely for the person who passes as well as the loved one left "alone." In their mutual descent into the water, a crossing of sorts, the girl becomes more deeply conscious of the ways in which her spirit is connected to her grandmother's as well as her mother's: "I wanted. I wanted my Amá. . . . The bathroom was filled with moths, and for the first time in a long time I cried, rocking us, crying for her, for me, for Amá. . . . There, there, I said to Abuelita, rocking us gently, there, there" (32). When the narrator rocks "us," readers can interpret the line in at least two ways: (1) that as her own body supports that of her grandmother, she rocks both bodies together, appropriating the maternal role, even as she longs for her own mother ("Amá"); and/or (2) that alongside the physical accompaniment she provides for her abuela, there is another interior, psychic sense in which the narrator realizes that her grandmother and her mother dwell entwined within her own self, so that "rocking us" refers to those generations of women within her body. This new awareness is, as Jean Franco asserts, a "knowledge that has been passed on from one generation to another, not through words but through touch" (xviii). Indeed, the protagonist's learning in this narrative is seldom transmitted verbally; more often it is transmitted through sensory engagement. In referring back to McClure's concept of ritual, the girl develops "an awareness of the divine" in ordinary life, for as she rocks together with her grandmother, she becomes aware of her "ontological inter-relatedness," developing a sense of herself as part of a larger historical narrative including her mother and grandmother and all women who have suffered (McClure 735–36).

Finally, it must be reiterated that the awareness this character achieves is at once painful and healing. Similarly, in her poem "i write," Elvira Prieto asserts, "i write because it hurts / to carry generations of suffering / in my skin" (7). Just as these words signal that the speaker's body and psyche painfully inherit the ongoing consequences of structural and social violence, Viramontes's protagonist comes to understand that her lived, embodied experience is part of a larger intergenerational story of suffering. Yet we are reminded that the ancestral memory that we carry in our bodies can also be a precious source of knowledge, for as she steps into awareness of her interconnectivity, she is released from the isolation that stunted her emotions and separated her from others. Through the spiritual work she undertakes, first in creative collaboration with her abuela, then as caretaker, and finally as priestess, she discovers her own authority—a highly developed subjectivity—to be a powerful force of witness and action in her own life as well as the lives of others. Through embodied ritual in alternative sacred spaces, she enacts a process of reciprocation, learning how to give of herself based on the acknowledgment of herself as loved. Chickasaw writer Linda

Hogan expresses, "Suddenly all my ancestors are behind me. Be still, they say. Watch and listen. You are the result of the love of thousands" (*Dwellings* 159). For the protagonist of "The Moths," it is the performance and creation of ritual that enables her to become aware of and responsive to the continued presence of the ancestors who stand behind her. Through this increased awareness that she is powerfully connected to others across space and time, she comes to know herself as both loving and loved, permitting the possibility of a new relationship with her mother. For to acknowledge and honor our ancestors' lives as inscribed within us makes a deep well of information accessible so that we might chart our own maps.

Conclusion: Reshaping Our Realities with Body, Spirit, Knowledge

In the introduction to *Rebozos de Palabras: An Helena María Viramontes Critical Reader* (2013), the book's editor Gabriella Gutiérrez y Muhs asserts that "a major void in the scholarship on Viramontes's creative writing still exists" despite the importance of her impact "in the area of the inscribed female body and subjectivity" (2). I hope the present examination might lessen that void by revisiting one of Viramontes's early works, "The Moths," and demonstrating the value it continues to hold for evolving scholarship regarding Chicana feminist thought. More broadly, I also intend this work as a complement to the growing body of scholarship regarding the link between spirituality and epistemology in Chicanx life and creative works. Thus I emphasize the critical contribution of such themes to the development of a transformative social consciousness. It is awareness of ontological interrelatedness in everyday life that signifies a conocimiento strong enough to transform the cyclical violence of patriarchy that isolates and divides not only women but society in general. This conocimiento, or spiritual awareness, is an embodied knowledge that links us to generations past, present, and future, with the potential to radically reshape our realities. For, as Suzanne J. Crawford writes, ritual can enable us to "re-create the world, re-create the self, re-create the body" (29). What I have thus tried to illustrate in my reading of Viramontes's work is that the link between body, spirit, and knowledge, as expressed through ritual, can signal a profoundly liberating politics with which to counter the generational trauma of patriarchy. As I turn to the next chapter, I expand the consideration of death, loss, migration of the spirit, and the disorientation of space and time addressed in this chapter; however, I more specifically attend to narrative depictions of the embodied experience of grief in the absence of a loved one. Further, as I transition to a focus on fables, I consider how encounters with the elements of nature provide space for the renegotiation and re-creation of the fragmented self, transcending Western binaries of life and death.

3

The Grieving Body

Radical Reorientation

Dressed in a huipil ornate with color, with a row of red flowers braided into her hair, Sandra Cisneros leans in to embrace fellow legendary writer Rudolfo Anaya, their smiles beaming into the camera. He is dressed in a suit coat, suspenders, and turquoise bolo tie, seated in a wheelchair, cane in hand. It is an affectionate pose, photographed on September 22, 2016, the day both were honored for their life's work, Cisneros receiving the National Medal of Arts and Anaya the National Humanities Medal. It is striking to see these two literary giants side by side and to imagine what their conversation might have been. Anaya is best known for his novel *Bless Me, Ultima* (1972) and Cisneros for her series of vignettes *The House on Mango Street* (1984), both staples in high-school and college classrooms as well as landmarks of Chicanx literature. Yet it is their more recent, lesser-known works that bring into view another layer of connection between these revered figures. Cisneros's 2012 short narrative *Have You Seen Marie?*, illustrated by Chicana artist Ester Hernández, and Anaya's 2013 novella *The Old Man's Love Story* both fuse autobiographical experiences of losing a loved one with fable, articulating an embodied shift in perceptive consciousness that can emerge from grief.

As with Helena María Viramontes's "The Moths," discussed in the previous chapter, these two short narratives may not seem on their surface to engage with the politics of social transformation commonly associated with Chicanx literature. However, these narratives model a consciousness that counters and contests the imperialism of Western ideological lenses. The epistemological and ontological disorientation that their protagonists experience initiates a process of inquiry about what it means to be in the world, as filtered through radically altered modes of perceiving and understanding. I read these two stories alongside one another for what they convey about the relationship between grief, spiritual knowledge, and embodiment, as well as for the resistant consciousness that they model for readers. As I argue, *The Old Man's Love Story* and *Have You Seen Marie?* depict grief as an experiential process through which embodied sensory perception of space and time is transformed and the individual is reconstituted in relationship to the natural, social, and spiritual worlds they navigate. For these protagonists in mourning must reorient themselves not only toward other people, but also toward their environments and the cosmos at large. In this sense, the narratives reflect on mourning as an act of stepping into a larger sacred story, the discernment of which is processed through embodied perceptions. I read these works as offering a unique perspective on, and approach to, broader human experience; rather than generalizing the particularities of grief, I am interested in how these two particular writers conceive of and express loss in ways that readers can learn from.

Each of these texts combines a fable-like narrative, lyrical prose, and characters strongly reflective of the authors themselves. I use the term *fable* to describe these stories because they each demonstrate lessons for the living and depict human protagonists interacting with forces of nature and spirit that possess their own agency. The natural elements, such as wind and water, take on particular significance in these works, animating a timeless force or presence that overpowers the individual lives of humans while unifying existence across temporal and spatial planes. Anaya's story of a nameless "old man" struggling with the loss of his wife (referred to only as "she") is told by an omniscient narrator and structured as a novella composed of twenty-seven brief chapters; here the living and the dead continue to converse, as the woman's disembodied spirit remains in constant dialogue with her husband. Meanwhile Cisneros's text is a collaboration with visual artist Ester Hernández, whose illustrations co-create a layered story told in the first person, in which an unnamed woman in the midst of mourning her mother emerges from her home to help look for a friend's lost cat; as the missing cat becomes increasingly indicative of the missing body of her loved one as well as her own sense of self, a maternal voice ultimately speaks to her through the river, wind, and stars. In reading these works in relation to one another, this chapter reflects on the ability of storytelling to express the inexplicable and, in so doing, transmit a sacred knowledge about grief as a human experience both transcendent and embodied.

Conceiving of and Giving Shape to Grief

In his 1917 essay "Trauer und Melancholie," translated as "Mourning and Melancholia," Sigmund Freud defines mourning as "the reaction to the loss of a loved person, or to the loss of some abstraction which has taken the place of one, such as one's country, liberty, an idea, and so on" (243). In the translation edited by James Strachey, Strachey's initial footnote specifies that "'Trauer,' like the English 'mourning,' can mean both the affect of grief and its outward manifestation" (243). Freud describes mourning as a condition separate from melancholia, though he argues that each presents the same "profoundly painful dejection, cessation of interest in the outside world, loss of the capacity to love, [and] inhibition of all activity" (244). For Freud, melancholia is discernible by the additional symptom of "the disturbance of self-regard" (244). Skeptical of clear-cut categorizations and characterizations, I am centrally concerned with his definition of mourning as a temporary state characterized by only the most profound responses to loss. Freud asserts: "Although mourning involves grave departures from the normal attitude to life, it never occurs to us to regard it as a pathological condition and to refer it to medical treatment. We rely on its being overcome after a certain lapse of time" (243–44). Here Freud suggests that mourning, unlike melancholia, is saved from a pathological diagnosis by being perceived as a temporary state that will naturally pass "after a certain lapse of time." This of course begs the question of whether the mourner can ever really return to the state of being that they inhabited prior to the loss. In an interview, Sandra Cisneros directly expresses such a sentiment, stating: "I truly believe you cannot overcome grief. You pass through it and it will always accompany you" (Terrero). In other words, even *if* the most profound elements of grief do dissipate, it might be truer to say that rather than overcoming grief, the mourner is transformed by it. Further, we might ask, When and if such a transformation takes place, might it impart some form of valuable knowledge?

Scholars such as Kathleen Woodward, Sara Ahmed, and Laura E. Tanner have taken up such questions in their work, engaging with and critiquing Freud's theory. In *Aging and Its Discontents: Freud and Other Fictions* (1991), Woodward expresses a central problem when she writes, "In 'Mourning and

Melancholia' Freud leaves us no theoretical room for another place, one between a crippling melancholia and the end of mourning. But some people come to terms with their grief by learning to live with their pain and in such a way that they are still *in* mourning but no longer *exclusively* devoted to mourning" (116). In other words, acknowledging a middle space between mourning and melancholia would more accurately account for the ways in which many people actually experience the loss of a loved one over time (125). Moreover, Woodward critiques not only Freud's theory but also, more broadly, theoretical discussions of mourning that do not effectively "combine the affective dimensions of the experience of mourning with theoretical descriptions of mourning as a process" (112). Thus, building a more satisfying theory of mourning would necessitate accounting for its processual nature while also taking seriously the various gradations and inflections of its felt emotions.

In *The Cultural Politics of Emotion* (2014), Sara Ahmed offers just such a theoretical discussion, productively highlighting the relationship between grief, affect, and process. Like Woodward, Ahmed critiques Freud's "Mourning and Melancholia," explaining, "The central assumption behind Freud's distinction is that it is good or healthy to 'let go' of the lost object (to 'let go' of that which is already 'gone')" (159). Ahmed problematizes the meanings of letting go by calling into question the degree to which the lost object (i.e., a loved one) is actually gone: "For the object to be lost, *it must already have existed within the subject.* . . . We can also think of this 'insideness' as an effect of the 'withness' of intimacy, which involves the process of being affected by others. . . . Each of us, in being shaped by others, carries with us 'impressions' of those others" (160). Thus, for Ahmed, grieving is not so much about letting go of what is gone as it is about preserving the impressions that we have already internalized and integrated, or, as she states, "keep[ing] one's impressions alive, as aspects of one's self that are both oneself and more than oneself, as a sign of one's debt to others" (160). I would suggest that such concepts of integration and indebtedness contradict the discourse of individualism (which is often precipitated by capitalism) and perhaps enable us to begin thinking about the relationship between spiritual interconnectedness and grief; for to recognize that the aspects that make up the self are also *more than oneself* is a critical step toward a spiritual worldview and a sense of being in the world.

Ahmed pushes her readers to consider that the impressions one carries are multidimensional: "Such impressions are certainly memories of this or that other, to which we return in the sticky metonymy of our thoughts and dreams, and through prompting either by conversations with others or through the visual form of photographs. Such 'withness' also shapes our bodies, our gestures, our turns of phrase" (160). As this chapter's analysis will discuss, the memories that we immerse ourselves in psychically are indeed only one element of the impressions that are marked upon us. In conjunction with the psychic imprints we carry, our expressive tendencies are also marked by our physical relationships, intimacies, and experiences with those we have loved, and, importantly, the body itself carries deep imprints of the lost loved one; these imprints, even as they may transform and undergo change, continue to be part of one who mourns, making Freud's injunction to let go of the lost object not completely possible. Yet there is another aspect to be considered, which is that if the self, including the body, is imprinted upon by the loved one, then the loss of that loved one can send the mourner's body as well as their psyche into trauma.

In *Lost Bodies: Inhabiting the Borders of Life and Death* (2006), Laura E. Tanner moves toward a critical inquiry of the body in grief, critiquing not only the "cultural injunction to move through grief" seen in Freud's theory but also "the tendency to define bereavement and its consolations in symbolic terms that obscure the bodily dimensions of loss" (13). Thus Tanner emphasizes the importance of acknowledging that even as the lost loved one remains, in the sense that the myriad impressions of them are kept alive, the loss of their physical body creates significant consequences for the griever; yet these physical aspects are rarely spoken or written about. Tanner draws from her own personal experience of grief when she writes, "Nothing that I read or knew before my father's death prepared me for this, most obvious of losses: the irretrievable sensation, the missing touch, the absent body that I sense but cannot locate, feel but cannot feel" (*Lost Bodies* 83). As she expresses here, despite the obvious fact of the body's absence in death, it is this physical absence that no discourse on grief had prepared her to anticipate or negotiate. Ultimately, it is a seeking of the absent body that Rudolfo Anaya and Sandra Cisneros (in tandem with Ester Hernández) express in their respective storytelling acts, as their stories give shape to the alienation of death, the sensory experiences of grief, and the irretrievability of the body. And it should be noted that literary narrative is a particularly fitting vehicle for these subjects. For whereas Tanner finds theories of mourning largely silent on the bodily loss experienced in grief, she remarks that "literary representations of grief render the corporeal experience of loss with surprising frequency" (*Lost Bodies* 83). I would add that literature has a particular capability to express dimensions often considered ineffable; thus the overarching framework of this book points toward literature's engagement with the spiritual, and in this chapter I more specifically focus on the articulation of the often-inexpressible experiences of grief.

In his 2014 collection of poems entitled *The Day of Shelly's Death: The Poetry and Ethnography of Grief*, Renato Rosaldo utilizes poetry to write about the traumatic and sudden loss of Michelle Zimbalist Rosaldo, who was his wife and a fellow anthropologist. As a poet and an ethnographer, he reflects on the particular capability of poetry to give shape to the confounding experience of grief: "Poetry has proven compelling for me because it allows me to dwell in powerful experiences and perceptions. It enables me to render these feelings intelligible, vivid, and present. In lyric moments, I seek the larger significance in these telling details. My task, however, is not to give clarity to feelings that are in fact unclear. . . . My task, as a poet, is to render intelligible what is complex and to bring home to the reader the uneven and contradictory shape of that moment" (Rosaldo 107). In his collection Rosaldo includes poems that relive, from various speakers' perspectives, the events surrounding his wife's tragic fall from a cliff in the Philippines while doing fieldwork. He frequently inserts small, seemingly unremarkable details that evoke a larger feeling not fully describable, such as the color of the pants and shirt he chose to dress her body in after it had been washed—"brown pants, / pale green shirt"—or the items he packed for his children, who were not yet aware of their mother's death: "diapers a toy truck pajamas / *Tintin in America*" (68). These details do not express a precise emotion or idea so much as conjure a moment, a memory, too unwieldy to be fully articulated.

Although the two works I focus on in this chapter are written as narrative prose rather than poetry, I argue that they are studded with what Rosaldo calls "lyric moments"; for Cisneros and Anaya use an often pared-down poetic language to "dwell in" experiences and perceptions of grief, and to vividly evoke and "render intelligible" meanings that might otherwise remain inexplicable. In other words, without trying to name or describe the experience of grief in its totality, they place a gentle frame around it, allowing the complex and vast "unevenness" that Rosaldo describes to become imaginable and thus take shape in the reader's mind. Through their own lyric moments, they each seek to communicate a larger significance that, while not fully comprehensible, can in some small way become momentarily and partially inhabitable.

In *Raising the Dead: Readings of Death and (Black) Subjectivity* (2000), Sharon Patricia Holland highlights writers and artists who engage with the subject of death and the questions surrounding it, and speaks of the importance of critics entering those discourses as well: "Because . . . societal fears [about death] are pervasive, discussions of death, and notions of the dead, have the potential to dissolve barriers between communities. Speaking about death and the dead necessitates that critics move beyond familiar country and into liminal spaces" (149). These liminal spaces, however partially inhabitable, offer the potential for a radical recognition of alternative ways of being and knowing. Specifically, as Holland points out, "embracing the subjectivity of death allows marginalized peoples to speak about the unspoken—to name the places *within* and *without* their cultural milieu where . . . they have slipped between the cracks of language" (4–5). Marginalized by death, the women-spirits in *The Old Man's Love Story* and *Have You Seen Marie?* find ways to "speak" to the living: while the old man's wife in Anaya's story speaks to him directly in a disembodied yet present voice, the departed mother in Cisneros's work speaks through the elements of nature. Both of these spirits offer their loved ones connection and knowledge from the other side, from somewhere within those "cracks of language" that Holland references, as well as from the cracks of permissible knowledge.

This potentiality to utter that which has been lost to language suggests the reclamation of displaced cultural epistemologies. Chickasaw writer Linda Hogan describes the artistic pursuit of expressing the *mystery* that overwhelms "a language of commerce and trade" that is too "limited, emotionally and spiritually" to fully describe the world's complexity (*Dwellings* 45–46). Rather than resigning herself to a silence imposed by an imperious language and culture, she asserts another way: "So we make our own songs to contain these things, make ceremonies and poems, searching for a new way to speak, to say we want a new way to live in the world" (46). Indeed, just as Renato Rosaldo's poems seek a new way to give form to the uneven contours of grief, the two narratives examined in this chapter emerge from the desire to articulate a transformational experience of grief that demands a shift in consciousness. Such utterances and reclamation of knowledge, as well as the insistence on new ways of knowing, can transform how readers themselves move in the world.

"I Wish Somebody Had Told Me. . . ."

In each of their narratives, Anaya and Cisneros centrally integrate something that might be thought of as the supernatural or mythic, but which they each refer to simply as "spirit." In the afterword to *Have You Seen Marie?*, Cisneros describes this as the "something" that exists "there . . . beyond our lives," which she recognizes as "love" (*Have You Seen Marie?* 94). Similarly, in the preface to his own book, Anaya emphasizes a love that "never ends" and frames his novella as "conversations with the departed" who continue to guide and shelter the living (*Love Story* vii). Indeed, both texts describe the attempt to seek out and even speak with the dead, as well as to describe the knowledge found in this quest. Reflecting on her own mother's passing as the inspiration for her story, Cisneros writes: "I wish somebody had told me love does not die, that we can continue to receive and give love after death. This news is so astonishing to me even now, I wonder why it isn't flashed across the bottom of the television screen on CNN" (*Have You Seen Marie?* 91). This astonishment about the possibilities of an ongoing relationality and reciprocity between the living and the departed suggests the discovery of a repressed or unspoken knowledge; more specifically, the reference to CNN reflects a public discourse that fails to disseminate such knowledge. Though the news network is not in the business of articulating spiritual epistemologies, Cisneros's assertion makes it clear that she deems such knowledge essential to living and being.

Ultimately, what she offers might be thought of as a counterknowledge that challenges dominant perspectives on grief and the process of mourning. She writes, "I wish somebody had told me . . . that death allows you the chance to experience the world soulfully, that the heart is open like the aperture of a camera, taking in everything, painful as well as joyous, sensitive as a skin of water" (Cisneros, *Have You Seen Marie?* 90). Here the author shifts away from conceiving of mourning as disinterest, detachment, or a form of shutting down; rather, she describes it as a form of opening up, becoming more vulnerable and sensitive—in other words, more perceptive. In an interview about the book, she also emphasizes the relationship she experienced between this increased perceptiveness and the potential for spiritual, creative growth: "During grief your heart is broken open and you become open to light, intuition, creativity and beauty. . . . And you should create, because it's a way to transform that darkness into light. . . . Otherwise you become stuck and deprive yourself of an opportunity to grow spiritually" (Terrero). Here Cisneros does not deny the pain and darkness of grief, but she also suggests that such sensitivity, if utilized well, can be a conduit for transformation, altering the ways in which we perceive and experience the world.

I find Jane Bennett's concept of enchantment useful for interpreting these ideas, as it emphasizes the kind of astonishment and sudden openness that

Cisneros describes. Bennett writes, "To be enchanted is to be struck and shaken by the extraordinary that lives amid the familiar and the everyday" (4). She adds further that "the overall effect of enchantment is a mood of fullness, plenitude, or liveliness, a sense of having one's nerves or circulation or concentration powers tuned up or recharged" (5). Taking into account the painfulness of mourning a loved one, it is also fair to venture that moments of enchantment are possible alongside that pain. For as Cisneros describes the opening of her heart during grief "like the aperture of a camera," she suggests the kind of plenitude that Bennett describes as the state of being "tuned up." Further, Cisneros's phrase "sensitive as a skin of water" is key to what Bennett argues about enchantment, particularly Bennett's description of the disenchantment symptomatic of modernity. Bennett writes: "The depiction of nature and culture as orders no longer capable of inspiring deep attachment inflects the self as a creature of loss and thus discourages discernment of the marvelous vitality of bodies human and nonhuman, natural and artifactual" (4). As this chapter's analysis of *Have You Seen Marie?* will show, the narrative expresses mourning as an experience through which one may attain (or regain) discernment, moving from being the "creature of loss" that Bennett describes to inhabiting a highly receptive and perceptive state in which one can be astonished by the "vitality of bodies," whether one's own or those found in the social and natural worlds. I would argue that to inhabit such a state of sensitivity and openness models a resistant mode of consciousness that moves toward a decolonization of knowing and being.

While Anaya's narrative predominantly emphasizes the experience of disorientation in mourning, it equally represents the process of seeking discernment that ultimately guides the lessons of both authors' texts. In his preface and acknowledgments, Anaya emphasizes his protagonist's "spiritual quest" as an epistemological search, explaining, "There are so many questions about life and death that the old man needs to answer," such as death's finitude, the existence of an afterlife, and what it means to find renewed purpose (*Love Story* vii). Significantly, however, Anaya emphasizes that his narrative is not about a man navigating these questions alone, but rather a man guided by the continuing relationship he holds with his loved one, even after her death: "These stories are only a small part of the daily conversations the old man has with his wife. After the loss of a loved one, we realize that conversations with the departed never end. Love never ends" (vii). As previously referenced, this is strikingly similar to Cisneros's evaluation in her afterword that "we can continue to receive and give love after death" (*Have You Seen Marie?* 91). This mode of consciousness resists the common ideological presumption in the West that reciprocal relationships can exist only between the living. Such reciprocity is further evidenced when Anaya speaks from his personal experience of mourning: "My wife's spirit has been constant, guiding and sheltering me. I pray daily to my ancestors who watch over me—so many guardian angels" (*Love Story* vii). Like Anaya himself, the old man in his narrative maintains a relationship with his wife's spirit even as he struggles with the absence of her material, embodied presence and the need for human touch.

Indeed, the "old man" of the narrative, who is also a writer, seems in many ways indicative of Anaya himself. The first lines of *The Old Man's Love Story* suggest this connection even as they reveal the fable-like nature of the book: "There was an old man who dwelt in the land of New Mexico, and he lost his wife. She died in his arms one night" (3). Readers familiar with Anaya's work will immediately suspect that this old man in New Mexico could be reflective of Anaya himself, for his writing is heavily linked to the region, and as the narrative progresses it becomes clear that Anaya's own life shares bountiful similarities with that of the protagonist. Yet leaving the old man nameless suggests a story larger than that of any one particular person. While Anaya might have written a formal memoir, he instead chose a strategy that highlights a common struggle against grief, loneliness, and old age, imparting the old man's lessons to his readers: namely, that despite the visceral painfulness of grief, our spiritual relationship to those we love does not have to end, even as we must continue to negotiate material needs and experiences.

While Anaya's story is told in the third person, Cisneros's narrative directly embraces the first person and is accompanied by illustrations portraying a character with a clear likeness to Cisneros. Those illustrations, drawn by Chicana visual artist Ester Hernández, who Cisneros explains had recently lost her own mother (*Have You Seen Marie?* 92), might tempt readers to strictly align the "I" of the narrative with Cisneros herself. However, as is the case with Anaya's text, the copyright page of *Have You Seen Marie?* asserts that the work is one of fiction, with "any resemblance to actual persons, living or dead, events, or locales" stated as "entirely coincidental." This emphasis on the narrative as representational rather than strictly autobiographical is reinforced by the book jacket, which describes the story as "a lyrically told, richly illustrated fable for grown-ups about a woman's search for a cat who goes missing in the wake of her mother's death." Thus, like Anaya's old man, the woman in this story both is and is not Cisneros herself.

Both tales render out of the authors' personal mourning a lesson at once intensely intimate and representative of grief as an experiential process of seeking and discovery. Cisneros explains that she wrote *Have You Seen Marie?* not only as a way to work through the experience of grief personally but also as an offering for others like herself: "Some people who heard me perform it out loud thought it was for children, but I wrote it for adults, because something was needed for people like me who suddenly found themselves orphans in midlife. I wanted to be able to make something I could give those who were in mourning, something that would help them find balance again and walk toward their rebirth" (Cisneros, *Have You Seen Marie?* 91–92). Similarly, Anaya also situates his story as a form of giving to others, stating, "This book is my way of thanking family and friends whose kindness and love have sustained me these past few years" (*Love Story* vii). Ultimately their stories, which emerge from transformative personal experiences of deep loss and mourning, are rendered as an offering; as each author reflects on alternative modes of perceiving existence and what it means to live with death, they offer a model of a resistant consciousness that potentially reconnects readers to a sense of enchantment and astonishment at the world's vitality. But further, each work highlights the ways in which such consciousness is perceived through the body.

The Old Man's Love Story: Grief, Memory, and the Lost Body

The old man's quest in Anaya's text, like that of the woman in Cisneros's work, narrates an embodied process of seeking that includes, even necessitates, moving through and conversing with various realms of consciousness in a process of gradual inquiry. In both narratives, the protagonists who seek their lost dead as well as a new understanding of the "lost" self must reorient their relationship to the universe and its elements. In *The Old Man's Love Story*, this initially becomes clear as Anaya describes the death of the old man's wife in relation to the wind: "A wind swept by, and she left the earth she loved so well—inevitable. Her soul rose into a world of spirits, the realm of those departed. A universe of spirits, all the dead souls since time immemorial, a mourning wind that circled the earth" (3). This "mourning wind" that circles and encapsulates the earth signifies a human relationship to temporality and existence, for the old man's wife now belongs to "time immemorial." And yet it is not only the departed who move into an alternative temporality but, in some sense, those left behind as well. For, as Anaya writes, the old man "had entered a time of grieving, not knowing if it had an end" (5). Thus, even as his beloved has transitioned into a disembodied unity with "a world of spirits" while he has not, his sense of time has shifted as he enters a deep state of "not knowing."

In *Arranging Grief: Sacred Time and the Body in Nineteenth-Century America* (2007), Dana Luciano argues that for nineteenth-century mourners who were enveloped in narratives of modernity, progress, and linear time, "the altered flow of time experienced by the mourner" was conceived of as "a version of sacred time, the regenerative mode that transcended ordinary time in a ritual revisiting of origins" (7). Luciano specifies that when she speaks of "origins," she points not to "beginnings" but to that which "rises above linear time and can be ritually perpetuated through it but never dissolved into it" (7). If we perceive the world of memories and spirit in which mourners may ritually dwell as that which "rises above linear time," then we must consider what happens to the body in grief, which is still living in a world of ongoing material conditions. Though Luciano's argument is specifically in reference to nineteenth-century mourners, I read Anaya's old man as experiencing a similar sense of sacred time; for if nineteenth-century mourners experienced the slowed-down time of grief in contrast to the rules of linear time as defined by modernity, contemporary mourners might have a similar experience in relation to the temporal pressures of globalization. Entrance into sacred time bears important influence on the old man's embodied experience, for inhabiting a new temporality means experiencing and sensing the world in a different way. As Luciano writes, "In grief, the sensory body does not rise out of time so much as fall behind it; everything but the past fades away and yet, at the same time, remains" (20). Thus, the sacred time of mourning does not merely apply to the mental, emotional aspects of human nature but affects the body as well, particularly as the body moves through and senses the world around it. In this particular understanding of grief as a state of being "out of step" with linear time, the potentiality for alternative forms of sensory perception that can disorient and reorient consciousness comes to the fore.

From the very beginning of *The Old Man's Love Story*, we see how grief affects sensory perception, particularly in relation to the natural world. After the old man's friends and family have come and gone and the ashes of his wife are left resting in an urn on his fireplace, "the old man move[s] into a new world, a deep silence" (Anaya, *Love Story* 4). That place of silence does not indicate motionlessness; rather, it pushes him into interactions with the universe and nature, enacting a form of inquiry and seeking. Relevant here is the concept of conocimiento, which Gloria Anzaldúa defined as a "form of spiritual inquiry" that "comes from opening all your senses" ("Now Let Us Shift" 119–20); however, the old man finds that such conocimiento is at least partially blocked by the trauma or susto of his wife's death. Anzaldúa describes such trauma as *una arrebatada*: "Cada arrebatada (snatching) turns your world upside down and cracks the walls of your reality, resulting in a great sense of loss, grief, and emptiness. . . . You are no longer who you used to be. . . . You feel like an orphan, abandoned by all that's familiar. Exposed, naked, disoriented, wounded, uncertain, confused, and conflicted, you're forced to live en la orilla—a razor-sharp edge that fragments you" ("Now Let Us Shift" 125). It is in such a state of disorientation and fragmentation that the old man seeks an answer to his grief, engaging in a search that is not only internal but also external. Anaya writes: "Early one morning as the sun rose, he fed the dogs, then walked to the river. He called her name. The wind in the trees moaned, but did not answer. The river swept south, indifferent" (*Love Story* 5). The wind, like the river, seems to ignore the old man's inquiries, leaving him alone and bereft, crying like a child (5). Despite his desire to make a connection and find answers in the land around him, he cannot make sense of what he hears; the trees "moan" but do not offer a clear answer, suggesting a form of indiscernible speech coming from nature. As will be discussed later in this chapter, the protagonist in *Have You Seen Marie?* engages in similar encounters with the environment around her, calling out her inquiries and struggling to make sense of the response. This confusion is related in both texts to embodied sensory perception.

In the midst of "empty space and silence," questions emerge in the old man's consciousness, revealing disoriented sensory perceptions: "Is she lost? Or am I the lost one? Why does the wind grieve as it sways the trees? Are those my cries I hear in the night? Are those my warm tears?" (Anaya, *Love Story* 5). This alienation from his own embodied sensations, specifically the sensation of crying, is paired with alienation from a rooted orientation in the world; it is as if the sudden absence of his wife's body, in its role as a relational point of existence, has disrupted his ability to cognitively register his own embodied presence. Laura E. Tanner poses a question about grieving that usefully relates to the old man's questions: "Given that we know ourselves and others not only through but as our bodies, how is grief structured around the unfolding of two bodies once intertwined?" (*Lost Bodies* 88). The arrebatada that he feels is a state of susto, in which his soul no longer feels unified with his body, partially because in his grieving he experiences both his soul and body as interconnected with that of his lost loved one. And yet this disruption is, at least in some sense, accompanied by a heightened perception of nature and its movements; for although he is distanced from his own bodily sensations, he exhibits enough perceptive awareness to at least notice the wind's "grieving" as well as enough curiosity to question why, even if he is not yet able to discern its message.

In *Ritual: Power, Healing and Community*, Malidoma Patrice Somé discusses the concept of grief in the Dagara community of West Africa, stating, "Death, and the sudden separation around it, puts the living in a state of emotional debt, loss and disorientation. The unresolved energy produced by the death of a loved one translates itself emotionally as grief" (97). Though Somé is here referring to the ethnically specific beliefs of the Dagara community, I would suggest that the concept of the disorientation caused by grief as a consequence of the "sudden separation" of death is helpful in thinking through grief in general, and this novella in particular. Anaya's old man repeatedly emphasizes the tension between eternal bonds of love and existential separation as he struggles to understand whether there truly exists a separation between the living and the dead. For the old man, the "world of spirits" and "the world they called real" are ultimately "separated only by a thin veil" (Anaya, *Love Story* 57); yet he feels the separation imposed by that veil sharply, reflecting that death has "cut the tether of love and unity" (56) and asserting, "Her soul was torn from mine" (58). It is useful here to turn again to Somé, who conceives that "death . . . produces a kind of sudden vacuum and loss of attachment that requires grief in order to heal" (97–98). In this light, the "empty space and silence" Anaya's old man experiences with the onset of his grief can be understood as the vacuum from which disorientation and its attendant possibilities for reorientation emerge. As Anaya writes, "Grief became his journey, a new reality" (*Love Story* 6); with this, readers begin to understand that the old man's disorientation signals not merely confusion but also a potential for reconstitution.

That journey, for the old man, means trafficking with the "world of spirits," and he determines early in the narrative to "look for her in that world, communicate with her, find her" (Anaya, *Love Story* 6). His material reality becomes deeply interlocked with a spiritual one: he feels his wife's warmth next to him when he lies in bed (13) and senses her so close by that he thinks he hears her breathing the "soft rhythms of the breath of life" (15). In this case, a heightened sensory awareness is intertwined with the power of his memories. Anaya writes, "She drew near. From across the great distance that separated them, her breath touched his face. He breathed in the fragrance of that unique perfume that was exquisitely her. Blindfolded, in a room with a thousand women, he could find her. He'd had a sense of her aroma from the time they met" (39). Dwelling in these sensory experiences in which her disembodied presence is deeply felt, he calls on his embodied memories of her living body, its smells and movements.

Further, he engages in remembrance of their travels and adventures together, which occur to him in "kaleidoscopic scenes" (Anaya, *Love Story* 14). These scenes transport him not only to different times but also to a different conception of space. Anaya writes, "When they first met she had carved rooms in his heart. They were in love. She had built beautiful chambers in his heart and named them" (14). The old man spends much time recalling these seemingly endless internal spaces within him, including the Room for Making Love and the Room for Kisses, but he spends most of his time in the Room of Loneliness (13–16). These internal rooms represent the vastness of the vacuum her death has left, as he remembers: "Daily and nightly, year after year, she led him into the rooms she had built. A sense of wonder filled him when he explored the chambers of his heart. Overwhelming joy. Love was constantly a new adventure, a learning, a going deep into body and spirit" (14). Here the old man characterizes love as an active and daily process of co-learning and of making space inside oneself to hold an expansive sense of joy and wonder. It is in the space of that expansiveness that he feels the ongoing need to venture deep into *both* body and spirit. For he cannot be completely satisfied with spirit alone, and even her disembodied voice admonishes him for spending too much time in the internal room of loneliness (39), reminding him, "So much of our understanding comes from our bodies" (42).

In many ways, the story narrates a disorienting push and pull between the spirit world his wife inhabits and the earthly world that repeatedly reminds him of his still-living body and its requirements. In the midst of this disorientation, the old man questions the nature of reality, memory, and existence, and this questioning dramatically reshapes his experience of temporality as well as spatiality. Retreating into memory becomes a process of "time travel" in which "images of the past [a]re a kind of freedom" from a reality that he trusts less and less, and yet he realizes that memory itself is suspect (Anaya, *Love Story* 9). For "the real question" that he seeks to answer is, "Where is she?" (55). The old man questions *where* precisely it is that she exists, and even as he holds ongoing conversations with her throughout the narrative, he wonders, "Could one live without form? Could one live as pure spirit?" and "Does soul move into a new body?" (41–42). These questions reflect the difficulty of understanding what one's own positionality in the world might mean without the body of the loved one.

Believing he can intervene in the world of spirits in order to be with his wife more completely, the old man attempts to materialize his wife's presence through a photographic image: "He needed her to be *in* the photograph, otherwise he didn't know where she was" (Anaya, *Love Story* 67). Underlying this statement is the suggestion that his own ontological state is dependent upon locating her precise presence in the universe. Thus, ritually meditating on one of her pictures, he deprives his own body of food and drink and speaks to her: "'Hijita,' he whispered, reaching for her. The room swirled, a vortex, round and round, making him dizzy. He groaned, closed his eyes, called her name. It was working, he was going into a trance. He could see her gliding across the garden, down the hollyhock path. . . . He raised his arm to take her hand, but instead fell face down. . . . Every bone in his body hurt. The room grew hot. He knew he was passing in and out of consciousness. The vibrations increased; he felt the earth trembling" (100). Here, the dizziness and earth-trembling vibrations the old man experiences in the swirling "vortex" of the room suggest a spatial disorientation, while a reckoning with his own continuing embodiment is reinforced through the pain of his bones. It is through this painfully embodied process of seeking the dead that he is confronted with two realities: (1) his wife cannot be brought back materially even as she already resides within him, and (2) he has a body that has not yet released him to the "world of spirits" and requires the nourishment of not only food and drink, but also human connection and touch.

"Silly man," she tells him, "I was always home" (Anaya, *Love Story* 100). And yet this idea that her continuing presence is around and in him is only partially satiating, for the scene reveals an intensely embodied need to make tangible contact. Tanner writes, "If American culture touts the consolation of memory and image as an answer to loss, understanding grief as an embodied experience demands acknowledgement not just of the failure of such images to render the body present but of their sustaining contribution to the taunting rhythms of grief. The verisimilitude of an image to a body taunts the viewer by asserting presence only to disrupt the exchange of intercorporeality that defines perception; a memory can be recalled but never held, the image of a body 'seen' but never touched" (*Lost Bodies* 89). In this sense, the above scene from the narrative can be read to represent the "taunting rhythms of grief" as mediated through the visual image of the old man's wife. Her photographic image suggests a physical presence that it can never actually produce; the presence of the past, contained in the image, leads the viewer to the enticing illusion that somewhere, somehow, that body still exists as it once was. The old man's willingness to put his own body through pain and suffering in his desperate desire to experience taking her hand one more time makes it evident that memory and image alone are not only insufficient, but can be haunting. For the image of a body cannot answer the real question the old man carries, which is, "Where is she?" While he may, in one sense, understand her as being always within him, the need to know through *touch* does not dissipate.

As the old man's need to go "deep into body and spirit" cannot be fulfilled by his memory alone, he finds himself desiring a woman's physical touch. And yet he questions his ongoing desires for physical intimacy: "Once in a while the need surfaced. He didn't know if he could trust his emotions. He felt the need to be close to a woman. Was it desire? A strange yearning? Or loneliness?" (Anaya, *Love Story* 13). Though sexual biology certainly plays a role in his desire, we must also consider the relationship between touch and a strong sense of self. In *Aging and Its Discontents*, Kathleen Woodward provides helpful context for understanding this desire when she writes, "The importance of touch is that it *places* you. It is the medium of the articulation of a relationship. Touch yields two different senses—that of connection and that of separateness. It makes for a sense of oneness, as with the body of the mother or nurse, as well as for a sense of difference. One thing is sure: if we are not touched, we might begin to suspect that we are not here. . . . We have a lifelong need to be touched" (175). I would add that, relevant to Anaya's narrative, this sense of both oneness and difference is also yielded by the body of a lover. As Woodward makes clear, touch not only enables us to feel deeply interconnected with others, but also confirms to us that there *is* a distinct "self" to be touched, and which can touch others, verifying one's existence. Thus the human need for touch is driven not solely by sexual desire but also by a desire for existential affirmation and embodied orientation to the world. Indeed, after her death, the old man begins to question whether it is really she or he who is lost. This idea is mirrored by Tanner's statement that "although the loss of loved ones may not erase our memories of their embodied presence, it necessarily undoes a chiasmic structure that depends upon the balancing force of a body that pushes back against our own" (*Lost Bodies* 89). In other words, to feel the pressure and sensation of another's body confirms one's own presence and place in the world.

While we might apply phenomenological concepts regarding consciousness and objects of direct experience, the narrative situates the push and pull between bodies in a specifically cosmic context. Drawing on concepts of spatiality and the cosmic universe, the old man conceives of his lonely and aging human body as a planetary body untethered, spiraling down in space: "He read that stars and planets affected each other's gravity. Push and pull. Massive stars ten times bigger than the earth's sun curved the fabric of space-time. The body was like a planet bending time until the person went spiraling down. He was spiraling down, lost in a vast space, unable to feel the gravity of those who circulated nearby. Maybe a woman would pull him back into a steadier orbit" (Anaya, *Love Story* 103). This need for a "steadier orbit" speaks to the relationality between bodies, particularly in terms of the way in which seemingly autonomous bodies are dependent upon the invisible gravitational pull of others.

Because the body of his wife no longer exists to steady his orbit, his has become a body "spiraling down, lost in a vast space." In other words, the once seemingly familiar space of the world around him has been thrown out of balance, and although he has not died, he cannot know himself as he once was or exist as he once did; thus he speculates about whether building an embodied relation with someone new will renew his ability to place himself in the world. James Krasner, in his work on literary portrayals of embodied grief, argues, "Any theory of embodied grief . . . must situate the survivor's body in a particular place and position," for, as he explains, "our grief becomes a series of slight physical adjustments based on the fact that a body that was always here, in a certain relation to our own, is now gone" (219). Ultimately, grief is presented not solely as a spiritual, emotional, or psychological matter, but also as a deeply embodied one, for all of these states are intricately interconnected. And if the mourner must reorient themselves in the world, that reorientation must take place on each of these planes.

For the lost body of the old man's wife leaves a vacancy that cannot be replaced by memory alone; even as he communicates with his wife, even as he feels her presence close to him, she remains divided from him by a thin veil, and the ongoing need for physical touch is acknowledged. In one scene of *The Old Man's Love Story*, the old man lies in bed contemplating his loneliness and engages in conversation with his wife's disembodied presence:

> She drew close, her shadow a comforting blanket, as it had always been. She knew what was bothering him. The loneliness was wearing him down.
>
> I use Bengay on my knees. Women don't like the smell of Bengay!
> She moaned, a sorrowful sound. She felt his loneliness, but what could she do?
> "A woman's body to hold—you know?"

She knew.

There is a Room of Kisses, she said. They had shared that communion, sacred as the taking of the Eucharist.

Everyone needs kisses.

Even old men?

Yes, even old men.

Me? Yes, you. The door to the Room of Kisses is open—don't close it. (16–17)

Here the beloved who has departed into the spirit world remains a "shadow," still present, able to draw close to comfort him, able to "moan" a sorrowful sound and be heard, still able to feel her living partner's loneliness, and still possessed of the ability to "know" and to advise. Regardless of whether this conversation is interpreted as a projection of the old man's grieving subjectivity or as a literal discourse between two sentient beings (one dead and one living), what is clear is that touch is established as not only a lifelong need but a "sacred" element of life. Specifically, the word "communion" suggests a sanctifying exchange that in this case is mediated through the body.

When the old man finally acts on his desires with a woman he reconnects with at a class reunion, the results reflect the challenges the body faces in carrying out such desires, for both of them are grieving a lost partner. As they clumsily make love, memories of their former partners and the loss of those bodies create a disorienting experience: "The old man felt confused. The world had somehow slipped away. Had they been trying for a few minutes or an hour?" (Anaya, *Love Story* 122). This temporal confusion is not due to ecstasy or bliss but to the intersection of old memories and new bodies. For even as they go through the motions, she whispers her husband's name and the old man longs for his wife's body: "Her body, her scent, hips, the sweat of their bodies, her warmth and love" (121). The body memory each of them carries associates the physical act of lovemaking with the particularities of their departed partners and the remembered sensations of their unique bodies. Krasner argues that "losing a loved one means losing not just a body but also one's bodily engagements with it," and he expands: "Our bodily habits place us in the physical world, where we have lived with other bodies. We shuffle and push in bed, reach for a hand that is always just down and to the left when we sit *here*. . . . And we feel the emptiness when that body can no longer be pushed against or held—that is, when our body's posture and motion recall a similar posture and motion we adopted to interact with the lost one's body" (222). Thus it is not simply that we long for the loved one's body, but that our own bodies have gradually become adapted to, and our bodily gestures shaped by, the body that is now missing. In this sense, then, it is not simply the physical presence of the other that is missed, but rather the understanding of one's own embodied relation to it. Due to the fragmentation of this learned way of being, one's own embodied subjectivity is thrown into crisis. As is made clear by the old man's lovemaking, we feel that sense of embodied confusion and loss when we engage in movements previously choreographed around a body now absent.

Despite the clumsiness of their initial lovemaking, the old man understands their attempts as "a human need" (Anaya, *Love Story* 121) as well as a shared struggle to "engage life" (134), a struggle by the living to make new embodied memories, because "mind, like flesh, needed harmony to survive" (131). Beyond this, he comes to accept that he no longer needs to seek out the spirit world, which after all resides within him and in some sense *is* him, or to obsessively fear forgetting: "The ghosts live in the blood. . . . Our human history writ in our cells. . . . Connected to ancient memories" (140). Thus he comes to understand that all his precious memories are stories written in his blood and cells, in his consciousness and in his body, which cannot truly be forgotten, just as with the ancient memories of ancestors he carries within him. Although the old man continues to wrestle with his sadness and spends much time reflecting on and dreaming of the past, he also takes small steps toward transitioning into a new phase of life. In this sense, the novella resolves that what letting go really means is simply making room for the possibility of more memories and experiences, as well as more love.

Engagement with nature forms a key part of the protagonist's developing consciousness of the meanings of existence and grief. In particular, he perceives the changing motion of the seasons around him as instructive with regard to the cycle of moods and emotions that he experiences: "Cycles of growth and rest, life and death imprinted into every living thing on earth" (Anaya, *Love Story* 141). His trust in nature, and in its mysteries and methods, enables him to conceive of life after the passing of his wife. As he sits in his garden, sensing his wife's presence beside him, he takes close notice of the movements of the hummingbirds that skim and buzz around him, the swallows that dance above, the appearance of a nighthawk, and the gathering clouds: "'Glory be,' he said. The world is charged with the grace of God. Ineffable" (142). This overwhelming greatness that he perceives but cannot name, and of which he is a part, enables a closer engagement with his own existence in the world. As he watches the gentle colors of sunset settle over the Sandia Mountains, he reflects on their source: "The glow comes from the heart of the mountains. . . . Everything has a heart, giving off light and heat. That's love" (145). Here the light and heat of the earth's geological bodies, radiated outward, are sensed as expressions of the pulse of life, which he does not merely witness but is actively involved in. It is based on this conception of an ineffable love that is "too big to be contained," which overwhelms the soul with its expansive spirit, that he determines the importance of ongoing participation in life and love as an expression of grace (153).

At the end of *The Old Man's Love Story*, the old man balances this attempt to engage himself in the world—spending time with family and friends, inviting his "lady friend" on a trip—with the reality of his own eventual death. That reality is signaled by the fatigue he feels and the preparations he has begun to make, such as creating a will and giving items away. He does not really know to what degree he should invest in a life that he senses is coming to an end: "Had he found a purpose in life? Or was it that no matter how sick the body, it just didn't want to die? Should he bother with the garden? Why plant anything if he wasn't going to be around to taste the fruit?" (Anaya, *Love Story* 159). Here, the body is conceived as having its own volition in its stubborn push forward, even as its impermanence is felt. This conscious questioning of a rationale for his continued investment in living despite the uncertainty of his own longevity is conceived through the lens of the garden; why "plant" during this season what one may not be alive to harvest? The old man resolves that "the only way out of an existential crisis [is] to get going," which would mean caring for others— family, community, earth, and those in need—and moreover that this care must be practiced "not to receive but to give, as long as he could" (164). This resolution to care and love not in hopes of return, but rather as a necessary element of an existence in which one has already received much, offers the reader a lesson drawn from the insights of an old man. As Anaya surely draws on his own experience of grief and the existential questions that come with advancing age to tell this story, readers gain knowledge about what it means to mourn with one's body and soul, question the conditions of one's own existence, and yet still participate in the fleeting pulse of life.

Have You Seen Marie?: Relocating the Story/Self/Body

The theme of grief as journey or quest is central to both *The Old Man's Love Story* and Sandra Cisneros's *Have You Seen Marie?* However, while the old man in Anaya's story mourns a late wife, Cisneros's protagonist searches for a friend's

lost cat while in the midst of grieving over her mother's death. The mournful-
ness of the narrative is announced by its epigraph, from Elena Poniatowska's
La Flor de Lis: "Es entonces cuando te pregunto, mamá, mi madre, mi corazón,
mi madre, mi corazón, mi madre, mamá, la tristeza que siento. ¿Ésa dónde la
pongo? ¿Dónde, mamá?" The question posed by this epigraph—where do I
put the sadness that I feel?—is directed at a mother invoked in alternating
modes that express the forlornness of the speaker. This sense of an overflowing
sadness that one does not quite know where to put is introduced early on in
Cisneros's narrative when the narrator-protagonist explains, "My mother had
died a few months before. I was fifty-three years old and felt like an orphan"
(*Have You Seen Marie?* 5). Her sense of abandonment is articulated not only as
a sense of suddenly being alone in the world, but also one of being ushered into
a *new* world. Cisneros writes, "I didn't know I would feel this way. Nobody told
me" (5). This line is perhaps purposefully ambiguous in its implication—is it
that nobody told her what grief would feel like, but someone should have, or is
it that nobody *could* have appropriately described what one feels in grief? The
gently drawn pink flowers surrounding the written text seem to be carried away
by a strong gust of wind, evoking at least two sentiments. As with the great
wind in *The Old Man's Love Story*, the wind here seems to suggest unseen forces
that carry life away into a distant territory; but further, the fluttering flowers
also indicate the ungrounded state the narrator inhabits in her new identity as
a motherless fifty-three-year-old orphan.

Those flowers flutter onto the following pages, as the narrator discloses, "I'd
been hiding in my house since. Most days I didn't even comb my hair, and most
days I didn't care. The thought of talking to people made me feel woozy" (Cisneros, *Have You Seen Marie?* 6). Framing these lines is an image of the purple
banister of the narrator's house, solidifying the reference to the house as a site
of refuge from a social world that the woman has withdrawn from. While her
lack of the will to comb her hair signals the shift in (or cessation of) expected
daily rituals, the "woozy" feeling she describes is particularly significant in what
it suggests about the instability and disorientation brought on by her grief, and
the implied need for reorientation. This enclosed and isolated state of mourning
might be interpreted through the lens of what Anzaldúa described as the Coatlicue state: "periods of being lost in chaos [which] occur when you're between
'stories,' before you shift from one set of perceptions and beliefs to another, from
one mood to another" ("Now Let Us Shift" 132). Immersed in a psychic state of
grief and feeling like an orphan, the woman finds that her story of herself and

her own belonging in the world has become unrecognizable. For as Anzaldúa asserts, "Tu autohistoria is not carved in stone but drawn on sand and subject to shifting winds" ("Now Let Us Shift" 142). In this narrative, the shifting winds of her mother's death require the protagonist to relocate and reconceive what Anzaldúa refers to as the "story/self/body" ("Now Let Us Shift" 142). Such reorientation requires the protagonist to emerge from her house and spring into action.

In this case, what moves the narrator outdoors and into action is the arrival of her friend Rosalind, whose cat Marie, disturbed by the long road trip from Tacoma to San Antonio, disappears promptly upon arrival. As Marie is the ostensible object of the narrative's search, it is worthwhile to consider the cat's fuller representational meaning. In one sense, Marie's missing body stands in for the absent body of the narrator's mother, a body that is also missed and sought out. However, in another sense, the cat in this story is directly intertwined with the psychic and emotional state of the narrator, who directly compares herself to Marie as she remarks that, just like the cat who cried during the entire drive from Tacoma to San Antonio, "I felt like crying and taking off, too" (Cisneros, *Have You Seen Marie?* 5). Marie's reappearance at the story's end further emphasizes her connection to the mourning narrator: "After three days, when her heart was smooth as river stone, Marie came out from under the house where she'd been hiding, and said, 'Here I am'" (86). Just as the woman in Cisneros's story (dislocated from her own ontological position in a world without her mother) initially hides away in the safety of her house, Marie hides beneath that same house, orienting herself in a new and frighteningly strange place. Marie's announcement at the text's end—"Here I am"—is an ontological statement not only declaring simply *that* she is but also affirming a situated sense of a self that is no longer lost.

Marie's heart, which must become "smooth as riverstone," signals the painful transformation the narrator's own heart must undergo; significantly, it is the search for Marie that enables the protagonist to reorient her relationship to her community, nature, and the broader universe. The question of reconnection to one's community is central to the narrative's middle, wherein the necessity of the search leads to a communion with others that the protagonist had previously avoided, enabling her realization that she is not alone in the grief of loss. As she moves through her San Antonio neighborhood alongside her friend Rosalind, making inquiries about the lost cat, she begins to observe and understand her own heartbreak within the wider arc of her neighbors' various experiences of pain and loss. Each time a neighbor responds to an inquiry about the missing Marie, the woman uses her previous knowledge of the neighbor's life to internally contextualize the response. For instance, when a neighbor named Carolina responds with a compassionate declaration that her heart would break if she ever lost her Yorkie, Coco, the narrator reflects on Carolina's past: "She knew about heartbreak all right. Her brother and mother had both died within a year and left her all alone" (Cisneros, *Have You Seen Marie?* 14). Similarly, when Roger and Bill, who live in the blue house across from hers, take a break from garden work to look at the flyer depicting the missing cat, they respond with a simple "We haven't seen nothing," yet the narrator internally interjects, "But I knew they had seen a lot," reflecting that "Bill had lost his oldest boy a few Thanksgivings ago, and Roger's sister was in the hospital again with cancer" (16).

Encountering another neighbor, Luli, who has the outline of a teardrop tattooed beneath her left eye (commonly associated with death or imprisonment), the narrator internally interprets the tattoo as proof that "Luli has witnessed too much grief for one lifetime" (Cisneros, *Have You Seen Marie?* 38). This reading of a body permanently marked by loss is reinforced by the way the page's words neatly curve around the accompanying illustration of a single brown eye with a teardrop below it and blue and pink eye shadow rising up to an arched eyebrow. On the adjacent page, the teardrop outline is pictured alone, visually bridging Luli's reaction to the missing cat, "Isn't it a shame to lose the one you love?" and the narrator's simple affirmation, "Yes it is" (39). Despite the outward brevity of this agreement, the narrator's revelation to the reader that her heart "felt as if someone squeezed it" (39) indicates that a gradual confrontation with her own grief is precipitated by these interactions. Encountering a woman knitting on her porch swing, the narrator's memory turns sharply toward her mother: "I thought about my mother and how she used to knit ugly scarves no one wanted to wear. Now I wish I had one of those ugly scarves, and my nose started to tingle" (42). These two lines are divided by a green-and-gold braided scarf, with tassels on each side, stretched out across the page; visually distinct from the plain blue scarf in the adjacent illustration of the knitting neighbor, this scarf, it is implied, is a memory of those her mother knitted. The tingling of the nose triggered by this memory, paired with the previously described squeezing sensation in her heart, suggests the awakening of her body to the loss that underlies the search for Marie.

However, just as Anaya's old man walks to the river to call his wife's name into the wind, receiving no discernible response, the pair of friends in *Have*

You Seen Marie? encounter a similar void—cats who "would not or could not say" (20) or simply curl their tails into question marks (45), and neighbors who offer to help and then forget, or who "sla[m] the door before we could say what we came for" (57). At times their search is conveyed in terms of disembodied voices projected into emptiness: "We sent our voices in places too dangerous to go ourselves. Beyond fenced driveways, into dark crannies sticky with cobwebs, between the floor planks of porches, into the mouths of scary hallways. But nothing and no one answered" (30). This passage is positioned adjacent to an image, on the neighboring page, of a large cobweb overlaying a black background with a single yellow door, suggesting that these abandoned domestic spaces are an abyss or boundary too dangerous to physically cross. At other times, their search is specifically physical: "'Marie, Marie!' We called up to trees. We crawled on our hands and knees and peered under parked cars. We walked behind houses and into scratchy, deserted gardens. But there was no Marie to be found" (49). As they walk and crawl through the neighborhood's open and hidden places, throwing their bodies as well as voices into the search, the narrator's personal grief continues to emerge as the missing cat becomes a placeholder for her missing mother: "'Marie, Marie,' we shouted. But, inside, my heart wheezed, '*Mama, Mama*'" (53). The narrator's internal sorrow is echoed by the universe itself, as "wind whirled the flyers we had left in dry hot circles, and big, sad drops of rain began as if to say, 'Despair, despair'" (53). While the old man's wife in Anaya's text becomes part of "a mourning wind" that endlessly circles the universe in a timeless embrace, this wind suggests a sentient power that mourns and despairs even as it overwhelms. Hernández's illustration evokes a stark and ominous mood, with vague black shadows rising from the land and the woman, herself a shadowy figure, advancing against rising circles of air and "sad drops of rain" as the lost flyers flutter away. This scene, which connects the narrator's internal state to the external elements, relates meaningfully to the final portion of the story, which shifts away from human sociality and demonstrates a deep encounter with nature and the cosmos.

As the day slips away, the narrator and her friend split up in order to cover more ground before nightfall, with Rosalind moving upriver while the narrator heads "downriver toward the Big Tex granary and the old Lone Star brewery" (Cisneros, *Have You Seen Marie?* 66). While she remains in familiar territory, a historically and socially significant geography, she ventures away from the confines of her neighborhood and into the open space of the river. There she enters into dialogue with the river, who is depicted as a wise and ancient presence:

"I asked the river, *'Have you seen Marie?'* River said, *'Mamita,* you name it, I've seen it.' 'Do you mean you've seen her?' 'I've seen everything, *corazón de melón.* Everything, everything, everything, everything, everything. . . . ,' River continued" (68; ellipsis in original). Unlike the "indifferent" river in Anaya's story, this river speaks, responding to the narrator's inquiry. However, while the woman asks about the lost cat, the river answers much more expansively, emphasizing through repetition the totality of what it has witnessed. Yet the woman cannot fully comprehend this answer, and thus, like the old man, she cries at the river's edge: "'But I don't understand what you mean.' There was something in my throat. I felt like I'd swallowed a spoon. I put my face under the water and cried" (70). In what becomes a baptismal scene, the woman is unable to comprehend the river's testimony of witness because she is not yet able to articulate her real question, which is blocked by the "spoon" of repressed emotion in her throat.

The river speaks again, this time in a long monologue: "River said, 'Don't you cry, *mamas.* I will take your tears and carry them to the Texas coast where they'll mix with the salty tears of the Gulf of Mexico, where they will swirl with the waters of the Caribbean, with the wide sea called Sargasso" (Cisneros, *Have You Seen Marie?* 72). Detailing all the places her tears will be carried, from Japan to Java and the Amazon, the Nile and the Danube, the Dardanelles and the Ganges, the spirit of the river vows that her tears will blend with "waters washing away the dead, and waters bringing new life, the salty and the sweet, mixing with everything, everything, everything, everything" (72–73). With an image spread across two full pages (74–75), Hernández illustrates the motion of the blue waters encircling the world's continents, which are marked with various pictorial icons; the movements of the water, indicated by various lines and arrows, carry the woman's tears until they intermix with all the waters of the world, moving in multiple directions simultaneously. Her tears seem to be symbolically represented by the same pink flowers that are scattered across the narrative by the wind, and in these waters flow living fish along with skeletal fish and small skulls that represent the washing away of the dead. Hernández's use of flowers to represent the tears of grief reminds the reader that there is still life intermixed with death, as they are part of the same continuum, which moves in circles and arcs rather than a single line with a specified end.

In the river's monologue, we find the affectionate names "mamita" and "mamas," which are terms of endearment often used to address children. In one sense, this signals the river as an elder; but when read even more closely, the monologue positions the river as an element of divine interconnectivity and duality, one that oversees both life and death—the "salty and the sweet"—and mixes the whole of it together. The illustration that readers see when the woman first encounters the river depicts a narrow flow of water surrounded by lush grass of green, yellow, and orange hues; a monarch butterfly glides above and several pink flowers float along its surface (69). Laid over this image is a woman's face sketched in monochrome blue, with long hair swirling upward and outward; she wears seashell adornments—as earrings, as a crown, and on her necklace—and seems to hold a staff with the symbol of a fish. While this deity image is not necessarily indicative of her per se, it is helpful to consider the nature of the mother goddess Yemayá, or Yemoja, in order to understand the implications of the river and its function in this story. Yemayá/Yemoja is "a deity known in Yoruba-based Afro-Atlantic religious cultures for her ability to dominate natural phenomena, especially aquatic zones of communication, trade, and transportation such as oceans, rivers, and lagoons" (Otero and Falola xix). In the case of Cisneros's narrative, we might interpret the sentient and wise river as similarly embodying a "zon[e] of communication" that intermingles with all waters of the world, both salty and sweet. Explaining that Yemayá/Yemoja is often "perceived as the water of life itself" (133), Allison P. Sellers offers the following example of a Brazilian praise song entitled "Yemayá's Song":

Siento un voz que me llama	I hear a voice that calls me
De lo profundo del mar	From the deep of the sea
Es la voz de mi madre	It is the voice of my mother
Di mi madre, Yemayá.	Of my mother, Yemayá. (qtd. in Sellers 143)

As Sellers explains, praise songs such as this refer back to specific myths which are "the sacred property of the *òrìsà*'s devotees" (142–43). In light of that mythic specificity, it may be more likely that Cisneros and Hernández are referencing a Nahuatl deity, or a more generalized deity concept. Nevertheless, the above praise song helps conceptualize how the river's voice in this story becomes an authoritative, ancestral voice, standing in for that of the literal mother and calling the woman to reorient herself. For just as this song's speaker hears a voice calling out from the sea and recognizes that voice as her mother's, Cisneros's protagonist is confronted by a divine river voice speaking affectionately as if she were its child. As yet unable to completely understand the river's message, she places her face beneath the water.

On the next pages, we see the woman's face, now above water and surrounded by splashing droplets; her expression is one of intensity, perhaps both anguish and relief, her face pointed upward and her eyes tightly closed. Cisneros writes, "I raised my face from the water and shivered" (*Have You Seen Marie?* 77), and readers might interpret that her body is shivering with a deeper understanding of the interconnectivity with which she is linked to all places and times through her grief. In this scene suggesting baptism, the sacred quality of water and its ability to reconnect us across space and time is invoked. In *Dwellings: A Spiritual History of the World* (1995), Linda Hogan similarly addresses the sacred memory of water from her perspective as a Chickasaw woman:

> Water seeps out of the rock canyon above me. It has been around the world. It has lived beneath the lights of fireflies in bayous at night when mist laid itself about cypress trunks. It has held sea turtles in its rocking arms. It has been the Nile River. . . . It has come from the rain forest that gave birth to our air. It brings with it the stories of where it's been. It reminds us that we are water people. Our salt bodies, like the great round of ocean, are pulled and held by the moon. We are creatures that belong here. (108)

Cisneros and Hogan both make reference to the circuitous routes of water and its ability to carry memory of the living universe; through migration and transformation, water carries consciousness of all the places it has inhabited and passed through, connecting us to sacred knowledge. And just as the voice of the river in *Have You Seen Marie?* takes on a nurturing, protective tone, Hogan's prose emphasizes the maternal aspects of water's "rocking arms" as well as its cycle of "giving itself back, everything a round river, in a circle, alive and moving" (108). This continuous movement and reciprocity, as well as the ability of water to carry stories that remind us of who we are and of our belonging in the world, are key to understanding the baptism scene that reorients the woman in Cisneros's narrative. For the shiver of consciousness the woman experiences as she raises her face from the waters of the river is a reminder of not only her spiritual but also her embodied connection across time and space. Just as the old man in Anaya's narrative senses his body only in relation to the pull of other bodies and must find a way to remind himself that he still belongs in the world, the woman in *Have You Seen Marie?* must also be reminded of her sacred belonging and orientation to the earth.

Interestingly, cypress trunks, which are referenced in Hogan's passage above, also appear in the next series of pages of Cisneros's narrative, as the protagonist's discernment takes firmer shape. Cisneros writes, "I sat on the giant roots of an ancient Texas cypress wider than thirteen people holding hands. . . . A tree so old it had been there since before Texas was Texas. Since before Tejas was Tejas. Since before me and my mother. Since before before" (*Have You Seen Marie?* 80–81). Paired with an image of two bare legs shown only up to just above the knee, with their pink-polished toes standing atop the large roots of a tree (figure 3), these words indicate a developing historical consciousness that places the woman, who in this image could be any woman, in a temporality that moves through history and beyond, "since before before." The image of bare feet touching the archive of the earth reflects a sacred relationship to the arc of time, which goes on and on, and which the protagonist realizes she is only one living part of. This visual expression of expansive temporality functions as tangible proof of a history that situates us and gestures toward the future as well as the past.

Reflecting on the awareness that emerges from the woman's bodily connection to the cypress tree, I find the work of Gloria Anzaldúa to be a helpful guide, as she theorizes an "awareness . . . not just in the mind, but also includ[ing] body knowledge" that "awakens some deep hidden memory or lost knowledge of times past" ("Flights" 24). Indeed, the protagonist in *Have You Seen Marie?*, as collaboratively presented in this scene through Hernández's image and Cisneros's words, is reminded through her body's tactile communication with the tree of a greater knowledge that had been previously lost to her—the knowledge that both she and her mother's soul are two parts of a greater continuum in which existence does not have an end. This directly relates back to Jane Bennett's discussion of a modernity that "discourages discernment of the marvelous vitality of bodies human and nonhuman" through its "depiction of nature and culture as orders no longer capable of inspiring deep attachment" (4). In this sense, we can read this scene as one of awakening, in which the narrator regains what the long history of conquest, colonization, and imperialism of thought has discouraged; through the awakening of her body awareness, she gains the ability to discern her own relationality to other bodies (here, the body of the tree) and also to the larger arc of time and consciousness.

Anzaldúa writes about the human relationship to trees, asserting that "we have a body awareness of trees and they of us" ("Flights" 24). Specifically, she describes a Monterey cypress in whose trunk the sacred image of La Virgen de Guadalupe appeared to her, and relates, "I sit on the knuckled roots of la

FIGURE 3 Ester Hernández, illustration of woman standing on cypress roots, from *Have You Seen Marie?* © 2012 Ester Hernández.

Virgen's tree and talk to it when I'm feeling jubilant or when painful memories take over and the whispering waves can't soothe the pangs" (23). As Anzaldúa states, "The Guadalupe tree reminds me of something I'd forgotten—that my body has always sensed trees' special relationship to humans" (24). It is in a very similar sense that the woman in *Have You Seen Marie?*, feeling orphaned by her mother's death, receives a sacred knowledge and memory that soothes her pain, specifically through her bodily contact with the roots of a cypress tree. Moreover, it seems specifically due to the sensitivity emerging from the pain of her grief—what Cisneros refers to as the heart broken open (Terrero)—that the protagonist is receptive to an awakening and embodied consciousness of this knowledge.

Anzaldúa addresses the perceptive aptitude of those who are particularly sensitive to their surroundings: "Spirit and mind, soul and body, are one, and together they perceive a reality greater than the vision experienced in the ordinary world. I know that the universe is conscious and that spirit and soul communicate by sending subtle signals to those who pay attention to our surroundings, to animals, to natural forces, and to other people. We receive information from ancestors inhabiting other worlds. . . . The soul forgets and must be reminded again and again by signals from nature whose spirits exist in fields, forests, rivers, and other places, and from arrebatamientos (traumatic events)" ("Flights" 24). Indeed, it is the *arrebatamiento* of her mother's death and the disorientation it causes that open up Cisneros's protagonist to sensing and perceiving a "greater" reality. She pays deep attention to the people she speaks to in her neighborhood and the signals her body gives after she converses with them, such as the squeezing of her heart or the tingle of her nose; but further, she pays attention to the natural elements around her, such as the river, trees, and wind, as she listens with her spirit, mind, soul, and body. It is as if, due to the trauma of her loss, she does not inhabit the "ordinary world" in the same way as before, but rather develops an embodied conversation with the signals around and in her. Just as she seeks Marie the cat, her soul asks to be reminded of something that it has lost or forgotten, and as she searches, the world around her increasingly offers information and knowledge.

Like Anaya's old man, who interprets the wind as a presence of time immemorial, this woman comes to understand her role in a time that has no end through her interactions with nature (as well as humans). And like the old man who, seeking an answer in the midst of his grief, calls out for his wife at the edge of the river, so the woman calls out for her mother. In the next set of pages, Cisneros writes, "And when the swirling inside me grew still I heard the voices inside my heart. *I'm afraid. I'm all alone. I have never lived on this earth without you.* Then I really felt sorry for myself and began to shake like branches in rain. *Mother, Ma, Mamaaaá"* (*Have You Seen Marie?* 82). Up to this point in the narrative, all of her interactions with humans and the elements of nature have contributed to her internalized swirl of ideas and emotions. However, I would also return to Somé's discussion of grief, in which he states, "Death, and the sudden separation around it, puts the living in a state of emotional debt, loss and disorientation. The unresolved energy produced by the death of a loved one translates itself emotionally as grief" (97). I would suggest that it is in this "state of emotional debt" that Cisneros's protagonist seeks a response to her call, and it is the "unresolved energy" produced by her mother's passing that swirls inside her. Just as the voice of the river assures her that it will carry her tears to mix with all the waters of the world, uniting geographic space and time, this swirling inside her reflects an internal landscape. When that energy stills, she is finally able to discern the fears that lie inside her heart. These internalized landscapes and energies are significant, for just as the old man reflects on the vastness of the spaces—rooms and chambers—inside his heart, so this narrative suggests an internalized universe indicative of the vastness of the spirit.

But further, it is notable that in this scene the woman describes her body in terms of a tree, recalling that she shook "like branches in rain" (Cisneros, *Have You Seen Marie?* 82). Here she not only possesses a bodily awareness, but she is aware of her body as something in and of nature, a natural body that, like the cypress tree, is its own archive of a specific and ongoing history. Returning to Bennett's concept of enchantment, this scene indicates enchantment's discernment of the vitality of bodies, in this case a link between human bodies and tree bodies. Unlike Anaya's old man, who in the early stages of his grief cannot make sense of the moaning of the wind in the trees or the "indifferent river" sweeping south, the woman in Cisneros's story has reached a state of discernment that allows her to hear a response when she calls out for her mother. "'Here I am, *mija*,' the wind said and mussed my hair. 'Here I am, *mija*,' the trees said and shushed me. 'Here I am, *mija*,' said the clouds grazing past. And when the night fell, the moon rose and blanketed me with her rebozo of stars. 'Here I am, I've been here all along, *mijita*.' 'Here, here, here,' said the little stars laughing. 'Here I am, here I am.' The light filled my bones" (82). The woman's cry to the universe, "Mother, Ma, Mamaaaá," indicates the search for her literal mother and an act of reaching out toward the universe as *madre*, mother, that which gives birth and, in this case, rebirth. And it is the wind, the trees, the clouds, the moon, and the stars that answer her, calling her "*mijita*"—my little daughter—an endearing expression of love. In one sense, her mother's disembodied soul speaks to her through the elements of nature; in another sense it is the variously embodied spirit of nature that speaks in the role of loving mother, of madre. In both interpretations the narrator is reoriented and reborn, in that she can once again sense herself as having a position in the universe—as being loved by the universe—due to her renewed ability to locate that love.

Just as, on the last page of *Have You Seen Marie?*, the missing Marie finally comes out from under the house and announces, "Here I am" (86), the repeated utterance of "Here I am" in the above scene locates what was lost as being present in the world around her, and *in* her, as the light fills her bones (83). The set of pages following this scene depict a black backdrop split horizontally by the horizon from which the rising white moon emerges; below the horizon, a stream of water runs from one end of the moon to the other in a semicircle, merging with it (figure 4). In the right foreground, unfilled blue outlines depict

FIGURE 4 Ester Hernández, illustration of woman wrapped in stars, from *Have You Seen Marie?* © 2012 Ester Hernández.

a woman's body wrapped by a rebozo of simple white stars that extend outward across the pages. As she looks toward the dome-like body of the moon, encircled by its own rings of stars, she places her hand over her heart, and her body is situated as yet another celestial body occupying the space of the universe. Here we might recall Linda Hogan's words that our bodies "are pulled and held by the moon," reminding us that "we are creatures that belong here" (*Dwellings* 108). Additionally, the illustration suggests the moon deity, Coyolxauhqui, who "personifies the wish to repair and heal, as well as rewrite the stories of loss and recovery, exile and homecoming, disinheritance and recuperation," along with "the search for new metaphors to tell you what you need to know" (Anzaldúa, "Now Let Us Shift" 143). In addition to the moon's pull, the stars that wrap around the woman and extend outward connect her to space and time. Hernández's decision to depict this image with simple colors—black, white, and blue—and simple lines, particularly as she leaves the woman's body unfilled, suggests not only the potentiality to be filled, but also the immensity of an expansive landscape and awareness that are both internal and cosmic. In this same way, Cisneros's seemingly simple, lyrical language suggests an expansiveness of the spirit and a deep experience of grief in broad outline, even as both defy full articulation.

Conclusion

In reflecting on these two stories for what they jointly and independently reveal about the experience of grief, I turn once again to Jane Bennett's thoughts on the concept of enchantment in modern life: "Yearning, yearning, and suffused with nostalgia for a lost cosmos, the modern self is a being with a hole in her center. . . . We long intensely for more time—time to become whole, to recover the theft of meaning, to locate our coordinates in the world" (78). As I have argued, Anaya and Cisneros use the "lyric moments" of their narratives to gesture toward an ineffable longing for relocation in the world, a longing that emerges from the embodied disorientation associated with the grief of loss. The old man and unnamed woman in these narratives indeed yearn not only for their lost loved ones, but also for an embodied sense of self that has been defined in relation to the other. Their nostalgia is not merely for the loved one's embodied presence, but also for the embodied relationship that provides a degree of orientation in the world. Who am I if I am no longer pulled to the earth by my mother's love and embrace? Who am I in the absence of a lifelong partner whose body my body has lived and breathed against? The quest to recover what has been displaced through grief's theft of meaning is also an attempt to relocate their own coordinates in the world.

In this quest, these characters simultaneously reach beyond the temporal and spatial limits of ordinary life and discover the miraculous within it, connecting and awakening their own bodies and spirits to a complexity that cannot be fully described. The old man conceives of himself as an untethered planetary body spiraling through space; throughout the narrative, he seeks a steadier orbit through the slow development of new embodied relationships, a reckoning with the spirit world, and a developing interpretation of his role in the ineffable grace observed in the earth's seasons, mysteries, and movements. Likewise, the woman in Cisneros's text searches for a lost body, only gradually awakening to her own embodied sensations of loss; through a series of engagements with natural bodies—those of water and trees, as well as the moon and stars—she is reborn into a renewed sense of herself as loved by and belonging to the universe. The "mourning wind" that carries away the loved one's soul into time immemorial is the same wind that destabilizes a rooted sense of self. And it is this very destabilization or disorientation that gives way to a painful process of discernment through which these characters gradually perceive their connection to a cosmos that transcends time and space. In the next chapter, I continue to consider narrative representations of engagement with the natural world in relation to radical self-reflection and an awakening consciousness. However, while the present chapter focused on adult narrators at midlife or older, chapter 4 considers the relational process of becoming that is experienced by children. Whereas *Have You Seen Marie?* is a picture book written for adults, I transition now to a consideration of the decolonial work approached in illustrated children's stories.

The Body Rooted and Flowing

Toward a Decolonized Spirituality

A queer Chicana artist, writer, educator, and activist, Maya Christina Gonzalez has approached children's books as a site of radical, transformational change for over twenty years. Since illustrating Gloria Anzaldúa's *Prietita and the Ghost Woman / Prietita y la Llorona* (1995), Gonzalez has collaborated extensively with Children's Book Press to create award-winning bilingual picture books that vibrantly acknowledge experiences and perspectives of people marginalized by dominant culture. In those collaborations, her illustrations have most frequently combined with the writings of Francisco X. Alarcón and, in several cases, Amada Irma Pérez. Also for Children's Book Press, Gonzalez has written and illustrated a trilogy of award-winning bilingual picture books, the last two of which are the focus of this chapter. The trilogy consists of *My Colors, My World / Mis colores, mi mundo* (2007), *I Know the River Loves Me / Yo sé que el río me ama* (2009), and *Call Me Tree / Llámame árbol* (2014). In 2009, she and her partner Matthew started Reflection Press, an independent publisher focused on social justice and inclusion, drawing strongly on Gonzalez's experience as an artist, writer, and classroom educator. In addition to creating and publishing accessible educational resources such as the *Gender Now Coloring Book* (2010) and its school edition (2011), the press released two anthologies (2015, 2016) featuring a diverse range of children's book authors and illustrators, and a self-care book for children, *When a Bully Is President: Truth and Creativity for Oppressive Times* (2017), written and illustrated by Gonzalez.

Additionally, in 2013 she launched an online learning environment, School of the Free Mind, working again with her partner Matthew to offer instructional courses for holistically creating and publishing children's books that place queer, Indigenous, and people of color's perspectives at their center.

These endeavors collectively reflect Maya Christina Gonzalez's passion for the revolutionary, even radical power of children's picture books to manifest change in the world through the imaginative acts of reading, writing, and making art. This approach can be further understood in the larger context of her early life and career. As she describes on her website, Gonzalez experienced a series of challenges in her life that taught her the healing nature of art: a childhood head injury that resulted in a coma and heavy medication for seizures; being disowned by her family at twenty-one after coming out; and heavy metal poisoning in 1996 that impacted her health for a decade (Gonzalez, "Bio"). As a result, her work as a fine artist, which reflects a deep engagement with her own consciousness as a queer Chicana and the experience of healing from racism, homophobia, and physical illness, also reflects her spiritual exploration (Gonzalez, "Bio"). In recognition of the significance of this work, her art has been featured on the cover of key texts such as *Living Chicana Theory* (1997) and *Contemporary Chicana and Chicano Art: Artists, Works, Culture, and Education, Volume 2* (2002). Her work with children's books may be viewed as an extension of this artistic process of healing and an attempt to pass on the knowledge she gained through the difficult challenges confronted in her own life. More specifically, she uses the domain of children's books as a productive space from which to generate discourses that respect children's complexity, enabling conversations about issues such as nontraditional gender identities, racial, linguistic, and cultural difference, and human interconnectivity. In other words, her works are uniquely situated to speak to a broad audience of readers across a spectrum of intersectional identities, offering as much learning for teachers and parents as they do for children.

In considering what a truly Chicanx children's literature might mean, we might consider a key phrase Gonzalez uses in her educational and promotional materials (e.g., website, posters, stickers, bookmarks): "Children's Books as a Radical Act." This motto reveals the underlying philosophy that guides her work; in advocating for more inclusive representation, she calls not only for stories with more diverse bodies and faces, but for narratives that counter dominant paradigms of thought and action, offering alternative ways to understand the world and one's relationship to it. A picture book is one of many venues through which children receive and make meaning out of messages about themselves and their worlds even before they can read; the messages they find in such texts enable reflection not only in terms of present experience, but also in terms of future potentialities that lie open. Reference librarian Brooke Manross Guilfoyle explains, "Picture books compete with many other influences to teach young children about the world. They inspire children to imagine and fantasize about who they are and who they may be as adults" (38). The introduction to counternarratives at an early age can radically impact the scope of our imaginations, which contour our development as people and the frames through which we interpret and inhabit our environments. Subsequently, the call this chapter makes for literary scholars to take children's picture books seriously is in part due to the political importance of co-identification in developing empowered subjectivities at any age.

More specifically, the works examined here reveal conceptually and aesthetically masterful treatments of challenging issues critical to contemporary scholarship across disciplines. Gonzalez's narrative and visual work offers innovative ways to approach concepts of spiritual decolonization, embodiment, and phenomenology from a specifically queer Chicanx perspective. More specifically, *I Know the River Loves Me / Yo sé que el río me ama* and *Call Me Tree / Llámame árbol* bring together word and image to represent the body as deeply integrated with the natural world via the spirit. Eduardo Duran writes that while "objectification of the land has allowed for the psyche of human beings to desecrate and wound the soul of the land," a resistance to such objectification integrates the realization that "[human] sense mechanisms are the only way that the land, which makes up our body, can express the pain it feels through our/its consciousness" (121). In this sense, if our pain is connected to the pain of the land, our healing movement toward wholeness must be situated in relationship to the land we are a part of. I argue that Gonzalez's stories provide radical decolonial spaces of encounter, situating decolonization as both epistemological and ontological, an ongoing process of reorienting the ways in which we think about and inhabit our bodies as they relate to elements of nature. Here I draw on Priscilla Solis Ybarra's assertion that the decolonial "prioritizes a non-Western theoretical basis and puts the body, a body politics of knowing, at its center" (12). In her work on Mexican American "goodlife" writing, which "integrates the natural environment as part of the community" (5), Ybarra writes that such literature "records a long history of active resistance to epistemic assault, preserving and generating a depth of connection and cooperation between humans and nature while it also challenges readers to move beyond the modern/colonial paradigms and toward decolonized knowledges" (36). In my examination of Maya Christina Gonzalez's picture books, it is precisely this kind of cooperation, connection, and knowledge that I focus on; for the children in these works are truly in community with nature.

Offering nonanthropocentric stories of existence, these books depict children encountering themselves in and actualizing conscious relationships with a living world of water and trees. In each book I trace the interplay between illustration and text, which playfully evokes a spiritual awareness that displaces Western binary assumptions of human/nonhuman. Gonzalez approaches her visual and written texts through an affirmative framework, emphasizing an epistemology of *belonging*; further, her characters' bodies are deeply engaged in a process of ontological becoming that enacts a form of spiritual decolonization. In *I Know the River Loves Me*, Gonzalez counters Western concepts of kinship and friendship, placing the child she portrays in an ecosystem of reciprocal care and loving action, such that she flows in harmony with nature. Meanwhile, *Call Me Tree* depicts children embodying nature, firmly rooted in their connections to one another, even as they see and acknowledge their racial and gendered variance. Thus, in both these works, children (as readers, viewers, and listeners) can freely imagine spiritual, embodied relationships unhindered by the Western binaries that fragment and rupture our conscious interconnections to nature.

Children's Books as Literature

As previously referenced, implicit in my analysis is the position that Chicanx children's literature can and should be part of broad academic discourse. Specifically, these works offer critical insight for scholars of literary studies, Chicanx/Latinx studies, gender studies, and ecocriticism. Marilisa Jiménez García explains that the academy has often approached children's literature "for and about people of color" through the lens of utilitarian necessity rather than with an appreciation of its aesthetic complexity, failing to perceive it "as *literature*" (111–12). Additionally, Jiménez García writes, "When it comes to Latino/a children's literature . . . we have a tendency to absorb this material as . . . invaluable for its cultural content—rather than seeing it as artistic, experimental, and intellectually challenging" (112). I would argue that in Gonzalez's picture books, cultural content moves beyond easily commodified traditions or aesthetics and looks toward ways of knowing and being that seriously challenge subject/object binaries of Western discourse (e.g., human/nature, spirit/body). Both of the texts addressed here show children learning to see past dualistic frameworks of reality and coming to understand their own existence through sensate experiences with sentient natural environments. Such stories are valuable to scholars as well as children for the innovative approaches they take to ecological problems and questions. Laura Barbas-Rhoden asserts that bilingual children's stories with ecocritical themes "bring new perspectives to bear on the landscape of American ecocriticism because they challenge children and scholars to conceive of an environmental ethics sensitive to diverse cultural perspectives and the realities of globalization" (359). Indeed, the shift away from Western divisions between humans and nature expressed in Gonzalez's books opens the way to an ecocritical perspective that places spiritually embodied fluidity with and rootedness in nature at its center. To acknowledge the challenge invested in such works is to recognize children's picture books as an important site of knowledge production and cultural memory, meriting scholarly attention not only for their value for early childhood education, but also because they negotiate timely issues in creative ways meant to inspire dialogue and reflective action.

Beyond these ecocritical contexts, literary scholars—not only those who focus on K–12 literature—can and should look to these sites as spaces of inquiry where we might find unexpected ways of perceiving our respective subjects of study. In an overview of children's literature in *The Routledge Companion to Latino/a Literature* (2013), Mary Pat Brady makes the assessment that although "literary scholars do not generally take children's picture books . . . seriously," the notable and "tremendous effort by a number of well-known writers to produce a new genre of picture books . . . suggest[s] that critics might well participate in this endeavor" (382). In this reference to "a new genre," Brady emphasizes stories that do not simply replicate or reinforce the dominant culture's narrative gaze but rather provide "visual and sonic" encounters that challenge it (382). Indeed, since the 1990s, well-known writers such as Pat Mora, Gary Soto, Gloria Anzaldúa, Rudolfo Anaya, Sandra Cisneros, and Juan Felipe Herrera have drawn attention to the field of children's picture books, and literary scholars are increasingly taking note. For example, in the case of Gloria Anzaldúa's children's picture books, literary analyses have been published across a spectrum of academic venues, including the *PMLA*, a journal of literary criticism (Tey Diana Rebolledo, 2006); *Aztlán*, a Chicanx studies journal (George Hartley, 2010); and the women's studies journal *Signs* (Isabel Millán, 2015). Thus the necessary work of establishing the relevance of children's picture books to the broader spectrum of Latinx literary scholarship has begun.

Of course, education and library professionals have extensively advocated for the importance of children's books that feature a diverse range of faces, cultures, identities, and experiences. With specific regard to broader depiction of Latinx cultural experiences in children's literature, this imperative is evident in the longtime work of advocates such as Alma Flor Ada, book awards such as the Pura Belpré Award, established in 1996 to honor writers and illustrators excelling at such portrayal, and current venues such as the National Latino Children's Literature Conference. Ada, described by Rosa Furumoto as the "modern giant of Latino children's literature" for her work as a writer, academic, and advocate (Furumoto 80), explains in the second edition of her book *A Magical Encounter: Latino Children's Literature in the Classroom* (2003) how several forces came together in the 1990s to encourage the development of a "little boom." These included the increased popularity of Latin American and Latinx writers; advocacy from the American Library Association for "authentic literature by Latino authors" and the creation of the Pura Belpré Award; federal and private funding for smaller publishing houses dedicated to Spanish and bilingual works; and educational publishers' interest in the bilingual market (Ada, *Magical Encounter* 46–47). Thus the development of the body of works that now exists is the result of the efforts of a web of figures including writers, illustrators, librarians, and alternative presses, as well as larger institutions. Brady affirms this perspective as she asserts the importance of "prizes for Latino children's literature [that] began to be established by activist-librarians and universities" in the early 1990s (378).

Tey Diana Rebolledo explains that small presses such as Children's Book Press, founded by Harriet Rohmer in 1975—which published both books featured in this chapter—have published works written and illustrated by authors and artists of color in response to the need for "cultural transmission to children through books written for them" ("Prietita" 280). According to Cary Cordova, Children's Book Press "was among the first publishers to challenge mainstream children's literature for its whiteness" (334). More specifically, Cordova outlines how Children's Book Press "participated in a publishing revolution to challenge the dominating literary and aesthetic canon and demand racial and cultural integration of Latinas, Latinos, African Americans, Native Americans and Asian Americans into the US educational system" (336). This educational advocacy was significantly tied to advocacy for bilingualism in children's books. As bilingualism provides teachers, parents, and children with more entrances to stories, increasing learning potential while acknowledging the value of both languages, bilingual children's literature is one form of epistemic resistance to English-language dominance. Barbas-Rhoden comments: "The bilingual stories from Arte Público and Children's Book Press seek to shape values and identities in ways that directly contest dominant ideologies in hegemonic US consumer culture, as well as the culture of Latin American elites" (365). Indeed, inclusion of both Spanish and English text can increase accessibility while inviting children and adults to perceive a story through more than one cultural and linguistic lens; in the process, assumptions and value judgments regarding monolingual identities can be contested and reshaped.

Reflection and Healing Through Visual Images

In tandem with this linguistic intervention, picture books do at least half their work through visual images, counteracting the social erasure of self that so many children experience. Maya Christina Gonzalez explains how this affected her as a child, stating, "I grew up during a time when I did NOT see ANY books that looked or sounded like me and my family or folks I knew. I think because of that, I used to draw my big, round Chicana face into the blank page in the backs of books!" ("Rainbow Alphabet"). Here Gonzalez underscores the utter absence of culturally affirming books in her life, as well as her clear desire to encounter stories that might reflect, through word and image, her individual and community experience. When she recounts drawing her own face into blank book pages, she acknowledges her early, intentional acts of inserting herself into the dominant narrative, remaking it in her image. Indeed, Gonzalez tells this story to explain the catalyst for her own artistic production as well as her activism around training others to create and publish so that more children can see themselves reflected in, and develop a sense of ownership over, the books they encounter. Notably, the images discussed in this chapter often feature children's faces, which sometimes fill whole pages as if to reinforce the importance of their very presence. In their study "Chicano Children's Literature: Using Bilingual Children's Books to Promote Equity in the Classroom," Laura A. Alamillo and Rosie Arenas write, "The importance of illustrations, as we look at Chicano children's literature, is for children to be able to view the illustrations as a vehicle to understand not just others, but particularly themselves. It is crucial that time be spent on 'reading' the illustrations since they play such an important part in the story being told" (57). Thus the images are not supplementary to the written story but rather form a corresponding and interlocking text that can also be read on its own, as in the case of children who have not yet developed literacy or language skills. In all cases, it is essential to pay careful consideration to the significant meanings conveyed in images, which create an interplay with and sometimes reach beyond what is immediately evident in the written words.

Images in children's picture books convey both surface representation and deeper symbolic meanings; in the case of Gonzalez's work, images can gesture toward a collective unconscious and toward existential concepts. Her artist's biography explains her engagement with art as "a lifelong, in-depth study of the nature of reality, consciousness and how these relate to creativity" (Gonzalez, "Bio"). As I demonstrate throughout this chapter, Gonzalez often gives shape to complex theoretical ideas through seemingly simple images of children inhabiting outdoor spaces and negotiating their embodied relationships to their environments. One of the primary elements of Gonzalez's artistic aesthetic, both in her fine art and her illustrations in children's books, is her thoughtful and productive use of the color palette. Elena Avilés writes about Gonzalez's use of color in her first self-authored picture book, *My Colors, My World / Mis colores, mi mundo* (2007), explaining that in this largely self-referential work, Gonzalez experiments with pink to upend assumptions about gender binaries and reclaim her own subjectivity: "She . . . uses pink to decolonize customs, traditions, and religious beliefs that show the force between visual and historical memory" (Avilés 39). While pink is not the predominant color in the subsequent two works I examine in this chapter, in each of them color is a "visual, figurative, and literal language . . . to speak to young readers" (Avilés 39). If color functions as its own language in these images, so does the quality of the lines, which are curvy and often swirling, avoiding sharp edges and closed terrains, communicating an ethic of flowing interconnection. This aesthetic accentuates an appeal to imagination, suggesting broad outlines that invite viewers to consider complex possibilities often rooted in spiritual concepts. I return here to Gonzalez's artist's biography, which explains that for her, images are "teachers from the soul" in that they are "by products of [a] creative process" that is also a "spiritual practice of allowing the image to slowly integrate and rise from a deep internal place and then become external" (Gonzalez, "Bio"). This philosophy of art as an exploration of spiritual consciousness from a queer, Chicanx perspective is clearly discernible in her children's books, which function as tools of education and healing, bringing sacred knowledge and memory to the fore.

Picture Books as Sites of Epistemological Encounter

Gonzalez explains that she wrote and illustrated her bilingual trilogy of children's books to demonstrate "just how valuable our connection to nature can be" (Nichols). Collectively, the three texts trace the progression from realizing a personal connection with nature to developing a fluid relationship with it, and finally to embodying nature; Gonzalez further asserts that the trilogy is marked by her conviction that "nature is a perfect resource to help us see through societal projections and feel powerful within ourselves" (Nichols). Relevantly, Gloria Anzaldúa refers to such societal projections as consensual reality, or the "assumptions and beliefs self/others/communities have about reality," which are imposed on us like cages; according to Anzaldúa, we must activate the imagination to "unlearn" these limiting assumptions ("Bearing Witness" 32). Gonzalez's narratives evoke the various ways that experiences in and with natural elements such as water, earth, and trees stimulate the imagination and expand conscious awareness of the self and existence. Her depictions of these experiences are thus not merely charming stories about children's playtime; they situate a decolonial shift in consciousness, revealing how the body's playful interactions with natural elements reconstitute perception, understanding, and experience. Chickasaw writer Linda Hogan similarly poses the problem of unlearning alienation from a balanced relationship to land as a question of sensory experience: "How can we listen or see to find our way by feel . . . ? How do we learn to trust ourselves enough to hear the chanting of earth? To know what's alive or absent around us, and penetrate the void behind our eyes . . . ?" (*Dwellings* 28). Hogan suggests that we must overcome this void, seeing past the consensual reality of societal projections, by learning to listen, feel, and know in alternative ways. I suggest that this work can begin with children's literature as a site of encounter—a site where children can be introduced to ways of being and knowing that offer alternatives to dominant Western dichotomies of body versus mind, human versus nature.

Regarding the importance of alternative knowledges, I turn to Boaventura de Sousa Santos's concept of epistemologies of the South, referring not strictly to a geographical place but "an anticapitalist, anti-colonialist, and anti-imperialist" framework. He writes, "By epistemology of the South I mean the retrieval of new processes of production and valorisation of valid knowledges, whether scientific or non-scientific, and of new relations among different types of knowledge on the basis of the practices of the classes and social groups that have suffered, in a systematic way, the oppression and discrimination caused by capitalism and colonialism" (Santos 51). Maya Christina Gonzalez's work offers its own creative retrieval, production, and valorization of spiritual knowledge that Western discourses of rationality have displaced, disregarded, and delegitimized. Importantly, her work not only teaches and models this knowledge but provides potential healing from the wounds of colonialist, capitalist erasure of a balanced and integrated subjectivity. Describing what he terms "the ecology of knowledges," de Sousa Santos adds: "Learning some kinds of knowledges may imply forgetting others and ultimately ignoring them. . . . Ignorance is not necessarily the original condition or starting point; it may well be the point of arrival" (57). Gonzalez actively resists this point of arrival, as her picture books imaginatively resituate relations between humans and nonhumans as fluid rather than dichotomous.

With this creative resistance, Maya Christina Gonzalez pushes against the damaging erasure of conscious interconnectivity—an erasure perpetuated and circulated through mainstream narratives as well as silences. Lara Medina recalls, "As a child, I was not taught that relationships matter the most, that my heart has intelligence or that my body can talk to me, that art is healing, or that the earth is alive and that plants and animals have spirit that can help us" ("Nepantla" 168). As implied here, a child's lack of encounter with such knowledge is not simply a lack but also a persistent colonial theft, resulting in psychological and ontological wounding. Gonzalez's intention in these picture books is to invest the viewer, reader, and/or listener with the ability to feel powerful within themselves, not through a lens of external domination but through a sense of self deeply integrated with nature. *I Know the River Loves Me / Yo sé que el río me ama* and *Call Me Tree / Llámame árbol* each offer vital lessons about a survival that does not position humans against or above natural environments but rather posits the self as fluidly related to and rooted in nature. While this is true of all three works in Gonzalez's trilogy, I focus on the last two for their specifically embodied narrative aspects.

Reciprocity and Kinship in *I Know the River Loves Me / Yo sé que el río me ama*

While the knowledge claim embedded in the title of this book emphasizes what the narrator knows, I do not read the story as primarily human-centered. The book's cover encourages a nonanthropocentric reading, featuring a girl drawn in plain black-and-white shading, while the environment she stands amid is fiercely colorful: green fish and frogs swimming in a swirling blue river; pink flowers with intricate patterns and green stems; and a sky of varied brown birds in flight against puffy white clouds outlined in blue. Indeed, Gonzalez does not depict the narrator with any color at all until the final page of the book. This strategy highlights the vibrancy of the world through which the narrator moves and to which she relates; in this light, the title's knowledge claim is much more about a relational sense of self than an individual one. In an interview with James Michael Nichols, Gonzalez discusses this second book in her trilogy, revealing two critical points: (1) she emphasizes the significance in the story's creation of her relationship with nature as a queer woman, and (2) she identifies the river as the book's source as well as its subject. Gonzalez states, "I found nature to be my true and constant friend when I was disowned by my family because of their homophobia. The river story rose at a time when I finally felt fully and unconditionally loved and supported in my life. The river actually told me the story!" (Nichols). Gonzalez's testimony that the story "rose" to her from the river credits the river as the original and sentient storyteller—a communicator and creative source of knowledge—while she becomes a conduit, allowing story to flow through her. Further, she posits the story's existence as the culmination of a loving relationship that flows over and beyond human sociality. As Gonzalez recounts the fracturing experience of familial rejection, she articulates the discovery of a meaningful friendship with her natural environment that ventures into kinship, yielding unconditional love and support. This conception pushes against the paradigm of superior humanity, or human as benevolent steward; for both friendship and kinship are defined by reciprocal bonds flowing in both directions.

Such a perception of human-environment relationships, emerging from Gonzalez's experience as a queer woman, offers an important ecological understanding that works to undo the consensual reality of supposedly rightful human dominance. In *Braiding Sweetgrass: Indigenous Wisdom, Scientific Knowledge, and the Teachings of Plants* (2013), Robin Wall Kimmerer, a plant ecologist and member of the Potawatomi Nation, addresses the importance of how we conceive of human relationships to land: "Knowing that you love the earth changes you, activates you to defend and protect and celebrate. But when you feel that the earth loves you in return, that feeling transforms the relationship from a one-way street into a sacred bond" (125). In this sense, the knowledge claim "I know the river loves me" enacts a spiritual context for the relationships humans hold to land, as spirituality lies at the basis of its acknowledgment of interconnection. Rather than inciting environmental consciousness as a one-way street of paternal protection, this framework shifts the discourse into an awareness of one's own participation in a sacred relationship. Lara Medina asserts, "Spirituality is fundamentally about being in relationship; being aware of one's interdependence or connectedness to all that can be seen and all that is unseen" ("Nepantla" 167). This understanding of spirituality represents a return "not to a romanticized past, but to ancient epistemologies that value and understand fluidity and change," as well as the power of relating to the world in a way that recognizes "the power of plant and animal medicines" (Medina, "Nepantla" 168). What is made clear in Gonzalez's interview but not explicit in the narrative of the picture book itself is that her ability to recognize a reciprocal relationship with the river functioned as medicine for her family's homophobia. The self-knowledge she attained was thus both spiritual and resistant.

Ecofeminism and the Decolonial

With this framework of fluid and spiritual interrelation in place, we must consider the question of gender as it operates in this narrative. On the first page, the dark shadow of a young girl emerges from the upper left-hand corner, walking down a curving tree-lined path along a swirling blue river in a green landscape; the entire scene is situated against a white backdrop of puffy white clouds outlined simply in blue. With the text appearing in the lower left-hand corner, Gonzalez writes from the perspective of the approaching child, whose face we cannot yet see: "I am here to visit one of / my best friends in the world—/ the river. She loves me" (*I Know the River* 2). Directly beneath this passage is a horizontal leafy green branch that visually separates the English text from its Spanish translation, written below the branch: "Estoy aquí para visitar a uno / de mis mejores amigos en el mundo / el río. El río me ama" (2). Firstly, this statement specifically asserts the river as a treasured friend, not an object of love but rather a sentient being capable of giving love. Further, the English text actively feminizes the river as "she" and does so throughout the entirety of the book, while the Spanish text maintains the standard usage of the masculine pronoun *el* in conjunction with the word *río*. Due to this linguistic distinction, the resulting connotation of the overall work becomes markedly different in English than in

Spanish, with the English version offering a perspective in which nature is not only sentient but also feminine. Yet what remains central to both versions is an emphasis on an epistemological and ontological framework that shifts away from and resists the separation between humans and nature.

This brings me to questions regarding ecofeminist discourses and their applicability to Chicana feminism, though I cannot fully flesh out an answer here. *Ecofeminism* broadly refers to a diverse range of approaches and perspectives regarding "the interrelated dominations of women and nature," emphasizing the "logic of domination" that emerged out of Euro-Western frameworks and the disproportionate levels at which women are materially affected by environmental problems (Eaton and Lorentzen 2). It is clear that Chicana feminist literature has long addressed such questions; indeed, María Herrera-Sobek proposed in 1998 that "Chicana writers have been at the forefront of feminist ecological concerns since the early 1970s" (90). Yet it is not entirely clear whether Chicana feminists themselves have wanted to take on the label of ecofeminism; for, as Christina Holmes explains, ecocriticism's "association with white Western feminism has turned some women of color away," and some have expressed "implicit and often explicit criticisms of racist and classist false universalisms . . . within ecofeminism" (34). Yet questions of ecofeminism as it intersects with Chicana feminism, and of Gonzalez's work in particular, merit consideration because, as Gwyn Kirk argues, ecofeminism does bear the *potentiality* to powerfully "[link] the oppression of women, racism, economic exploitation, and the ecological crisis" through its concern "with personal and planetary survival" (2).

One of the more contentious questions in ecofeminism centers on the dangers of romanticizing nature (e.g., the river) as feminine or essentializing women as inherently closer to nature. In the context of Gonzalez's work in particular, I would argue that the spiritually based interconnectivity she premises does not romanticize the feminine (in either English or Spanish), but rather proposes the feminine as fluid and unrestricted to rigid, simple gender binaries. Thus, though it is unclear whether Gonzalez would claim the title of ecofeminist, texts such as this one might substantially contribute to the development of ecofeminist discourse. As Holmes writes in *Ecological Borderlands: Body, Nature, and Spirit in Chicana Feminism* (2016), "The too-easy dismissal of ecofeminist work forecloses important questions that ecofeminism raises. . . . We need to consider how our relationships with each other and with the environment shape efforts toward justice or risk being left out of the conversation even as we challenge some of the shortcomings of ecofeminist theory production" (2). Certainly, *I Know the*

River Loves Me / Yo sé que el río me ama is a book that, at its heart, pushes us to consider our relationships with the environment in ways that challenge and potentially reshape assumptions about our embodied actions and perhaps our obligations toward the world we live in.

To return briefly to the first page in the story, an additional component of the image is notable for its gesture toward the decolonial work the story will do. The girl is positioned at the beginning of a blank pathway that is outlined simply in brown against a vibrant landscape, while her own image is almost entirely filled with heavy black shading. The shadowed occlusion of her figure suggests a concept of identity that can be developed and realized only through active, relational engagements as the story progresses. For, after the opening page, the remainder of the narrative substantiates the narrator's knowledge claim that the river loves her as one based on embodied and sensory experiences; significantly, these depictions orient young readers, viewers, and listeners to nonnormative ways of being in and with the world. In this way, the story not only decenters human domination over nature but destabilizes the very assumption that we are separate from it or, as Laura E. Pérez states, that "we are unrelated, gulfs apart from nature, from other people, even from parts of our own selves" ("Crooked Lines" 23). For as the narrator engages with and encounters nature, she encounters an increasingly developed sense of self as well. Thus Gonzalez's story powerfully reinforces Pérez's assertion that countering the dominant narrative of rupture and isolation from nature is "perhaps the most pressing ideological and political work, the heart of the 'decolonial'" ("Crooked Lines" 24). Though this short children's picture book may appear simple on its surface, the work it does is indeed decolonial, political work of unlearning the separation from nature that fragments the spirit.

Sensory Experience as Evidence

As the story evolves, the protagonist's claim that the river loves her is evidenced through an evolving series of interactions that posit a fluid relationality between human and nature. The narrator hears the river calling to her as she moves closer in proximity. Once the girl arrives at the river's edge, she asserts that the river "jumps" and "sings" upon seeing her there; the assertion that she is *seen* by the river emphasizes that she is subject to the river's conscious gaze and welcome greeting (Gonzalez, *I Know the River* 7). Not only does the narrator sense herself as seen, but as she enters the water, it reflects the narrator back to herself. Gonzalez writes, "I know the river loves me because when / I look into her face, she's happy to see me," or, "Yo sé que el río me ama porque cuando / lo miro a la cara, está contento de verme" (11). This mirroring, combined with the ascription of seemingly anthropomorphic aspects to the river's movement—such as jumping and singing—might at first glance suggest a narcissistic human desire to inscribe the self onto nature. Yet I argue that Gonzalez portrays this mirroring as a relational one in which the narrator does not dominate nature but rather finds herself deeply immersed within it and, as such, is able to dissolve the boundaries between herself and the river. For the girl does not describe the river as a mere mirror of her own image; rather, she acknowledges the river as a sentient being with a face (*cara*) of its own.

The image that accompanies this scene spreads out over two pages. On the left side, the girl is drawn in black and white, immersed in the blue and green wavy lines of water up to her chest. Her face is drawn large, emphasizing her eyes' contented gaze into the water that reflects her image on the right-hand page. Most notable in this illustration is the girl's long black hair, which extends across the pages until it seems to belong to the water image, such that one cannot be easily disconnected from the other. Significantly, both faces smile calmly as they look at each other. Rather than the girl simply seeing herself in the water, this illustration seems to portray the river's own sentient spirit and ability to gaze back. The intertwined relationship that is ultimately portrayed, signified by the hair that bridges the two faces, reflects the need to situate ourselves within an ecological system of relationships. On the subject of ecocriticism and literature, Grisel Y. Acosta asserts, "We need to explore, in our literature, what it is that we invest in our landscapes and how it aids in our survival. After all, we are looking at our literature not only to get closer to nature and to understand our environments, but to also understand ourselves and our role in said environments" (202). To understand our environmental role, in other words, necessitates a confrontation with ourselves and a reckoning with the reciprocal relationship that requires us to give and invest in that relationship as well as to recognize what it is that we receive. Thus, when Gonzalez's narrator sees herself reflected in the water, she is at the same time sensing herself as loved and appreciated, seen for who and what she is in a way that human society often fails to do.

This emphasis on relationality rather than domination is reflected in Gonzalez's own words when she states her intention: "I wanted to share with kids the notion that nature is a constant resource not only to see ourselves, but also to feel held when we need it" (Nichols). This framing of an affective relationship with nature reaches new and more embodied levels toward the middle of the narrative, when the protagonist dives beneath the surface of the waters of the river, which figures simultaneously as playmate and protectress: "When I jump on / her back she holds / me up. When I leap / into her arms she takes / me in" or "Cuando brinco sobre / su espalda, me sostiene. / Cuando salto a sus / brazos, me acoge" (Gonzalez, *I Know the River* 12). The protective envelopment described in these lines indeed emphasizes the natural world not as a merely utilitarian resource but as a vital source of support that can hold us up and take us in. Beyond this, the images literally framing the written text depict an expansive and playful joy, as the girl swims through the water that fills the pages. Depicting her in four different bodily postures, the illustration emphasizes the narrator's joyful movement through the river; smiling, she swims alongside green frogs, as the lines of the water curve and swirl in all directions.

This relationship further evolves in the following pages, in which we see the young girl transition from active play to blissfully floating through calm turquoise waters, her body gracefully gliding in the center of the two pages (figure 5). As two multicolored fishes swim beside her, the girl stretches out her arms, delicately treading water while her long black hair swirls upward, pulled by the water's movements. With her eyes closed, she bears a look of utter contentment upon her face. On the lower left-hand page, the English text appears: "She tugs on my hair and my arms / and we flow together" (Gonzalez, *I Know the River* 14). And on the lower right-hand page is the Spanish text: "Me acaricia el pelo y los brazos y fluimos juntos" (15). This scene highlights the distinction created through the feminization in the English text, which seems to suggest a feminine water deity such as the river goddess Oshun. Here the river provides a sensual balance, embodied as physical pleasure that takes on a spiritual level. And while the Spanish text does not feminize the river, "me acaricia" suggests a loving caress in a way that does not entirely come across in English. Relevant to the sensations depicted in this scene, Laura E. Pérez asserts, "The body regenerates through the circulation and exchange of spiritual or vital life-force energy within itself and between itself and other life forms" ("Crooked Lines" 27). It is precisely such an exchange that is ardently depicted in Gonzalez's image and text, a replenishment and regeneration that results in joyful pleasure.

Here I turn to the phenomenological perspective of Mark Johnson, who states, "*In our experience of movement, there is no radical separation of self from*

FIGURE 5 Maya Christina Gonzalez, illustration of girl underwater, from *I Know the River Loves Me / Yo sé que el rio me ama*. Text and illustrations copyright © 2009 by Maya Christina Gonzalez. Permission arranged with Children's Book Press, an imprint of Lee & Low Books Inc., 95 Madison Ave, New York, NY 10016.

world" (20; italics in original). This statement eloquently translates the implications of integration embedded in the image above; as the girl swims, she registers equilibrium with the forces that she is experiencing in her body. But further, the narrator's assertion that she and the river flow together emphasizes the unison reached through movement. In a spiritual context, Johnson discusses a spirituality that "involve[s] a capacity for horizontal (as opposed to vertical) transcendence, namely, our ability both to transform experience and to be transformed ourselves by something that transcends us: the whole ongoing, ever-developing natural process of which we are a part" (14). The horizontal position of the girl's body in the water illustrates this capacity both to be transformed and to be active in the process. This phenomenological approach, focusing on consciousness and the objects of direct experience, is helpful in understanding the embodied aspects of Gonzalez's text and illustration. Here I highlight the scene's engagement of "our sensorimotor capacities" (Johnson 19), such as "proprioception (our feeling of our bodily posture and orientation)" and "kinesthetic sensations of bodily movement," in knowing the world (Johnson 276). The girl's closed eyes and expression of serenity suggest the sensations that she is processing in her body as she moves in harmony with the water, which tugs at her hair and arms.

The Ecological Body in Flow

Emphasizing the importance of environmental exertion and force in knowing the world, Johnson describes the "ecological body": "There is no body without an environment, no body without the ongoing flow of organism-environment interaction. . . . The trick is to avoid the dualism of organism *and* environment, [which] falsely assumes the existence of two independent entities. . . . Instead, we must think of organism (or body) and environment . . . as aspects of one continuous process" (276). Thus, through submersion in the river, Gonzalez's narrator is able to experience this "ongoing flow" of interaction between herself and the water, such that in their harmonious flow she can sense her body in a different way, as an ecological body. Significantly, this embodied experience that allows the narrator to sense her interrelationship with nature and feel her body as more expansive and more permeable affects her actions out of the water as well. Later, as she sits at the water's edge, with only her feet in the water as she reaches into the river full of swimming frogs and floating flowers, we see the bottles and plastic six-pack rings she will pack in her open backpack before she leaves. The text reads, "The river takes care of me and I take care of the river. / I only leave behind what already belongs to her" (Gonzalez, *I Know the River* 18), or, in Spanish, "El río me cuida y yo cuida al río. / Sólo dejo atrás lo que ya a él le pertenece" (19). This reciprocal relationship of mutual caring, alongside the image of the litter that the girl has collected, signals a conscious sense of obligation and respect toward the river. This sense of mutuality also signals a relationship to nature characterized as friendship, but perhaps even further enacts a level of kinship—family members who actively take care of one another. In this sense, the book directly suggests implications for environmental action and justice.

However, this obligation of loving action toward the environment is not based only on embodied experience or philosophical imperatives; more specifically, the narrator's relationship to the river is clearly shown to be a spiritual one. This is most strongly emphasized in the last scene of the book, in which we see the girl wearing her backpack, which signals her impending departure as she stands upon a bridge overlooking the river (Gonzalez, *I Know the River* 22). Whereas she has been drawn only in black and white throughout the rest of the narrative, in this image blue lines drawn upon her dress swirl outward from her chest, over the bridge, and down into the water, becoming large waves that crash and meld into the river (figure 6). This image succinctly reflects the organism-environment interaction that Johnson describes, illustrating that "the body" also means that which is "outside" of it, because it can only be fully known and actualized via its fluid interaction with this outside. In this case, her body is drawn as literally conjoining with the body of the river, through an implied flow of spirit. Further, I read the image of the bridge upon which she stands as the "epistemological 'bridge' between nature and culture" described by Mary Mellor, the domain of "those women (and men) who are able to break out of [the] framework" of "dualist structures" (19). For, as Gonzalez emphasizes throughout the text, the narrator's reciprocal encounters with nature allow her to dissolve the boundaries that separate or isolate her from it as she increasingly actualizes her role in the larger ecosystem, one in which she is active and also acted upon.

FIGURE 6 Maya Christina Gonzalez, illustration of girl on bridge, from *I Know the River Loves Me / Yo sé que el río me ama*. Text and illustrations copyright © 2009 by Maya Christina Gonzalez. Permission arranged with Children's Book Press, an imprint of Lee & Low Books Inc., 95 Madison Ave, New York, NY 10016.

Thus, returning to the narrator's earlier statement "fluimos juntos," asserting that she flows *together* with the river, I reflect on what is accomplished in that flow. As Pérez writes, "The natural world is in constant motion—fluid, porous, changeable, inexhaustibly enigmatic" ("Crooked Lines" 23). Such fluid and porous motion combined with the image of the bridge strongly evokes the conceptual work of Gloria Anzaldúa, who wrote extensively about sensory awareness and embodied relationships to nature that alter consciousness and action in the world. Brena Yu-Chen Tai theorizes what she calls Anzaldúa's "permeable body paradigm" as involving a "rethinking [of] the self-other relationship in a liquid and porous sense as 'self~other,'" arguing that "*liquefying* the space between the self and the other is crucial to the process of becoming whole" (Tai 1). It is just such "liquefying" that we see illustrated and expressed in the final scene of Gonzalez's narrative, as the girl's body extends over and across a bridge, into liquid, via a spiritual connection that transcends the traditional parameters of her physical body. This illustrated porosity illuminates the concept of the "permeable body" as well as Johnson's concept of the "ecological body." But further, such fluid porosity offers readers, viewers, and listeners a decolonial framework that empowers them to see past the void of, and begin to heal, epistemological and ontological wounds. For the last page in the story repeats the title's statement—"I know the river loves me," or "Yo sé que el río me ama"—but further adds, "and I love the river," or "y yo amo al río" (Gonzalez, *I Know the River* 23). The sacred bond expressed in this statement of engaged reciprocity and conscious awareness assumes an intimate relationship between humans and nature that offers a different kind of sociality and kinship in which the narrator articulates her love for the environment as well as her sense of being loved by it in return.

In conclusion, these kinds of literary encounters can potentially model for children as well as adults a radical spiritual relationality capable of producing regeneration, pleasure, and healing. The story not only depicts an ongoing encounter with the natural world in which the narrator sees and feels herself as interconnected with the living sentience of nature, but also sets up an encounter for the child experiencing the text. Ada describes the encounter between a child and a book as "magical" because "books broaden young people's view of the world and enlarge their experience," and also "enrich children's minds while strengthening their spirits" (*Magical Encounter* 1). As I have tried to show, the epistemic shift encouraged in this children's picture book is not unconnected to the potential for spiritual development; for spirit is central to the narrative and visual work in this text, and is articulated through embodied interrelationship. This is equally true of the last book in Gonzalez's trilogy, which I examine next.

Nature as Teacher in *Call Me Tree / Llámame árbol*

In *Call Me Tree / Llámame árbol*, Gonzalez crafts the interplay between illustration and text to playfully communicate a spiritual awareness, unsettling binary paradigms of race, gender, and being. More specifically, the narrative visually and textually embraces "seeing" ontological and embodied difference while asserting a shared belonging and interconnected "rootedness" in the earth. Gonzalez presents a child narrator, drawn recognizably brown and purposefully gender-free. Dressed in blue jeans, a striped T-shirt, and red overalls, this character features rosy cheeks and lips and short black hair. Gonzalez explains that while some reviewers have interpreted the narrator as a cisgender boy, her intention was to provide "a much needed break from the constant boy-girl assumptions and requirements" and "a moment to pause and consider those assumptions, requirements and their impact" (Nichols). This intent to turn away from an immediately legible gender identity, as well as the binary frameworks undergirding a demand for such legibility, is reinforced by the written narrative's disengagement from gender-specific pronouns. Not only is the book written without male or female pronouns, but Gonzalez also requested that the publisher use only the terms "child" or "kid" to refer to the main character in press materials for the book (Gonzalez, "Gender Free"). These active choices shape the story as one that affirms children who do not fit into or identify with binary categories, while encouraging every person who encounters the text to think beyond the limits of those categories.

Significantly, Gonzalez emphasizes human gender expression as reflective of the diversity found in nature: "ALL of nature reflects multiple levels of gender expression. As a part of nature, so do humans. Because *Call Me Tree* is about kids embodying nature, open gender identity and expression were built in!" (Nichols). Thus, in visualizing and describing human embodiment of nature, the narrative works to naturalize an open gender identity. In its modeling of natural diversity, nature functions as a source of knowledge, or teacher, providing valuable lessons with which to deconstruct and reconstruct social systems of thought and practice. Importantly, this emphasis on natural diversity, as it plays out in the narrative, relates to gender and race alike; for the child narrator, who grows from a seed into a "tree," reaches toward and interconnects with other trees/children who reflect a broad spectrum of variations and inhabit various modes of being and spatial locations. As I will argue in my analysis, *Call Me Tree / Llámame árbol* narratively describes a developmental, spiritual consciousness based on an identity that is relational to the environment.

Earthen Knowledge

The very first pages of the story provide immediate insight into the spiritual basis of the narrative. As the story opens, the landscape is visualized as a golden-brown womb, and thus a mother to the child narrator, who is depicted as a seed comfortably enveloped within the earth (figure 7). Above the horizon is a night sky of blues and swirling indigos and bright white stars. Rather than being separate and independent from the land, this child is intimately related to it, resting in child's pose (as described in yoga) within the earth's body. The illustration spans two pages, with the child as seed depicted on the right side and the written text laid over the landscape on the left side. The English text appears first, in a downward-sloping style, followed by the Spanish translation below it. Gonzalez writes from the child's perspective, "I begin / Within / The deep / dark / earth," with the first line, "I begin," signaling a story of origin (*Call Me Tree* 1). While *I Know the River Loves Me / Yo sé que el río me ama* does not list a translator, Dana Goldberg is credited as the translator for this book. The translation of the first line, "I begin," as "Nazco" (I am born) indicates not only origin but more specifically birth. The next lines, "Within / The deep / dark / earth," or "Dentro / De la tierra / profunda / y oscura," trace the earth not only as a site of origin and birth, but also one of encapsulation and hiddenness. In this written text, as well as in the visual image itself, readers may intuit not only the sense of *tierra* as mother/womb—a place of origin and connection—but also as the ground of sacred knowledge and deep, profound memory.

On this first point regarding sacred knowledge, I would point more specifically to scholar Patrisia Gonzales's discussion of "earthen knowledge," in which she writes: "From the natural world emerges natural knowledge and earthen knowledge. The land and the natural world are alive and imbued with a life force and spirit, so much as we may make and create meaning, land also creates our meaning as a living entity" (xxi). Reading the first scene through this lens, we can interpret a message about an ontological and epistemological tie to

FIGURE 7 Maya Christina Gonzalez, illustration of child as seed, from *Call Me Tree /
Llámame árbol*. Text and illustrations ©2014 by Maya Christina Gonzalez. Permission
arranged with Children's Book Press, an imprint of Lee & Low Books Inc., 95 Madison
Ave, New York, NY 10016.

the earth; in other words, the scene expresses that through our origin in and
embodied connection to the land we derive meaning, and, in turn, it is through
this same earth-tie that we create and negotiate meaning. In the image, a pink
swirl in the approximate shape of a question mark appears directly above the
narrator's resting head, suggesting thought process and inquiry even while this
child-seed sleeps and grows within the earth. This representation of land as
site of original knowledge is complemented by an indication of land as site of
ongoing sacred memory. For "nazco" (I am born) uses the present tense, unlike
the more typical phrase "yo nací" (I was born), which uses the past tense. "Nazco"
suggests that this birth is not a matter of a now-finished past, but rather a
birthing that is never quite over. Likewise, "I begin" indicates a present tense
in which the point of origin is always now. The power of these simple words
reflects what Alma Flor Ada means when she states that even in children's
literature, "language is taken to its highest and deepest dimensions," offering to
those who encounter it "the possibility of seeing in new ways, and entering new

realities" ("Foreword: Literature" xii). This scene uses both word and image to communicate an ongoing origin, resituating linear assumptions of reality that separate past from present and self from earth.

The creation of an entrance into a nonordinary conception of reality reflects the sacred role of story itself. In her scholarship on traditional Indigenous rites of birthing and healing, Patrisia Gonzales explains that birthing stories can be medicine, as stories are "forms of remembering natural laws" because they "contain original instructions and encoded knowledge" that can be "'felt' in the body" (39). In this sense, a story can allow us to "remember" something we already sensed as true but had not yet brought into consciousness or did not previously have language for; further, stories allow us to process knowledge through our felt and embodied senses. Understanding the power of stories in this way reaffirms that from the first page, *Call Me Tree / Llámame árbol* is far more than an entertaining story; indeed, it utilizes image and text to communicate complex ideas about human existence. Even for children with undeveloped language and literacy skills, the visual signs and bodily postures presented in the illustrations make this a story that children may feel in their bodies.

Ultimately, the story asks us to remember our embodied interconnection with the earth, in terms of what can be seen as well as what is unseen or hidden. The lines "deep / dark / earth," or "tierra / profunda / y oscura," indicate to children the value, richness, and depth held in darkness, which is also a mother and site of origins. To understand how the narrative's complex communication takes place, I draw on Gloria Anzaldúa's theory of *el cenote* as a well of images, or a "dreampool." She writes, "I taste a forgotten knowledge triggered by an odor or some trivial incident and suddenly out pours ancestral information stored beyond the files of personal memory, stored as iconic imagery somewhere in that deep dreampool, the collective unconscious" ("Llorona Coyolxauhqui" 297). The first page of this picture book, which draws on iconic birth imagery, functions to remind us of forgotten knowledge, which is not simply personal knowledge but part of an underground, ancestral, collective unconscious, triggered by the interplay of image and language. The unnamed child lies in a dream state, a seed within the earth, extending one hand upward through the multiple layers of earth and atmosphere, a golden tree growing around it: "I dream / I am reaching / Dreaming and reaching / Reaching and dreaming" (Gonzalez, *Call Me Tree* 5). The paired alternation and repetition suggest that dreaming and reaching are one and the same, intertwined acts, *soñar y extenderse*; when we dream, our consciousness reaches out toward some as-yet-unfulfilled reality, and when we reach, actively extending ourselves outward, we express a dream at the core of the soul. Thus the origin story expressed in this mythic image is a story about the nature of existence.

Awakening to an Ecosystem

Upon awakening, which is also a birth, the child emerges above ground, with eyes open to witness the watercolor sky with puffy pink clouds and yellow birds flying. Reaching and rising, the child stands in front of a tree whose body is also the child. Unlike in *I Know the River Loves Me / Yo sé que el río me ama*, the child in this book is not drawn in black and white but rather appears in vibrant color throughout the entire story. With bare feet touching earth, outstretched arms, and eyes closed once again in a meditative state, this child appears in perfect harmony with nature—indeed, the child *is* nature. In the middle of the narrative, we are met with the child's face drawn wide across two pages, a seeming gesture toward Gonzalez's own experience of never finding her face in books as a child. Surrounded by blue sky, green leaves, and more pink clouds, the child's face is round and golden brown with rosy cheeks and small brown open eyes that gaze at the viewer. The child asks, "And what do I see / With my eyes / As I rise?" or "Y qué veo / Con mis ojos / Mientras me elevo?" (Gonzalez, *Call Me Tree* 11–12). This image of the awakened self signals a shift from the unconscious to the conscious self, which strives to discern its surroundings. Anzaldúa describes this effort toward discernment: "World of uncanny signs. A secret language shared with the spirits of trees, seas, wind, and animals. . . . The shock of waking to other realities—same world, new eyes" ("Llorona Coyolxauhqui" 297). The new eyes the child uses to read the "uncanny signs" of the world above ground invite the reader into a shared gaze. The language shared between the elements of nature is not a language of words but a language of signs, attunement, and recognition.

On the next set of pages, we learn what the child sees: "Trees! More and more trees / Trees and trees / Just like me!" or "Árboles! Más y más árboles / árboles y árboles / Iguales a mí!" (Gonzalez, *Call Me Tree* 13–14). This text is laid over an illustration featuring four "trees" that the child sees, different from each other in color, shape, and flower: a tall blue trunk with yellow flowers and orange leaves; a short brown trunk with a full pink bush of leaves; another brown trunk with green leaves and pink flowers like starbursts; and a trunk of light brown whose leaves are hidden from view. In front of each tree stands a child, each of whom has different hair, skin color, dress, and posture, with at least two in yoga poses. Despite these clear variations, the narrator exclaims that the trees are "just like me!" This is not meant to indicate a message of color blindness, for the child's eyes are wide open on the previous page, and, as becomes obvious on the following pages, the child recognizes the many differences between these trees. Firstly, the child acknowledges its own ontology as tree: "A tree I am / A tree I stand," or "Un árbol soy / De pie estoy" (15). Simultaneously, the child acknowledges the distinct spatial locations of the other child-trees it sees: "On a sidewalk / En la acera," "On a mountain / En la montaña," and "By a river or a road / Junto al río o al camino" (16). Just as each tree grows in its own unique site, visually distinct in color and type, a child stands in front, embodying an expression of race and gender that distinguishes it from the others. Further, these children move and inhabit their "tree" bodies in different ways; for example, one stretches and arches with the wind, hair flowing with the leaves of its tree, while another dances upon a single foot, arms stretched as wide as the branches they reflect.

This diversity of movement is reaffirmed in the following set of pages as the narrator acknowledges not spatial location but the actions of the tree-children it sees. "Some trees reach / Some trees teach / Some trees stand so still," or "Algunos árboles se extienden / Algunos árboles enseñan / Algunos árboles se quedan / tan quietos" (Gonzalez, *Call Me Tree* 18). Thus the tree-children not only look different from one another but also function in unique ways, creating space to honor difference in the minds of readers. Importantly, the recognition of seeing, speaking, and honoring these differences does not undercut the concept of interconnectivity or the narrator's earlier statement that these trees are "just like me." Toward the end of the narrative, across two pages, Gonzalez illustrates the concept of interconnection across difference (figure 8). On the left-hand page stand three tree-children who are swaying in the wind, mouths agape and hair blowing along with the leaves. On the right-side page we see our narrator, arms outstretched in front of a large, green, bushy tree. All of these children possess their own observable characteristics, yet swirling brown lines extend from their feet and down into the ground, finally meeting with one another. Thus this scene simultaneously visualizes difference and interconnection. Here I turn back to Anzaldúa, who describes her idea of an embodied identity that encompasses more than sex and race, writing, "When I think of 'moving' from a sexed, racialized body to a more expansive identity interconnected with its surroundings, I see in my mind's eye trees with interconnected roots (subterranean webs)" ("Geographies of Selves" 66). These subterranean webs might look very

FIGURE 8 Maya Christina Gonzalez, illustration of tree-children, from *Call Me Tree /
Llámame árbol*. Text and illustrations ©2014 by Maya Christina Gonzalez. Permission
arranged with Children's Book Press, an imprint of Lee & Low Books Inc., 95 Madison
Ave, New York, NY 10016.

much like the swirling lines found in *Call Me Tree / Llámame árbol*. Anzaldúa
expands, "We are responsible participants in the ecosystems (complete set of
relationships between a network of living organisms and their physical habitats)
in whose web we're individual strands" ("Geographies of Selves" 67). In this
sense, we can read the children in Maya Christina Gonzalez's work as individual
strands, each inhabiting their own field of difference within an interlocking web
of relationships. Thus the narrative depicts for its readers and viewers a concept
of humanity as existing within an ecosystem of natural diversity; further, the
image of underground roots connecting a network of organisms and habitats
can help children to understand the concept of mutual support.

The Roots of Ancestral Knowledge

Writing about the fruiting processes of pecan trees, Robin Wall Kimmerer
explains: "If one tree fruits, they all fruit. . . . Not one tree in a grove; but the

whole grove; not one grove in the forest, but every grove; all across the country and all across the state. . . . What we see is the power of unity. What happens to one happens to us all. . . . All flourishing is mutual" (15). While the trees in *Call Me Tree / Llámame árbol* are not all pecan trees, the image of interconnected roots offered by the story clearly conveys a similar message of mutual coexistence and the kinship, or at least sociality, of trees. In *The Hidden Life of Trees* (2015), forester Peter Wohlleben makes this direct comparison between trees and people, asking, "But why are trees such social beings? . . . The reasons are the same as for human communities: there are advantages to working together. A tree is not a forest" (3–4). Relating this to Gonzalez's narrative, it becomes clear that she draws on the reference point of trees as a way to teach readers, viewers, and listeners to embrace individual differences as strengths, while remaining conscious of the often unseen ways in which we are connected to one another and have integrated lives. Thus the narrative works to undercut binary frameworks of gender and race, presenting a story in which people who are different from one another are also tied to each other without collapsing, sacrificing, or erasing that difference.

Significantly, the message that this interrelatedness emerges from a connection to nature performs important decolonial work, challenging subject/object binaries of Western discourse by drawing on non-Western knowledge forms and potentially reorienting how readers and viewers think about their relationships to the earth, other people, and their own identities. With the iconography of the root, Gonzalez invokes not only a society of mutual support and interconnection, but also a source of ancestral knowledge and strength. For, as Wohlleben writes of literal tree roots, "it is in the roots that centuries of experience are stored, and it is this experience that has allowed the tree's survival to the present day" (81). If, as Gonzalez's narrative suggests, we are trees with underground roots that connect us to one another, then those roots connect us not only to others who are living in the present day but also to the experiences and knowledge of those who have come before us, and who can make us stronger.

The healing quality of this story is perhaps most potent when we recall that it begins as a birthing story, for in that light these underground roots might also be perceived as umbilical cords. Patrisia Gonzales describes Indigenous practices that ritually treat the *ombligo* (which "connects to—and is—the center of the world") as sacred, sometimes involving its burial or return to the earth (142, 148). Regarding these practices, she writes: "These acts return the child to a living relative, mother or grandmother, the mother of all. The body is also a sacred ground . . . linked to stories and metaphors. . . . Through such practices, the body becomes a mediator of the landscape and yet part of it, part of sacred communication that expresses a sacred medicine" (148). In *Call Me Tree / Llámame árbol*, the sacred connection between bodies, spirit, and land is recalled through a practice of storytelling that involves both words and images. The child born from the womb of the earth is related to it as kin, and also *is* the ground from which it grows. These tree-children's bodies, locations, expressions, and functions are distinct, and yet, even as they stand in difference, they take part in a form of sacred communication, not only through their roots but also through the medicine of song. For in the abovementioned image of three children swaying in the wind, their mouths are open to sing. As the text proclaims, "Some sing songs / Some sing along / All trees have roots / All trees belong" or "Unos cantan canciones / Otros se unen al coro / Todos los árboles tienen raíces / Todos los árboles tienen un lugar" (19). This sense of ontological belonging to and rootedness in the landscape is interlocked with an epistemological understanding that every being has a place within the sacred chorus of song.

Conclusion

These picture books draw on written and visual text to restore sacred memory and knowledge about our relationships to land as kin—best friend, playmate, protectress, and mother. Through iconography and image, Gonzalez's stories work to heal the wounds of the epistemic and ontological violence that ruptures our felt sense of interconnection to others across space and time, including the spirit and bodies of the natural world. By resituating the framework of our relationships to ourselves, each other, and nature, her books intervene in the consciousness of those who encounter them. Even for children who have not developed literacy and language skills, these stories are clearly about the movement of our bodies, and more specifically the knowledge and memory of interconnectivity that are transmitted through that movement. These are narratives that push us to think beyond the notion of our individual human bodies as isolated by gulfs, even as they distinctly honor the marvels of those bodies and what they can do. In other words, these works inspire us to consider how our bodies can only be fully known through our engagements with and in nature, and also how our bodies *are* nature, are land. While librarians, K–12 education scholars, and children's studies practitioners have emphasized children's picture books as a critical site of knowledge formation, I have sought to show the complex work these narratives perform and the value they hold for literary scholars more generally. In particular, I suggest that scholars of Chicanx studies will find an exciting body of work in children's literature, one that is thematically and theoretically challenging and strongly linked to the discourses of the field, such as spirituality, memory, landscape, and embodiment. Indeed, these are all evident concerns in the next chapter, which is focused on a more traditional genre, the novel. Yet I will return to an idea that I have addressed to a lesser extent in this chapter—dreaming as a site of embodied knowledge.

5

The Dreaming Body

Resituating Time, Space, and Knowledge

I n examining embodied spirituality in Chicanx narrative, this study has
focused on noninstitutional sites of encounter: the ocean's shoreline, the
riverbank, a community of trees, the garden and home, and the stage. Yet
this chapter considers narrative representation of a site typically thought of as
uniquely *disembodied*: the dream space. As I suggest here, dreaming can be a
space in which to experience—and thus better understand—complex relationships between body, environment, spirit, and one's own soul. Specifically, I attend
to the depiction of embodied states of dreaming as they relate to dream work as
a method of learning and a form of knowledge in Luis Alberto Urrea's historical
novels *The Hummingbird's Daughter* (2005) and *Queen of America* (2011).* Based
on twenty-six years of research by the author, these novels imagine the life of
Teresa Urrea, a popular healer also known as La Santa de Cabora.† The first of
these works depicts her life in Mexico, the country of her birth, detailing her gift
(*don de Dios*) and training as a curandera, in particular a *partera* (midwife); the
novel also relates the brush with death that transforms her into "La Santa," an

---

*In my use of the phrase "dreaming body" in this chapter's title, I refer to the body in
dreams and the body that dreams. Though Arnold Mindell used this phrase frequently in his
writings, it is not my objective to invoke him or his work here, but rather to refer to embodied
states of dreaming in a broader sense.

†For the purposes of this chapter, I use "Teresa Urrea" to indicate the historical figure
these novels are based upon and "Teresita" to refer to the character featured in these works.

uncanonized saint believed to possess miraculous healing powers. For the many pilgrims and followers who sought her out during the Porfiriato era in Mexico, Teresa Urrea was not a representative of Rome or the official Church's priests, whom she strongly criticized;[‡] rather, she embodied the regional particularities of a Catholicism marked by distinctly non-Western frameworks—namely, the principle of mindbodyspirit integration and the prioritization of environmental relationships.

The Hummingbird's Daughter ends with her political exile from Mexico under the orders of Porfirio Díaz on the charge of inspiring the Indigenous uprisings carried out in her name. *Queen of America* presents her life in exile on the other side of the U.S.-Mexico border, traveling across the United States, where she lived up until her death at the age of thirty-three. While elsewhere I have written on the more overtly political and historical contexts of spirituality in *The Hummingbird's Daughter*, I focus here on the representation of dreams as an embodied spiritual and epistemological practice in that novel and its sequel.[§] Further, it is my contention that although dream discourse in these novels may not read as overtly political, its epistemic contexts frame dream work as decolonial practice. Specifically, I address these concepts through the relationship of apprenticeship between "Teresita" (as she is referred to in the novels) and Huila, the curandera who "follow[s] an invisible map made of dreams and stories" as she teaches and guides Teresita in her own development as a skillful dreamer (Urrea, *Hummingbird* 212). The "dream time" they each experience suggests mysteries of the body, both in terms of the body that dreams and the body in dreams—for example, the body in flight. Dreams and visions in these narratives provide alternate conceptions of time and space in which discourses of disembodiment and embodiment are in productive conversation with one another.

I begin by offering useful contexts through which to approach the narrative representation of dreaming as a form of embodied experience and intelligence, specifically decentering the Western perspective. Moving into narrative analysis of *The Hummingbird's Daughter*, I focus on Teresita's childhood dreams, which

---

[‡] As Raphael Brewster Folsom explains: "The presidency of Porfirio Díaz (c. 1876–1910) saw the expansion of a national network of railroads, the reform of education, the centralization of state power, and a steady assault on practices of collective landholding" (1). Amid this modernizing mission, widespread abuses were perpetuated by the state, and in particularly heinous fashion toward Indigenous groups.

[§] See Christina Garcia Lopez, "This Land is Holy!"

initiate the reader into the world of dreams as a composite of experiential, spatial, and temporal landscapes; her training with Huila; the night-flying trips she takes with her friends that signal her proficiency as a dreamer; and the dreams and visions surrounding her temporary death, Huila's actual death, and eventually Teresita's exile. Transitioning to the novel's sequel, *Queen of America*, I consider the implications of Teresita and Huila's continuing bond via powerful dreams and visions, and the lessons the novel attempts to impart regarding conscious awareness, perception, and the crossing between life and death. Across the two novels, dreaming is depicted as a form of travel or flight of the soul, a temporary dislodging of the soul from the material body. As Gloria Anzaldúa explains, "According to Mexican indigenous spirituality, el alma es una entidad que puede desprenderse del cuerpo" ("Flights" 29). This cultural understanding of the soul as an entity that can break away from or fly out of the body is discussed in chapter 1 in the context of susto, as the unintentional result of fright or trauma. However, this chapter examines such splitting as the result of skillful dream practice that allows the soul to take flight, discover hidden worlds of knowledge, and carry this knowledge back to the material body. I consider these representations with a specific focus on the degree to which they imply an embodied spirituality, even when the soul is separated from the material body. Further, I analyze the significance of natural environments in these dream states and flights in relation to an embodied intersubjectivity.

The Intelligence of Dreaming

In her influential collection of essays on radical Chicana feminism, *Massacre of the Dreamers: Essays on Xicanisma* (1994), Ana Castillo reflects on the relationship between dreaming and politics through a Mesoamerican lens. She recounts the legend of the Mexica ruler Moctezuma, who ordered the massacre of mystic dreamers who predicted the fall of his empire. As she explains, from Tenochtitlán the ruler "called on the thousands of dreamers who were sharing the same premonition" and, out of "his own sense of despair and because of his abuse of power," ordered them murdered in addition to "having their wives and children hung and their houses destroyed" (Castillo 14–15). I recall this story, which is recurrent throughout Chicanx discourse, to consider the usable information it might offer us now regarding the political contexts of dreams as intelligence. To understand the contemporary relevance of this legend, we must examine the implications of the dreams and the undercurrents of Moctezuma's murderous impulse.

If we consider dreams as stories that arise from the collective and personal unconscious, they are stories not only about ourselves but also about our interpersonal and collective relationships. As Castillo conjectures, the shared dream of those who predicted the fall of Tenochtitlán "may not have been a sign of premonitory gifts but the fact that much of the populace knew their nation was in trouble"; yet their ruler sought to extinguish the dreamers, their families, and their dreams in an attempt to salvage his power (Castillo 15). The attempted denial and delegitimization of stories that threaten both the dominant national narrative and those it empowers continues to resonate today. Dreams present a potential counternarrative that serves the needs of the spirit over, for example, those of the state. Grouping dreamers with poets and visionaries, Castillo warns that such figures are "banished at the point when [their] society becomes based on the denigration of life and the extinction of the spirit" (15). Willingness to seek guidance in the messages of dreams, visions, and the artistry they inspire may counter the blinding nationalism that criminalizes the act of imagining otherwise. Whether we conceptualize *dreamers* as literal dream practitioners or, more broadly, as those who dare to imagine alternative possibilities—such as the DREAMers of today who likewise struggle against extinction of spirit—dreams compel us to make present individual and shared memories. However, this chapter treats literal dream work as knowledge carried in our bodies and accessed during dreams, stretching across space and time.

Jungian psychoanalyst Clarissa Pinkola Estés, who has also written about the legend of the massacre of the dreamers, closely considers the relevance that dreams continue to have for us in the context of a collective well of memories. From a Jungian perspective, she emphasizes the common images, figures, stories, and ideas that repeatedly appear across cultures, geographic spaces, and temporal periods, considering them recurring aspects of the human psyche. While we are prone to consider our dreams entirely our own, Estés offers a different viewpoint. Positing the psyche as "a universe unto itself," she asserts, *"Maybe we dream new dreams just for ourselves. But, for certain, we also dream old dreams, recycle dreams dreamt by others who lived long before we were born"* (Estés, *Untie* 52–53; italics in original). From this perspective, one of a collective unconscious that never entirely deletes ideas even as peoples, cultures, and societies pass away, we might begin to consider dreams as mediators of information once held by previous generations. Further, we can inquire how such information might be useful not only in a personal sense but in an interpersonal context as well. In her discussion of the Mesoamerican legend of the massacre of the dreamers, Estés explains that "night dreams were considered intelligence then" (*Untie* 57) and "tribal dreamers took their callings to dream 'for the people of this world' as their serious troth with the holiest of Holy—to care for, educate, and protect the wisdom of souls" (59). This perspective on dreaming as holy work that can serve one's broader community provides an important basis for understanding the discourse of dream work in Urrea's novels. For while the historical figure Teresa Urrea lived centuries after Moctezuma and the dreamers of this legend, and certainly in different cultural terrain, the lessons her teacher Huila passes on to her in these novels reflect related principles about the work and possibilities of dreaming. Thus I am concerned with the epistemological and ontological intervention that such a conceptualization offers to contemporary consciousness, particularly with regard to a healing subjectivity.

Scholar Patrisia Gonzales describes herself as "a granddaughter of Kickapoo, Comanche and Macehual peoples who migrated throughout the present-day United States and Mexico" ("About Patrisia Gonzales"). In *Red Medicine: Traditional Indigenous Rites of Birthing and Healing* (2012), Gonzales discusses dreams as a continuing part of her personal medicine (169), while also reflecting on the historical persecution of Indigenous peoples who engaged in dream practices in the territories now known as Mexico. As she explains, "During colonial times, dreamers could be persecuted for their *don*, or gift," and were "recorded as targets of Inquisitorial efforts" (178). Importantly, such targeting focused on both the dreamers themselves and the collected and represented knowledge of dreaming, the written sources of which were at least partially destroyed: "Colonial records acknowledge the existence of the Nahua book of dreams, *Temicamatl*, as well as similar books among the Maya, none of which survived the massive book burnings overseen by the Catholic Church during the early colonial period" (Gonzales 175). This destructive impulse exemplifies the epistemic violence and repression exercised toward dream practices and emphasizes the importance of oral tradition. Furthermore, this targeted repression continues into the present, for, as Gonzales asserts, "during various periods from the 1950s to the present, Mayan dream interpreters and dreaming have been targets of state repression and religious conservatives" (180). Acknowledging this ongoing history situates dreaming as an epistemological practice that has been struggled over across cultural identities, temporal periods, and spatial locations.

Thus, relevant to this chapter's analysis, even where dream discourse in these novels does not seem overtly political, the characters' engagement with dream knowledge is in some sense politicized by the cultural, historical, and epistemic contexts framing it. Indeed, as related by Yolanda Broyles-González, the historical figure of Teresa Urrea was "born at the intersection of Mayo and Yaqui territories, and she rose to prominence at a time when a new wave of armed Mexican soldiers, along with *hacendado* land-grabbers and sexual exploiters, occupied the Yaqui/Mayo homeland (today's Northwest)" (Broyles-González 127). Teresa Urrea was the illegitimate daughter of a wealthy white landholder and a poor, young Native girl, and her rise to spiritual prominence reflected the complex intersections of the Porfiriato era, which itself was marked by an ongoing struggle for survival amid genocidal violence against Indigenous peoples, political corruption, and widespread poverty and suffering among the masses. Luis D. León writes that she became "a symbol of indigenous agrarian resistance to the Americanizing forces of . . . Díaz, who attempted to eliminate the Sonoran Indians through his *scientífico* programs, which allowed North Americans to mine Mexican land" (*La Llorona's Children* 143). Importantly, this symbolic status was rooted in her perceived healing gifts, as well as spiritual and land-based epistemologies and practices.

To contextualize these ideas, popular spirituality in rural northern Mexico at the time took on what might be described as a veil of Catholicism while "shielding and camouflaging the indigenous ways within the hide-and-seek of the new nation's *mexicanidad*" (Broyles-González 121). Specifically, the healing practice of curanderismo at hand in these narratives is a central example of the syncretism melding Catholicism and Indigenous beliefs and practices. Though Teresa Urrea eventually came to be known to her followers as a miraculous healer called "La Santa de Cabora," her practices, including her purported engagement in dream work, were often in contradiction and resistance to the official Catholic Church. George Hartley explains the syncretic nature of curanderismo: "Despite being superficially transformed by the monotheistic traditions of Islam and Christianity, the practices and belief systems of curanderismo stem primarily from polytheistic tribal-indigenous sources. Curanderas often use Christianized elements, but these elements themselves are primarily pre-Christian, given a Christian veneer through various syncretic influences" ("Indigeneity" 190). It is in this way that we must approach the complications of the language in these novels, which regularly refers to "God" in what seems to be a Catholic or more generally Christian context, while at other times referring to "the creator" and "the four directions," suggesting an Indigenous context; indeed, the character of Huila uses all of these terms. Further, practices depicted in these texts, such as soul flight or even the investment of significant meaning in dreams, would likely be rejected by the Catholic Church as superstition. Indeed, León writes that even as Teresa Urrea was popularly known as a saint, she was excommunicated from the Church (*La Llorona's Children* 145). Given these political and historical circumstances, I argue that although dream work is not necessarily an inherent aspect of curanderismo, Teresita's engagement in dreaming as a meaningful form of knowing in these novels, alongside her work as a healer, suggests dream space as one possible site or contributory source of healing from the violence of colonialism and its ongoing effects.

In my analysis of dreaming as epistemological practice in these novels, I am concerned specifically with the embodied experience of the soul. While it is the strongly disembodied aspect of dreaming that shifts us beyond the normal parameters of bodily confines, I am interested in how the act and meaning of dreaming relate to the interrelationship of the mindbodysoul. In their co-authored book *Integral Dreaming: A Holistic Approach to Dreams* (2012), Fariba Bogzaran and Daniel Deslauriers explore "how the dream and bodily/somatic life intersect" (210), arguing that dreams are "fully bodied experience" (216). More specifically, they situate the body as a space through which the dreaming self can move: "In a sense, the body, like the dream, becomes a landscape through which consciousness can travel and glean meaningful insights accrued by the (re)experience of embodied states" (207). From this perspective, the body functions as a kind of geographic space that holds memory of countless experiences within its muscles, bones, ligaments, and cells; accordingly, these experiences might be accessed and felt again via the work (or play) of a traveling consciousness during dream time. Further, if we connect this thinking to Clarissa Pinkola Estés's discussion of dreams as ancestral memory, we might consider how the experiences stored in our bodies may not be limited to those we have embodied ourselves but may potentially include the embodied experiences of those who came before us. Taking this intersection between dream and body a step further, Bogzaran and Deslauriers consider how dreams may leave "traces" or "subtle impressions" in the body that continue to be felt and negotiated even after a dream has ended (216). In other words, we might conjecture that dreams are embodied in that they (1) draw on memories of previous embodied states; and (2) create new states of embodiment in which the awakened dreamer must manage felt residues of emotions and sensations left in the body, even if unconsciously.

While dreams provide a working medium through which to explore the depths of consciousness and embodied experience, a longstanding challenge to the legitimation of dreams as knowledge within dominant discourse is their incongruence with Western notions of reality. Gloria Anzaldúa approached these questions of reality by confronting the Western tendency to delegitimize acts of the imagination as false or unreal. For example, she describes what she calls her *ensueños* in terms of an active, waking practice of processing images that sometimes emerged from her own consciousness and other times from a universal consciousness (Anzaldúa, "Flights" 35). In addition to this waking practice of ensueños, she asserts, "Dreams, too, are a form of experience, a dimension in which life and mind seem to be embedded" (35). For Anzaldúa, engagement with images through the creative process of imagination is a method of accessing "another type of reality" not marginal to or lesser than ordinary reality but rather parallel to it; yet, she argues, overemphasis on whether dreams and other acts of imagination are sufficiently "real" only distracts from the tangible effects they render in one's life (35–37). In specific, she focuses on the embodied aspects of imagination: "The body does not discern between different kinds of stimuli; the body doesn't distinguish between what happens in the imagination and what happens in the material world. Every time you have a nightmare or think about meeting someone, your mental/emotional scenario makes you nervous and flustered. The body responds. The body mediates these two realities; it is in the body that they coexist. There's frustration in trying to separate the two" (Anzaldúa, "Creativity" 108). According to this thinking, the body acts as a meeting place or nexus, mediating a continuum of realities communicated through images and ideas. Thus, regardless of whether one considers a dream *real* or not, the embodied responses stimulated by the emotions and ideas it renders bring that dream space into material reality. In this sense, then, the dream is an embodied experience even as it allows one to transcend the space of the physical world. Reality thus becomes a mediated idea played out in the materiality of the body. Further, this perspective strengthens understanding of why and how the body, as a meeting space of multiple realities, can be considered sacred terrain, for, as Gonzales asserts, the body is the "re-search instrument" through which we process the "phenomena" accessed through dreams (182). In this chapter then, my interest in Teresita and Huila's dream work is not merely about their individual psychic experiences, but more broadly about the embodied mediation of reality and collective knowledge.

Initiation Dreams

The actual Teresa Urrea was alternately viewed as a healer, a saint, a heretic, and a dangerous subversive during her lifetime (1873–1906), resulting in her political exile from Mexico at age nineteen (Romo 23). As the first in this pair of novels, *The Hummingbird's Daughter* covers the period from her birth in Sinaloa to her exile. After she drew thousands of pilgrims in Sonora, Mexico, with her healings and questioned the authority of the Catholic Church, Teresa Urrea's name was taken up in Indigenous uprisings in northern Mexico with the cry "Viva Santa Teresa" (Romo 23–24). Luis D. León explains that while "efforts to hold Teresa responsible for the Yaqui and Mayo revolts were futile," the Mexican government, in its fervor to take control of Indian land, "imprisoned her for a brief time in 1892," ultimately forcing her and her father, Tomás Urrea, to board a train to Arizona under orders never to return (*La Llorona's Children* 146). Her life in the United States would take her not only to Arizona but to a great many other places including Texas, California, and New York, as she toured the country surrounded by a kind of celebrity; she settled in Clifton, Arizona, prior to her death from tuberculosis at the young age of thirty-three. Her life in exile is the subject of *Queen of America*, which I cover to a lesser extent than the first book due to the particularities of my focus, though it merits its own extensive analysis. Certainly a significant aspect of Teresa Urrea's continuing resonance as a historical figure is her appeal to a broad variety of people on both sides of the U.S.-Mexico border.

The Hummingbird's Daughter is divided into five sections (or "books"), beginning with "Book I: The Initiation of the Dreamers," which relates the story of Teresita's birth on the Santana ranch in Sinaloa, Mexico. As the story opens, we meet her mother Cayetana Chávez, nicknamed La Semalú, or "the Hummingbird," on the day she gives birth. Later in the novel, she is described as being of Mayo, Tehueco, and Yaqui descent, with a Catholic father and a mother who "followed the old ways" (Urrea, *Hummingbird* 70). At fourteen years of age she gives birth to Teresita, a child fathered by the ranch's wealthy white *patrón*, Tomás Urrea. We are also introduced to Huila, the old *partera* (midwife) and *curandera* (healer) on the ranch, who delivers Teresita and is known to the *patrones* in whose home she works as María Sonora. The historical figure of Huila is referred to as a "Yaqui" in Romo's scholarship (Romo 27) and a "mestiza" in the work of Paul Vanderwood (Vanderwood 166), while both affirm her identity as a *curandera*. In Urrea's novel she seems to negotiate these identities smoothly, praying from two different perspectives that somehow coexist: "She paused to offer up a prayer to the Maker. As María Sonora, she prayed to Dios, as Huila, she prayed to Lios. Dios had doves and lambs, and Lios had deer and hummingbirds. It was all the same to Huila" (Urrea, *Hummingbird* 16). As a central character in *The Hummingbird's Daughter*, she is a wise and respected figure in her community and a teacher to "Teresita," who is left behind after her mother Cayetana leaves the ranch when she is only a child.

As an "illegitimate" daughter, Teresita is left to live with her aunt, an unkind woman named Tía. With an absent mother and no knowledge of her father, she asks Tía about her identity; in response, Tía sarcastically suggests that she ask Huila, the midwife who delivered her. When Teresita, a member of the peasant class, sneaks into the main house where Huila works in order to do just that, Tía rages at the girl for putting them both in jeopardy by transgressing the social order of the ranch; she beats her with a wooden spoon and tosses Teresita into a pigpen as punishment. Here the first dream occurs, an initiation to the world of dreams as a place of power for both the reader and Teresita. For the dream is the first in a series that present an alternate experience of space and time, requiring readers steeped in Western consciousness to make a significant shift in perspective in order to make sense of the whole.

As the girl passes out in the pigpen, covered with welts from the beating she has just received, she closes her eyes: "Then she was falling. Falling through the earth, through the spaces between the stones, into the deeper nothing of the sky. Falling, where the sky itself became small again and was contained inside her own eye. Falling through her eye into the place where dreams harden into stones and become the ground" (Urrea, *Hummingbird* 68). Here an ordinary sense of space is inverted as she falls through earth *first* before reaching sky and ultimately falls through her own eye, suggesting the unconscious. Importantly, it is here that dreams become solid material (stones), grounding rather than ethereal or inscrutable. Additionally, the fragmented phrases "Corridors of flame" and "Obsidian rooms" that immediately follow the description of her fall indicate an unconscious that surpasses the individual psyche to include an ancestral and cultural context. Discussing "obsidian's place in Mesoamerican cosmovision and ideology," Marc N. Levine emphasizes "how obsidian and people came together through embodied ritual and everyday practices" such as the mining and crafting of the volcanic glass, as well as its use for bodily adornment (14, 16–17). More specifically, Levine highlights how "histories of embodied experience become rooted in memory or the landscape" (16). Thus the rooms and corridors that

Teresita passes through in her dream seem to signal spaces reflective of not only her own mind but also a living ancestral memory. Here the obsidian rooms of her dream gesture toward the embodied practices of her ancestors and the larger ecology and "cosmovision" of these practices.

Alongside an alternate conception of space, her dream offers an experience of all time as simultaneous, for "her days rose about her, from womb to playtime, from this moment to far ahead of herself: womanhood and mirrors" (Urrea, *Hummingbird* 68). In this dream time, past, present, and future present themselves to her simultaneously, such that she can observe her own life through the mirror of the dream's reflection even as her physical body continues to lie in the pigpen. Next the "sparks" of her sputtering brain flash in a series of fragmentary scenes: herself carrying a water jug atop her head, dark hands loading bullets into rifles, laundry foam sliding down river stones, and women's hands slapping maize dough into tortillas (69). The emphasis on body parts—the head, the hands—highlights embodied activities, not only her own but those of anonymous figures. The representation of the daily rituals of transporting water, preparing tortillas, and doing laundry highlights women's embodied labor, particularly among the so-called "peasant" classes. Placed alongside images of dark hands loading bullets, these images might allude to the Mayo and Yaqui land-based rebellions that would eventually use her name as a battle cry, or possibly to the activities of the Mexican Revolution later. Stylistically, the majority of this section of the dream looks and feels more like a poem than prose; the spacing and cadence express each image as partial and incomplete, with each fragment visually delineated on the page by dashes and flowerlike asterisks. Additionally, the white space of the page gestures toward the ambiguous quality of the dream space. Overall, this stylistic alteration reinforces the dream's differentiated mode.

Importantly, Teresita sees in this initial dream figures of very intimate relevance as well. First she sees the familiar figure of Huila, who is walking through trees, reminding the reader of the curandera's ongoing movement through and relationship to the land and nature. She also sees her mother's image: "Though she had no memory of seeing the Hummingbird, she knew who it was. 'Mother,' she whispered" (Urrea, *Hummingbird* 69). Teresita has no conscious memory of her mother, as Cayetana left the ranch when Teresita was only two years old; yet Teresita observes her mother in the dream space, an occurrence that happens several times in both novels. Indeed, prior to the end of the sequel, *Queen of America*, Teresita's dreams are the only spaces in which she encounters her mother, each time evoking a powerful sense of witness to what she longs for. The absence of her mother is particularly important to both narratives, serving as a catalyst for much of the action. The ability to overcome such distance within the time-space of the dream is indicated in the simple last line of chapter 8 of book 1: "In the dream, she traveled far" (Urrea, *Hummingbird* 69). This assertion indicates a movement through both space and time, even as her body lies aching within the pigpen where her aunt has thrown her. As she awakes, she finds herself next to a sleeping mother pig, who "lazily offer[s] her fourteen nipples to this small human shoat" before returning to her own pig dreams (70). This image of the girl as a "shoat," or young piglet, reinforces her state as an orphan, motherless and tossed aside with the animals. This image of Teresita suffering from bruises, open wounds, and mosquito bites provides a reference point of pain that she will not only be healed of, but from which she will grow to heal others.

Significantly, it is while the curandera Huila treats Teresita's wounds with a medicinal remedy of crushed *cuasia*, or bitter wood, that she senses sparks of warmth indicating the presence of "the gift" in the girl (Urrea, *Hummingbird* 77–78). It is thus that Teresita spends the night in the main house with Huila, where she has a second dream, in which "she thought she was awake, but she was not" (80). Barefoot in a field of flowers, she is observed from a distance by "three old men" who are "of the People," which indicates them as members of local Indigenous groups (80). These old men appear repeatedly in Teresita's dreams, and readers come to learn later that she too is a figure in theirs, suggesting a dreamscape that is to some extent shared. As this second dream progresses, the relationship between dreaming and the body in dreams comes to the fore. Barefoot, Teresita turns, sees a hill of blossoms, and walks up it. "Her feet hurt from the pebbles in the ground, and the path turned to a clear stream of water, and the water cooled her feet. . . . She thanked the ground for its mercy" (81). These seemingly simple details demonstrate a complex dreamscape in which the dreamer experiences embodied sensations in direct response to the environment. Both the registering of pain and the cooling sensation of water suggest Teresita's bodily awareness in the terrain of her dream. More specifically, Teresita experiences a felt sense of an environment that, in turn, responds to her sensation and alters to give her body within the dream comfort and relief. This reciprocity between dreamer and the landscape of her dream is further accentuated when she offers thanks to the ground in her dream for its mercy. Ultimately, this dream allows her an experience of harmony and balance with an environment that is alive and responsive to her needs, and which she respects as well. In this way, the dream provides a knowledge that is not merely observed, but felt and embodied in such a way that its residue may inform her future work as a healer.

The final part of this dream emphasizes awareness not of her own body but of an external one. As she sits upon a rock, she becomes aware of a hummingbird "made of sky," which is "too small to be seen, yet she could see it" (Urrea, *Hummingbird* 81). The ability to see beyond what is ordinarily possible suggests the increased power of perception in dreams, and an alternative type of knowledge. Further, the contradiction held in the hummingbird's body is significant, as this creature that is "too small to be seen" is made up of sky, which is too immense to be taken in wholly. This ability of the bird's body to contain and express spatial contradiction is reasserted, as "its blue breast reflected the world as it descended" (81). Thus the hummingbird's body becomes a mirror in which to perceive the unperceivable world, suggesting that its own sacredness reflects that of the larger world from which it emerges. Further, even as the hummingbird vaguely alludes to Teresita's mother, known as La Semalú, it clearly signals the myth of hummingbirds as spiritual messengers, for it descends "from the heavens," landing on her knee, and, turning to the left, drops a feather into her hand as she reaches out toward it (81). When Teresita later reveals the dream to Huila, the old woman listens carefully, asking questions, and interprets the dream, explaining that hummingbirds come from heaven, feathers are sacred, and left is the direction of the heart (96). Upon assessing Teresita's lack of knowledge regarding these principles, she expresses dismay at the girl's lack of education:

> "What does it mean, Huila?"
>
>> "Well—the hummingbird is the messenger of God."
>
>> "He is?"
>
>> "You didn't know that?"
>
>> "No."
>
>> "Has no one taught you anything?"
>
>> "Only you, Huila." (96)

For Huila, spiritual skills of observation and interpretation are essential to everyday life; her assessment that the girl has been deprived of these skills demonstrates a cultural politics regarding what constitutes valuable knowledge and education. For in the query "Has no one taught you anything?" lies the implication that without sacred knowledge, she has no real understanding. This marks the beginning of Teresita's dream training under Huila and, I argue, her entrance to a critical site of knowledge formation, allowing readers a complex understanding of the mindbodyspirit relationship.

Entering the Geography of Dreams

The tutelage in dream work depicted in *The Hummingbird's Daughter* makes a distinction between regular dreams and the medicine worked in "a dream that is not a dream" (125). Regarding this second type—the exceptional dream—Huila explains that while everyone can have them, "not everyone learns to enter the dream and work with it" (126). Thus the narrative posits dreaming as work that one must develop an aptitude for, and dreams as spatial environments that can be entered, inhabited, and exited. The imperative for such work is represented as being intimately connected to the sacred, and thus an essential undertaking. Huila declares, "We must—we have no choice. It's simple: without the dreams, we cannot converse with the secret" (126). Here dream work is conceptualized as *communication* with the larger universe of power that lies beyond ordinary perception; this conception frames Teresita's previous dream of the hummingbird hovering above her as an encounter with the sacred, in which the hummingbird expresses the world itself and bestows a message. Such a perception of dream work is reflected in Patrisia Gonzales's discussion of dreaming, in which she writes, "Dreamtime is one place where relationships to continuities with the life source are expressed. Through dreams, we find the unity of the multiverse" (173). Thus, rather than passive observation of images or engagement solely with one's own individual psyche, dreaming is understood as an engaged interrelationship with the universe on its multiple levels, which can be entered into in search of usable knowledge. It is in the same vein that Gloria Anzaldúa once wrote regarding her ensueños, or "awakened dreams": "I am playing with my Self, I am playing with the world's soul, I am in dialogue, between my Self and *el espíritu del mundo*. I change myself, I change the world" (*Borderlands* 92). This interpretation of dream work as actively engaged, productive dialogue fits well within the context of the narrative at hand, for in Teresita's dreams she is one player within a field of participants, and the work she does there yields knowledge and understanding applicable to waking life and its material conditions.

To elaborate on the spatial and epistemic intersections of dream work, I draw on Linda Hogan's conceptualization of dreams in *The Woman Who Watches*

Over the World (2001). She writes, "Dreaming articulates the terrain of night, the range of a human soul, the geography of the holy, and draws a path to the divine. It is a map of sorts, one unknown to us by day. Dreaming is the point at which we begin to know. We are the dreamed, as well as the dreamers" (136). In this sense, dreaming is a way of knowing as well as a felt *place* of knowing, one in which we both come to know and are known in a divine sense. Thus working within the geography of dreams becomes a sacred task as well as a migration or border crossing of sorts, not without spiritual dangers. Even as Huila explains that angels and souls travel the regions of dreams, where "God can speak to you," she likewise acknowledges that "the devil" may do so as well (Urrea, *Hummingbird* 126). These potential encounters with beneficent or malevolent forces, which scare the young Teresita, highlight the special role the dreamer holds in taking up the task of dream work, underscoring the dreamer's value to their community. While Huila doubles as a housekeeper in the home of Tomás, the patrón who cares nothing for dreams and spirit, she is respected among the rest of her community as a powerful healer and midwife. Just as she works on the material level, using her hands and herbal remedies to sustain the lives of those around her, the spiritual is likewise a key aspect of her work. In conversing with the "secrets" of creation through the dream mode, she glimpses hidden aspects of the universe and its reality, gaining a more complex consciousness; it is this skill that she seeks to teach Teresita, whom she has identified as having "the gift." While Teresita's father Tomás, whom she comes to live with during this time, does not approve of such "peculiar enthusiasms," Teresita nevertheless undergoes tutelage with Huila and emerges as a powerful dreamer in her own right (251).

This training reaches an apex during the long journey from the Santana ranch in Sinaloa to the Cabora ranch in Sonora, after Tomás is forced to move his operations due to his political activities and the feared retribution of the dictator Porfirio Díaz. After a long day of travel, their entire party stops to rest for the night, and Teresita lies about ten feet away from Huila. "There was no way to know when the dream began. She didn't know, even, if she really was dreaming" (Urrea, *Hummingbird* 136). The third-person narrator describes her watching the stars and beginning to see a fleck growing larger and larger, "until she realized that it was Huila, walking down the sky as if it were a stairway" (136). Smoking a pipe, Huila "walked down in a spiral, coming from a place far up in the night, and she saw Teresita and smiled down at her" (136). Teresita witnesses Huila's spiraling descent from a faraway place, indicating Huila's own dream work as travel and movement through the dream space, the deeper realms of which she is returning from. Her smiling acknowledgment of Teresita again gestures toward the dream as a place of meeting and communication, which is emphasized when the two engage in discussion. The girl asks Huila what she is doing, to which Huila replies, "I'm flying," and informs her, "You shouldn't be watching me. It's rude to watch people fly" (137). In addition to the soul flight suggested here, this exchange implies that the dream world is a place with its own social rules, with which Teresita is not yet familiar. Further, this interaction signals the dream as an intersubjective, relational space. Defining intersubjectivity as the "dynamic field that is produced and enacted when one's own 'interior' self encounters another's," Bogzaran and Deslauriers assert that "by putting attention mostly on the individual and private aspects of dreaming, one often fails to see how dreaming stems from relational and communal life" (119). Thus the dream world might be more productively considered as a space of interrelational encounters and experiences in which one participates or takes part. In this sense, the question of whether Teresita is dreaming of Huila or Huila is dreaming of her is too simplistic, particularly as the next part of the dream reaffirms the dream space as shared rather than autonomous.

Just as in Teresita's previous dream, in which she noticed three Indigenous men observing her from a distance, Huila, in this dream, calls Teresita's attention to "skinny men in white running from sleeper to sleeper" (Urrea, *Hummingbird* 137). Identifying the skinny men as Yaquis, she explains, "The Indians are dreaming about us again" (137). This statement articulates a distance between Teresita and Huila as an "us" observed by Indigenous consciousness and "the Indians" who dream of them. This differentiation is of interest, given that both Teresita and Huila seem to be at least of mixed descent from the Yaqui people and both share with the Yaquis the Cahita language. According to Huila's statement, they have entered a dream space in which one is both subject and object, both knowable and in search of knowing. For those skilled in collecting data from the dream space and bringing it into waking awareness, the dream becomes an entrance into a larger cultural or even world consciousness. Thus the dream is represented in the narrative not as something imagined by the individual mind but as another point of access to awareness.

This is reaffirmed later in the novel when they encounter Yaquis who recognize them in waking life: "The old leader of the village looked at the girl and said, 'I know you,' in the old tongue. 'I saw you when the old woman was flying'" (Urrea, *Hummingbird* 186). Thus Teresita and Huila are known entities for the

Yaquis who have observed them in dreams, and, we learn, these Yaquis have also "seen [Tomás] coming in dreams," suggesting dreaming as a mode of tracking or mapping the literal movements of bodies over land (186). Such skill would be of clear value under Díaz's regime of modernization, which involved the exploitation of Mexico's resources by U.S. land and business interests, resulting in large-scale displacement from the land, starvation, and government-endorsed massacre for Indigenous people. Raphael Brewster Folsom explains, "In the last decade of the nineteenth century and the first decade of the twentieth, the Díaz government launched a brutally effective campaign to liquidate the Yaqui threat, killing hundreds of Yaquis and deporting thousands more to the henequen plantations in Oaxaca and to Yucatán as slaves" (2). While Tomás and those who accompany him are not an army, the coming of a Yori (white man) does signal potential danger to the Yaquis; thus dreaming becomes a defensive mode, a way of seeing in the dark. As for Huila and Teresita, who share with the Yaquis the Cahita language, or "the old tongue," their status as "mestizos and half breeds" who live on a hacienda controlled by a wealthy and powerful Yori marks them as distinct and at least partially other (Urrea, *Hummingbird* 186).

Further, while these different figures seem to circulate in shared dream spaces, each participant holds a different level of knowledge and aptitude; Teresita has yet to acquire the expertise to work with dreams in a meaningful manner. This education continues in the next portion of the dream in which Huila, having descended from the sky, hovers above her own sleeping body as in an out-of-body experience. In this scene, the relationship between the soul in flight and the material body is illustrated in the form of a direct encounter with the self. Huila hovers above her sleeping body and looks down at it while her student, Teresita, witnesses the reunion or merging of these two aspects of self: "Huila bent down and took hold of her own shoulders. She shuddered once, as if stepping into cold water, and pulled herself toward her own body. The body kicked once and rolled over. Huila was inside, hidden from view within Huila. Teresita watched her sleep. The body said, 'Good night, girl.' 'Good night, old woman,' Teresita said. Then, 'Is this the dream?' 'It is.' Huila started to snore" (Urrea, *Hummingbird* 137). As described in this passage, "the body" is the physical self with which the soul-self must come back into alignment. As Huila's soul has flown from her body and these two parts of herself are temporarily out of union, she must return to it and reenter. Thus, to say that Huila "was hidden from view within Huila" is another way of expressing that the soul-self has reentered the physical self and that each is an integral part of a whole mindbodyspirit. In this sense, the dream provides a learning experience for Teresita and an image that allows the reader to conceptualize the relationship between the integrated parts of oneself. Regarding the body's role in a complex subjectivity, M. Jacqui Alexander writes, "Since body is not body alone but rather one element in the triad of mind, body and spirit, what we need to understand is how such embodiment provides the moorings for a subjectivity that knits together these elements" (298). Witnessing Huila's soul reentering her body is just such a lesson, illustrating that, outside of soul flight, a body is *not* just a body but rather a carrier and mediator of the parts of oneself that transcend what is materially evident (Alexander 298). Accordingly, Teresita senses that this is precisely the kind of dream that Huila has described to her—a dream that is not a dream—a concept the girl could not understand until she experienced it. In this way, dreams are positioned in the narrative as a space in which to experience and thus understand complex relationships between body, environment, spirit, and one's own unique soul.

Far more than a projection of the psyche's desire to transcend the limits of the body, I suggest that the dream described above expresses dreaming as a site of education, in which conceptions of existence and reality might be productively challenged and reshaped. Not only is Teresita educated in this dream, but the reader is also offered a reeducation regarding the elements of the self. Writing from a non-Western perspective, Patrisia Gonzales asserts that dreams "erase borders of experience" and "defy accepted notions, in much of non-Native society, of what constitutes the space of reality, the body-space of what many people accept as a fixed spirit that inhabits the body and remains there until death" (179–80). Thus the dream described above can be read as representing a form of unbounded spatial experience in which spirit, or more specifically one's unique soul, may undergo a form of travel beyond the body, even as such travel is mediated through the body. Further, while *The Hummingbird's Daughter* is a fictional narrative, this representation reflects specific cultural contexts, for as Gonzales explains, "It is often held in Indigenous medicinal knowledge of Mexico that the soul . . . may travel to the underworld, to mountain shrines, to visit other people, to visit ancestors or other spirits" (177). This conception of the possibility of out-of-body experience pushes us to reconsider the boundaries of consciousness; and in tandem, the potentially embodied aspects of such soul flight are equally remarkable. In this particular dream, when we, like Teresita, observe Huila's out-of-body soul shuddering "as if stepping into cold water" and reentering her body, we are reminded that existing in a body is a felt experience to which we constantly acclimate (Urrea, *Hummingbird* 137). In other words, an out-of-body experience (or the witnessing of one) may enable us to reconsider the dynamics of our waking embodied experience and its connection to another plane of existence.

At the end of this dream, the Yaqui dreamers and Huila's sleeping body pass out of view, and Teresita observes people "far from her, yet right beside her," reading books and newspapers; "she knew they were reading about her," but they are "too far in time to hear her" (Urrea, *Hummingbird* 137).[¶] Here, "future" events are close enough to be witnessed even as they remain far away in both space and time. Teresita's ability to sense this contradiction in her dream suggests the special quality of the dream world. Such spatial and temporal contradictions are frequent in the dreams I have discussed thus far, and they exemplify the dream world's challenging of assumed boundaries, not only with regard to the mind-bodyspirit relationship but also in terms of temporal and spatial reality. In this sense, the dream itself is Teresita's training ground, a space in which she learns both how to work within dreams and how to question the assumption of fixed realities in waking life. Through such learning, she becomes a skillful dreamer, capable of extraordinary forms of travel.

We Are Water, We Are Clouds, We Are Air

As Teresita grows and develops in her abilities, she becomes adept at manipulating temporal and spatial experience through her body, allowing her soul to travel out of her body with intention. This soul flight, a willful out-of-body experience described in other contexts as astral projection, is elaborately depicted in the novel, though neither of these identifying terms are used. The practice highlights Teresita's clear distinction as a figure outside the boundaries of the Catholic Church, and while for some readers this depiction may invite the interpretation that the novel is a work of magical realism, historical accounts reflect that, whether reality or rumor, such powers were attributed to Teresa Urrea during her lifetime. As described by David Romo, two friends of hers—Mariana Avendaño and Josefina Félix—separately claimed to have traveled with Teresa in these out-of-body journeys to distant places and times, with

---

[¶]Amy Robinson offers a compelling discussion of this scene in relation to the subject of literacy in the novel. See Robinson 240–63.

Avendaño describing flying "hand in hand" with her and Félix simply asserting, "She would wake me up . . . , invite me somewhere and we would find ourselves there instantaneously" (29). These accounts are almost certainly the basis for the scenes in *The Hummingbird's Daughter* in which Teresita takes her friends on nighttime flying trips. Further, it should be noted that historical accounts also include the political context of these abilities. Romo writes: "In the fall of 1896, when a rebellion broke out in several towns along the U.S.-Mexico border waged in Teresita's name, rumor had it that the young miracle worker had used her powers of astral projection to lead the revolt against the soldiers of Porfirio Díaz. Although she was hundreds of miles away in El Paso, federal soldiers claimed they saw Santa Teresa leading a group of rebels at Nogales, Sonora" (29). That her contemporaries ascribed these powers to Teresa Urrea may not establish them as facts, but it does reveal a late nineteenth-century conception of the potential to transcend and collapse linear space and time. Further, the account of federal soldiers who reported witnessing her lead the rebels at Nogales indicates the belief (and, importantly, fear) that her powers, or the public perception of these powers, could be put to political ends. In this light, the scenes of soul flight with friends can be read with an additional understanding of the material significance of the abilities portrayed. For indeed, Teresa Urrea's political exile in 1892 branded her as the "most dangerous girl in Mexico" (Torres, *Curandero* 93).

In a scene in which Teresita lies in bed between her two best friends, Josefina ("La Fina") and Gabriela (who later falls in love with her father Tomás), the development of her powers under Huila's tutelage becomes clear: "It had come to her as a realization a few months before. She simply knew one night that she could capture their dreams and direct them. She could not explain how it happened, or why. But if she concentrated, she could take the girls on journeys as if they were flying in the wind" (Urrea, *Hummingbird* 253–54). The capability to direct not only her own dreams but those of others demonstrates Teresita's growth and particular skill as a dream worker. Importantly, this skill, as represented in the narrative, is marked by embodied aspects even while the flight itself might seem to be a predominantly disembodied experience. Firstly, the girls' preparation for the journey is physical: "[Teresita] reached out to them under the covers. They put their hands in hers. La Fina wrapped her legs around Teresita's leg. . . . No number of assurances from Teresita made her trust that she wasn't going to fall" (255). Here the girls do not merely brace themselves separately, they interlock their bodies and clasp hands, creating a physical connection as they prepare for the felt experience of flight. Though their material bodies will not leave the room, they anticipate, based on previous journeys, a felt experience so strong that Josefina fears falling while in flight. Interrogating the question of embodiment (and disembodiment) in relation to dreaming, Jennifer M. Windt explains, "The connection between vestibular sensations such as flying and lucid dreams may indicate that lucid insight into the fact that one is dreaming is related to a heightened awareness of the sleeping body, as well. Moreover, the process of losing touch with the sleeping body may actually *enhance* the phenomenology of (bodily) presence in dreams" (367). In other words, the very fact that Teresita and her friends are entering a dream state in which they are aware that they are dreaming enhances the intensity of their embodied sensations, more specifically their sense of movement. Thus Josefina's fear of falling results from an extremely strong sense of bodily awareness experienced in the dream state, as directed by Teresita.

As they continue to prepare for their flight, Teresita coaxes their bodies to sleep by speaking directly to their various body parts: "Feet—go to sleep. Go on, you've had a hard day. Now sleep" (Urrea, *Hummingbird* 255). As she uses speech to gradually convince each body part of its lethargy, her friends grow drowsy until they feel themselves becoming lighter, and their sensation of the mattress below them alters until they finally feel themselves rising into the air. Teresita continues to guide their embodied sensations with her spoken words: "We are rising, rising, can you feel it? We are light now as cottonwood fluff. Feel it. The earth falls away. We have been prisoners of the ground, and now it releases its grip on us. Yes. Yes. The air moves us freely. We are like water. The air is like water. We are water. We are clouds. We are air'" (255). As if performing a guided meditation or a form of hypnosis, Teresita manipulates their embodied sensations through a series of spoken suggestions and commands emphasizing their lightness of being. Notably, she conjures their felt experience of lightness by invoking nature and its elements; they begin light as cottonwood fluff and, as they rise, they gradually come to embody water, air, and the combination of the two as clouds. Unlike in her initial dream, in which the dream becomes a solid and grounding force, Teresita conjures this lucid dream state as a liberation from the earth's ground (and their material bodies), such that they are no longer "prisoners" to the limits of the flesh. To be water, to be air, is to be free of the constraints of one's own body.

In "Now Let Us Shift . . . Conocimiento . . . Inner Work, Public Acts," Gloria Anzaldúa writes about a similar experience of flight, which she initially describes as one of being pulled from her body, using the second person "you" to describe her own memory: "Cool and light as a feather, you float near the ceiling looking down at your body. . . . As you float overhead you bob into a white light—the lightbulb or the sun? You could glide out the window and never return" (134–35). In this experience of extreme lightness, compared to that of a feather, the limits of the room, like the limits of her body, begin to dissolve; the light around her could be sun's light or the light of a bulb, suggesting a transition into a different dimension of experience. Anzaldúa's sense that she is not confined to the room in which her body lies but could fly out the window—a departure of the soul—at first troubles a central conception in her work, that of an integrated mindbodysoul. She writes, "Leaving the body reinforces the mind/body, matter/spirit dichotomy that you're trying to show does not exist in reality" (135). Importantly, Anzaldúa resolves this question, both ontological and epistemological in nature, by understanding her experience as an affirmation of the intertwined nature of mindbodyspirit and by resituating what a body is: "If the body is energy, is spirit—it doesn't have boundaries. What if you experienced your body expanding to the size of the room, not your soul leaving your body?" (134). Thus the felt experience of the dream, where boundaries fall away, enables her to reconceive her own existence in dramatically different ways, departing from her previous sense of the body. Describing the knowledge she has gained and its effect upon her waking life, she reflects: "Besides the mortal body you have a trans-temporal, immortal one. This knowing prompts you to shift into a new perception of yourself and the world. Nothing is fixed" (135). In the same way, just as Teresita and her friends sense themselves rising above the imprisonment of the ground through the directed dream state, they also potentially rise with their trans-temporal bodies to another place beyond that of waking life. When one rises to that other place, the boundaries around thought and being can be potentially surpassed, however temporarily, in a way that offers new perception.

More specifically, *The Hummingbird's Daughter* posits dreaming as a site of powerful ancestral knowledge both collectively inherited and learned. While everyone dreams, and those dreams can be understood as emerging from the well of the collective unconscious, it is only through tutelage with Huila that Teresita, a particularly talented student, learns to skillfully navigate the dream world. Further, it is Huila who teaches her how to pray and perform the rites of birth, and additionally imparts plant and animal knowledge that has been successively passed down: "Huila taught Teresita all the secrets that could be taught," including the power and strength of "blood time" (menstruation) and childbearing, as well as "dangerous prayers," "secret foods," and the language of rattlesnakes (Urrea, *Hummingbird* 275). The passing down of secret knowledge is framed as an intentional and purposeful act in which the teacher bestows privilege upon a gifted student as well as a sacred obligation to be responsible with this knowledge. We might conjecture that such knowledge is described as secret, even dangerous, for two reasons. Firstly, within the specific historical context of Porfirian Mexico, spiritual practices perceived as Native without a Catholic veneer could be seen as a threat to the state's version of *mexicanidad*. As Broyles-González explains, "To be publicly identified as Yaqui (or any other tribal affiliation) in the late nineteenth- or early twentieth-century Americas was an almost instant death warrant," which pushed Native forms of spirituality "underground" (120). But more broadly, the secrecy around such knowledge likely refers to the great power it conveys and thus the responsibility it requires of the one who wields it. From Huila's perspective, to enter into that world of power is to enter into danger.

Upon Teresita's admission that she "make[s] Gaby and Fina fly," taking them on trips to far-off cities, Huila delivers a dire warning: "You are in danger, and those around you are in danger. You have chosen a way fraught with danger. Be careful" (Urrea, *Hummingbird* 275). This warning serves to remind Teresita that the knowledge she is gaining affords power but also requires discipline, because it is not her own: it originates in a spiritual universe larger than herself and beyond her total control. In her discussion of "nightflying," Aurora Levins Morales similarly writes about the "forbidden heights" reached through such flight, which "requires a willingness to leave the familiar ground and see what is meant to be hidden, a willingness to be transformed" (48). In other words, the willingness to venture into normally hidden realms carries the potential to be transformed by a power greater than oneself; such witnessing thus becomes a risk as well as a gift. As Teresita's powers grow, she at times terrifies others and herself, such as when she unintentionally throws her half-brother into a catatonic state through the sheer power of her anger at his taunts. While her tutelage under Huila transforms her consciousness of the world and her relationship to it, such knowledge ultimately isolates her from those who fear her power, including her family and friends such as Gaby and Fina. Teresita has chosen the pursuit of a "secret" knowledge, an understanding of divine and earthly forces, and the development of her own agency; thus she has sharply diverted from the accepted path allotted to young women in her community.

Theresa Delgadillo writes of *The Hummingbird's Daughter*, "The novel imagines an intrepid, fierce, confident character with a spiritual calling whose schooling in native healing and worldviews stands in contrast to Western gender norms and religiosities" ("Spirituality" 244). Indeed, Teresita is a character who upends the social strictures placed upon her and frequently pays a price. Thus the novel emphasizes her chosen work of healing, which includes her dream work, as a sacred duty and vocation that comes at a cost—namely, the intimacy and friendship of others her age.

Of Death and Dreams

The historical figure of Teresa Urrea is primarily known for healing abilities that she is said to have acquired after a physical trauma; these abilities were deemed so miraculous that they drew throngs of pilgrims to the ranch where she lived, leading to the moniker "La Santa de Cabora." As Desirée Martín explains, "In 1889 Teresa suffered a cataleptic fit or seizure that caused her to go into a coma for thirteen days," and when she awoke during her own wake (for her family believed her to be dead), she "appeared to have acquired telepathic and teleki-netic powers" (37). In *The Hummingbird's Daughter*, Luis Alberto Urrea depicts Teresita's seizure and coma as the result of an attack by a man named Millán, a former miner prone to violence and sexual depravity. This reflects William Curry Holden's representation in the biography *Teresita* (1978), which tells of a man of the same name who "became insanely infatuated with Teresita" and "attempted to rape her at Cabora" (51). While explanations of what caused the seizure vary, her perceived awakening from death after bodily trauma added a significant element to stories that would later circulate about her powers, mak-ing Cabora a popular site of pilgrimage: "Claiming to be inspired by visions and voices of God and the Virgin Mary," she began curing pilgrims through "a combination of touch, herbal remedies, and mixtures of soil and her own saliva or blood" (Martín 37). In the novel, her encounter with "the Mother" and "Itom Achai" (Our Father) in the midst of her temporary death is depicted as the source of her miraculous powers, and the scene is written entirely in italics, suggesting its significant nature.

In this temporary death, she finds herself in a lush environment of leap-ing deer, flowers, and coyotes drinking from pools of water, highlighting the ecological aspects of her soul's travel. This environment seems to allude to the place Yaqui myth refers to as *sea ania* (flower world). In *Yaqui Deer Songs / Maso Bwikam: A Native American Poetry* (1987), Larry Evers and Felipe S. Molina explain: "Located in the east, in a place 'beneath the dawn,' the *sea ania*, flower world, is described as a perfected mirror image of all the beauty of the natural world of the Sonoran desert. It is filled with flowers, water, and natural abundance of all kinds. And it is home to the prototypical insects, birds, and animals of the Sonoran desert as well. Chief among these is the deer known to Yaquis as *malichi* [little fawn] or *saila maso* [little brother deer]" (47). Thus this scene of Teresita's temporary death, through which she develops a miraculous ability to heal, seems to be a strong reference to her Yaqui heritage. That her development into "La Santa de Cabora," with its popular Catholic inflections, is facilitated by an encounter in the Yaqui flower world is perhaps not so contradictory as it might seem. For, as Folsom notes, Yaqui religion during this time "mix[ed] elements of Catholic belief and native ritual" (1). Likewise, Evers and Molina assert that the Yaquis "made . . . Catholicism . . . into something distinctly their own"—for example, through stories of "how *Jesucristo*, Jesus Christ, himself, roamed through Yaqui lands creating mountains and pointing out medicinal herbs to the Yaqui people" (40). The strong relationship between Catholicism and ecology in Yaqui spirituality is accentuated in this scene in which Teresita initiates her transformation from curandera to popular saint.

As the Mother embraces her and escorts her to meet Itom Achai, Teresita "sees the three old Yaquis from her dreams walking in the distance" (Urrea, *Hummingbird* 326). Their continued observation of her movements through this sacred plane emphasizes that even death is sociocultural rather than strictly individual. Itom Achai, who is also referred to in this scene as "God," speaks to Teresita in the Cahita language and embodies nature itself, with "a long braid of waterfalls, honeysuckle, comets," and eyes in which she sees eagles (326). Here God's body is not only a geography unto itself but an entire cosmos, and as he hands her a cup to drink from, in which she sees stars reflected, ordinary rules of spatial reality are deconstructed. Finally, God announces to Teresita, "I have a gift for you," and hands her a rose, which alludes to her healing powers as a gift given directly by God (326). However, the rose also gestures toward Teresita's embodied sanctity in a very specific way. Regarding the historical figure of Teresa Urrea, Martín points out that "like all saints, her body is the vehicle through which her sanctity is transmitted"; in Teresa's case more specifically, that sanctity was largely associated with the perfumed scent that pilgrims claimed was emitted by her body and bodily fluids (42). Historian Paul

Vanderwood writes, "Pilgrims soaked their handkerchiefs and bandannas in water she used for her work, saying that it smelled sweet" (169). Thus the gift of the rose in this sacred encounter signals her embodied state of sanctity, which comes from God but flows through her body to the people she heals. Regardless of whether readers differentiate between her dreams, visions, and out-of-body experiences, this particular encounter represents the receipt of a very specific embodied knowledge and healing capability that will carry over into her waking life, forever transforming it.

Yet before the healings at Cabora begin, a different "miracle" occurs. According to accounts of what followed immediately after she awakened from her apparent death, Teresa Urrea predicted a death within several days, and, proving her own foresight, "her teacher Huila passed away and was buried in the coffin intended for Teresita" (Cisneros, *House* 317). In the novel, Huila's movement toward death is strongly linked to a discourse on dreams. Even prior to Teresita's prediction, Huila's aged condition is described in terms of increased sleep and decreased engagement with her usual rituals of waking life: "Huila no longer rose early. For the first time in her life, she slept through dawn. She no longer knelt to her prayers, nor did she go out to her grove to address the Creator and the Four Directions. When Huila awoke, she would lie, sometimes for an entire hour, as if her dreams had taken too firm a grip on her and refused to let her go" (Urrea, *Hummingbird* 308). In this description, the term "Creator" is used instead of "God," revealing the slippage between these terms from Huila's perspective, as at other times she uses the latter. Her aging is depicted as a transition or crossing from living in one realm to residing in another, as she slips away from the activities of daily life and lives more and more in the dream realm that grips her.

When Teresita, risen from her catatonic state, attends to Huila on her deathbed, she lovingly reassures the old woman about the transition, calming her fears and likening death to falling asleep and awakening in another world. She prays while Huila moves in and out of sleep, her pulse growing weaker: "Her dreams were full, Teresita knew, of her dead parents, her dead brothers and sister, her dead lover. All the doorways unlocking before her, all the hallways swept clean, the lamps being lit. The gate to Huila's garden coming unlatched" (Urrea, *Hummingbird* 338). In this passage, dreams are described in spatial terms, as an entrance, a pathway to another realm of being, a threshold that one crosses. More specifically, movement into death, facilitated by dreams, is described as a ritual of reunion rather than a departure, one in which those loved ones who have already made their crossing welcome us into their presence. As such, the afterlife, evoked here as a garden entered through the gate of dreams, denotes a place of richness and growth. In this sense, death may be likened to falling asleep, but it is paradoxically also depicted as a form of awakening to another existence. Having made the crossing herself, if only temporarily, Teresita proclaims to her father and her friend Gabriela, who is now a stepmother figure, "You are awake when you sleep," and, "The flesh is the dream" (341). This reversal of common conceptions presents an alternative view of consciousness that fundamentally questions the root of reality, causing them to think her mad and furthering her isolation. With her teacher gone, Teresita enters a new stage of her life, becoming an object of pilgrimage, at the center of an ever-expanding community yet always at its margin.

When, at the novel's end, Teresita and her father are exiled by Porfirio Díaz as treasonous enemies of the state, heretics against the Church, and abettors of Indigenous uprising in Sonora, Sinaloa, and Chihuahua, they are placed on a train heading north to the United States (Urrea, *Hummingbird* 477–78). It is on this train that Teresita is reunited with Huila once again through the medium of a dream, wherein Huila offers needed wisdom as Teresita crosses the border into exile. Teresita dreams of "the sacred spot where Huila once prayed" and the "old forgotten she-pig" from her initial dream in the novel, then experiences what seems to be a false awakening, finding Huila sitting in the train car. As they converse, Teresita suddenly finds herself transported outdoors, "walking in a blue stream, on smooth white stones" (485). The sudden shift between environments reinforces dream time as unbound by the ordinary rules of space and time. Further, the natural environment of her dream builds an association between the natural elements and the wisdom received in dreams. Additionally, the same three Yaquis who repeatedly appear in her dreams observe her and Huila from a distance, while a hummingbird circles above her, speeding away to the left; these elements of previous dreams integrated into this one suggest both change and continuity over the course of her life.

As Huila and Teresita "clim[b] through a tissue of cloud," they reach a blue sky filled with stars "creating a grid in the sky, spreading out away from her until they became invisible in every direction" (Urrea, *Hummingbird* 485–86). Huila directs Teresita to watch the stars as they swell and form millions of silver globes, and tells her: "I had to die for God to teach me this. But I am teaching you now. Look" (486). Returning through the dream to share sacred knowledge with Teresita just when she needs it most, Huila directs Teresita's attention to the globes, each of which reflects an image of Teresita at a different point in her life, past, present, and future. Images of motherhood, marriage, mourning, childbirth, laughter, weeping, sleeping, and many other life scenes cover the sky. Huila tells her, "It is you. Every you, every possible you. Forever, you are surrounded by countless choices of which you are to be" (487). Explaining that this is what one's life looks like to God—a series of choices—Huila warns that in this "universe of choices," one must "learn to choose" and "learn to see" (487). This emphasis on learning as an imperative for a life well lived is illustrated through the images in the dream in a way that would be impossible in waking life. The silver globes of possibility spreading across the sky in this scene illustrate Gloria Anzaldúa's assertion of reality as a composition constantly under construction: "Knowledge is relative, and reality is a composition. You reconstruct yourself and, to a lesser extent, your culture, society, and world by decisions you make. It basically comes down to . . . awareness of yourself, of your acts, of the acts of others, and of the world" (Anzaldúa, "Flights" 43). This knowledge about the reconstruction of reality and her own agency in that process is given to Teresita through her dream just as she enters into an unknown terrain where she must make choices that will affect herself as well as others. Huila's assertion that she must learn to see suggests that in order to make conscious choices she must be aware of her circumstances, and thus she must learn to be attentive and perceptive in this new life. As Teresita's train speeds northward, away from all that she has known, Huila's visitation enables her to understand a profound truth, that her future is not foreclosed but rather has been struck open. With this, Huila spreads her arms and suddenly slips from view, commanding Teresita to wake up, which she does, to find herself back in the train. This lesson from her old teacher, imparted across the divide of death, emphasizes the dream as a space of encounter and a site of learning, particularly for those who know how to pay attention.

To and Through the Silver Sea

As Luis Alberto Urrea continues Teresita's story in *Queen of America*, the sequel to *The Hummingbird's Daughter*, he presents her life in exile as a process of learning amid displacement. The narrative highlights a series of misfortunes in her life—assassination attempts, a marriage that quickly turns to violence and betrayal, alienation from her family, and commercial efforts to exploit her gifts. Each of these misfortunes leads her further away from her original calling. During these trials, her dreams continue to be potential sources of information, though she does not always understand them: "In America, you needed different dreams. And she did not yet know their language" (Urrea, *Queen* 5). The "language" of dreams alludes to their potential for conveying knowledge, as well as the implied need to "speak" or translate that language into meaning that is useful in waking life. As Anzaldúa once wrote, "Each reality is only a description, a system of perception and language" ("Flights" 45). Exiled to a new geographical, cultural, and linguistic location, Teresita needs new dreams that will enable her to draw the maps for her life and understand the challenges and failures she confronts in the United States. Yet she also uses dreams to travel the terrains of the homeland she can no longer enter by ordinary methods. Dreams allow her to follow her mother, now only "a small shadow of memory" (Urrea, *Queen* 78), from town to town in Mexico, watching her from a distance and whispering her name, unseen and unheard: "Teresita would fly through clouds and rain, under ice-cold stars and under the orange Mexican moon, to find her" (79). Regardless of exile's disorientation, her continued dream practice allows her to sense and seek out the mother who will always be a missing part of herself until her mysterious arrival at Teresita's front door at the end of the novel. As Teresita lies on her deathbed, she senses the arrival of Cayetana, the hummingbird, who stands outside, now an old woman come to ask forgiveness and say goodbye: "Teresita had felt her shadow all these years, had sensed her far away, knew she was not dead. Saw her on some nights, during her most vivid dreams. And here, on the long unlikely mystery road, she had come back" (477). This fortuitous reunion with her mother provides Teresita with great happiness and contentment before her death, alleviating the great loneliness of her life.

However, it is Huila who provides Teresita with guidance and support through many of her struggles and who teaches her the sacred work of herbs, birthing, and dreaming. As discussed in the previous section, Huila reaches across the chasm of death to continue her role as teacher at the end of *The Hummingbird's Daughter*; likewise, she appears to Teresita in several parts of *Queen of America*. When Teresita and her father make the journey to the high country of Clifton, Arizona, to escape the threat of assassins in El Paso, she catches a glimpse of Huila in a dream and runs after her, but receives only a wave before the old woman slips out of view (Urrea, *Queen* 179). However, in Clifton some time later, Teresita receives a night visitation from Huila in the devastating aftermath of her shotgun wedding to a man who turns deranged and violently attacks her.

Having run away from her father's home to wed and no longer welcome there, she departs Arizona—the scene of so much sadness—for California, but not before she has "a very odd little dream" in which Huila appears to assure her that, despite her pain, she must awaken to the work God still calls her to do (267–68). The nature of that work comes into question as she travels from city to city in the United States with a consortium that conspires to profit from her healings. During this time she has two children with a man named John Van Order, with whom she eventually parts ways, and becomes increasingly enmeshed in her own celebrity status among upper-class Anglos. Finally she leaves it all behind, returns to Clifton with her children after hearing of her father's passing, and resettles there until her own premature death. In my brief analysis here, I focus on Huila's final visitation at the novel's end, when she arrives to usher Teresita into death and present her once again with a vision of her life.

With her loved ones (including her mother Cayetana) surrounding her bed at dawn, Teresita experiences a false awakening and surveys the room, finding them all asleep. One detail in the room that catches her attention is the wad of bloodied cloths at her bedside and the bowl placed there for her to use during coughing attacks: "The terrible porcelain bowl where she spit up clots had mercifully been emptied while she slept. Of all the horrors of this illness, it was that bowl of blood that most filled her with dread. Its ugliness, the fact of it, erased all illusions" (Urrea, *Queen* 479). The "terribleness" of the bowl and the blood it holds resides in what it implies about her body in its illness: that it is no longer capable of sustaining the force of her life. Soon she hears the click of the door, and, as it swings open, cottonwood fluff and sunlight pour into the room, causing her to experience spatial disorientation: "She was confused for a moment—didn't that door open to the hallway? She'd thought so. Wasn't she on the second floor of her father's house? Had she forgotten that it opened to the outside world?" (480). Suddenly she becomes less sure of the space she inhabits and its orientation to the "outside world," signaling that Teresita is not in the reality she thought she was in. As Huila enters the room, in an old dress, apron, and rebozo, Teresita expresses her joy at seeing her teacher once again and kisses her hand: "Teresita put the old one's knuckles to her lips. Her hand smelled of cilantro and mint" (481). Teresita's gentle gesture yields a sensory experience of the curandera's presence; her body smells of the tools of her work even after death, reminding the reader of Huila's embodied relationship to the natural environment. Even as Teresita emits the smell of roses, a mark of the sacred gift that flows through her, Huila emits the scent of herbs, the tools of her trade throughout her life. Thus their bodies carry the mark of who and what they are, and yet Huila's body is not a material one. She has come to escort Teresita to the world of spirits, where she will not be limited by the material bounds of her flesh; however, Teresita does not yet realize this.

When Huila beckons Teresita to come with her, Teresita insists at first that she cannot, as she is too physically ill to get out of bed. Huila responds with what at first seems a strange remark: "You are not your body. You were never ill. It was ill. It has nothing to do with you" (Urrea, *Queen* 481). Coming from a curandera whose lifework was based on the integration of the mindbodysoul triad, Huila's statement is striking for its distinction between the "you" of the soul and the "it" of the body. Here Huila speaks specifically within the context of death, in which Teresita's soul will permanently depart from her body. Still, this departure from the body is depicted *as* embodied, as Teresita maneuvers her way out of bed: "Teresita slipped her legs out from under her mother. Cayetana never stirred. She swung her legs over and contorted herself to get around Gaby. She managed to rise without bouncing the bed. Not an eyelid fluttered" (482). She is able to slip out of bed without waking her loved ones because her material body is not moving; yet it is as if Teresita's soul is embodied, even as it departs the body that she will leave behind. When Huila asks her, "How do you feel?" Teresita takes a breath and finds that she is now able to breathe without coughing up blood, free of the complications of her illness (482). Thus this scene suggests death as a liberation of an embodied soul from the material body; Teresita is able to move, feel, and breathe in ways that her material body would no longer permit her to do. Finally, Huila explains that she has something to show Teresita and, assuring her that her loved ones will be all right, instructs her not to look back; with this, they step beyond the room of her deathbed.

The world they enter together is described as "a brilliant spring morning" in which Teresita's senses are overwhelmed (Urrea, *Queen* 482). With deep attention to the environment, she feels the grass, "luxurious against the bottoms of her feet," indicating that her soul is able to experience a distinctly embodied pleasure (482). She is stunned by the beauty of the garden in which she finds herself, and she takes in each detail as if at an endless feast: "They were looking all round them at columbines and foxgloves, daisies and cosmos. Sunflowers, morning glories. Wild irises were purple, yellow, and white—butterflies that erupted from the blossoms looked like more blossoms suddenly animated" (482–83). This first stage of Teresita's passage into death is amazingly alive and vibrant, marked by movement and color; however, she is stunned not only by the sheer variety of life in her garden of death, but also by the magic of its details. Butterflies fluttering about irises are perceived as extensions of the flowers themselves, blossoms erupting into flight. This new perception of seemingly ordinary objects (i.e., flowers, butterflies) signals Teresita's deep attention to the world's movement and receptiveness to the information it conveys. Looking out at a group of aspens, she calls out to Huila with a sense of urgency, "Look how they tremble in the breeze! They look like coins in the light" (483). Teresita's exclamation demonstrates that she is seeing these trees with new eyes, noticing with fresh vision the miracle of their movements, the golden color and roundness of their leaves.

While this increased attunement to and perception of her environment may seem insignificant, they are evidence of a shift in consciousness of the kind that enables us to rethink our relationship to spirit, nature, and the everyday worlds in which we move. Christina Holmes emphasizes that when critics disregard the ecological themes in Chicana feminist art and literature in favor of more explicitly social themes, we overlook the intersubjective understandings that these themes invoke (Holmes 73). Though *Queen of America* is not Chicana feminist literature in terms of its authorial context, the argument Holmes makes remains relevant. Specifically, she asserts that through elaborate narrative elements that highlight the ecological, writers "destabilize our given understandings" in ways that "disrupt our sense of selves and orient us toward critical reflection and the formation of new (inter)subjectivities" (Holmes 73). By writing Teresita's garden in terms of awe as well as sensory and embodied pleasure, Luis Alberto Urrea enables readers to reflect on the failure of ordinary perception to recognize the movement of spirit through all things. As Teresita marvels at the life blooming and trembling around her and the luxurious sensations she experiences, she is reoriented by the ultimate destabilization of death. In this, the author does not so much romanticize death as depict it as a rebirth, or crossing over, into a new awareness, which may provoke readers to critically evaluate their own degree of attunement.

Despite Teresita's desire to linger in the garden, Huila urges her on through the trees until they are "hit again by glorious light on the edge of a great precipice" (Urrea, *Queen* 483). From this precipice, which indicates Teresita's passage into another realm, she again witnesses the vision Huila showed her at the end of *The Hummingbird's Daughter*. The great light that strikes them suggests the illumination of knowledge delivered through this vision: "The sky was full. Every part of it taken up by a shining silver globe. Mirror-bright. . . . Receding into the infinite distance. Hundreds of pure silver spheres. Thousands. Each globe shimmered" (Urrea, *Queen* 483). Teresita recognizes this vision and knows that the globes represent every possible moment and choice in her life. As she leans in, she sees her face in each sphere; however, Huila explains that, unlike the last time she showed her this vision, Teresita has no more choices left: "This is the culmination, child. . . . There are no more paths. There are no more choices. In the end, you are left with this. Yourself" (484). The composition of her life's choices is projected onto the sky like a map, no longer under construction but complete, a representation of herself. The conception of one's life and self as defined by one's choices integrates a specific ethics into the narrative, a lesson the story imparts to its readers. This is particularly true when Huila addresses Teresita with the following injunction: "You must ask yourself—do you like what you see?" (484). Importantly, the narrative does not situate perfection as an imperative, for *Queen of America* plainly displays the series of ill-fated choices Teresita makes during her life in the United States, struggling between her sacred calling and her desire to simply be a woman on her own terms. When she speaks her concern over her failures, Huila assures her, "That was part of your job," indicating imperfection as part of the job of being human and alive (484). Thus the ethics the story offers is not a lesson in a life free of error, but rather the awareness that we must look at our choices as a culmination of ourselves. Accordingly, this is the point at which Teresita begins to realize (though it has already been clear to the reader) that this dream is actually a crossing into death.

In the last scene of the novel, the thousands of silver globes reflecting Teresita's life choices begin to absorb into a single central sphere; at first they move gently, and then more wildly, accumulating one by one into a "globe of quicksilver" (Urrea, *Queen* 484). The reference to the liquid metal quicksilver suggests not only the relationship between Teresita's life and the elements of nature, but also life's quickly changing circumstances, which are fluid and never fixed. "When all the silver spheres had fallen into it, it burst silently. Its silver tide spread out before them in a vast, shining horizon. 'Oh!' Teresita cried. It was a silver sea" (484). In this rushing movement toward the center, Teresita's individual choices accumulate into one shining entity before the globe bursts, alluding to the fullness of life, for its "silver tide" cannot be held or contained. That her completed life becomes a free-flowing sea emphasizes the transformation of lived experience into the natural movement and energy of the universe. Significantly, Huila is present for this last lesson, ushering Teresita into the next realm without fear. Realizing that she has died, Teresita looks to her old teacher for instructions on what do next, and Huila responds that they should swim. Though Teresita has never been able to swim before, Huila assures her that this sea is different and that she will not let her slip away.

Importantly, in these last lines of the novel, readers are presented with a scenario of death in which we do not proceed alone, but rather may be guided by loved ones—our teachers—who have died before us. In this scenario, then, death is not a slipping away but a crossing into another reality. Additionally, the final transition into death is depicted as embodied, one in which Teresita's soul can swim through the precious river of her own life: "They took each other's hands. They stepped into the calm silver tide. It was warm. Teresita shivered once. She could see stars and moons reflected in the infinite water. 'When you get tired,' Huila said, 'float.' They waded deeper, and when they were fully immersed, they swam toward the other shore" (Urrea, *Queen* 485). When they take each other's hands, the scene mirrors the way in which Teresita once clasped the hands of her friends before taking them on nighttime flying trips, assuring them that they would not fall while under her guidance; now it is Teresita who needs Huila's guidance and instruction. Huila prepares Teresita for the crossing, advising her that when she becomes tired, she can float and will not sink; she provides the lessons that Teresita needs to know in death, just as she did in life. Significantly, the warmth of the water, like Teresita's shiver, reinforces the depiction of death as a felt experience, alluding to the soul's embodiment even in the absence of a physical body. Swimming, they are immersed in "infinite water" that reflects the cosmos, just as Teresita once saw the cosmos in God's cup during her first death experience. Thus, swimming to "the other shore" means to become immersed in, and flow through, the immensity of an existence too infinite to be grasped in life.

Conclusion

Left with this last image of Teresita and Huila disappearing into the distance together, readers who know how to pay attention may sense themselves as recipients of knowledge to pass on to others. This knowledge of the crossing is not simply about what happens after death, but about the relationships that we build in life and the learning that ensues on both sides of that border. In *The Hummingbird's Daughter* and *Queen of America*, Luis Alberto Urrea presents a concept of the soul that can pass in and out of different realities, and in and out of the physical body, to discover new experiences and understandings; significantly, the soul is depicted as embodied in its experience of movement through space and time. As Teresita receives an ongoing education in the spiritual skills of observation and attunement to her shifting environments, she learns to negotiate the boundaries of everyday life so as to transcend them. While her life is marked by suffering, exile, and the alienation of loneliness, she draws on the gifts of ancestral knowledge that Huila teaches her, and which she possesses a special capacity for exercising, in order to heal herself and others. Though she performs much meaningful work in waking life, it is through dream work that she learns to perceive (and reconceive) existence outside of ordinary domains. Even as readers may be unfamiliar with the specific cultural contexts of these novels, Western assumptions about what constitutes learning, education, and knowledge will be productively challenged, opening the door to the development of a decolonizing consciousness.

EPILOGUE

Can the stories we tell, and those we take in, meaningfully contribute to social and spiritual transformation? And how are social and spiritual transformation interlinked? In my work as a scholar and in the classroom, my concern is to convey why literature matters to lived experience and how it can transform us as people, making us more conscious in our relationships to and engagements with society, the world, and the cosmos. As a space that invites and even requires some degree of reflection, literary narrative is always engaged in the formation, and potentially the reshaping, of consciousness, sometimes in ways directly resistant to the dominant social narrative that propagates the needs of the nation-state, capitalism, and the ongoing residues of colonialism. Even when a story does not seem overtly political on its surface, it can productively challenge us to rethink assumptions about the ways we move and exist in the world, our interconnectivity and its implications, and whatever it is that we think we know.

As I have argued throughout this book, this capability is often a result of the sensory, embodied experiences that a story expresses and mediates. Through a story's imaginative evocation of a body (or bodies) not literally present, the reader, using their own embodied knowledge to process what they are reading, can in some sense enflesh the story as something carried in their body. This intimate connection to characters, narrators, feelings, and environments outside of one's immediate reality can become a form of travel in time and space that powerfully affects the reader's consciousness. In this way, reading narrative can function as an epistemological, decolonial practice when it challenges ways of knowing that have been standardized through long trajectories of colonial and imperial projects, as well as the erasure of other forms of knowing that have been subject to those same forces. In direct relation, this epistemological work can substantively alter our ways of being in the world.

The works I have examined suggest a fundamental interconnection among all existence and highlight the spiritual fragmentation that emerges from the erasure of the consciousness of this interconnection on an individual and collective level. In doing so, these narratives encourage readers toward a more holistic perception. Yet, with the great exception of works circulated so widely that they alter the social fabric and public consciousness, the transformation that I am describing mostly happens at the level of the individual writer, reader, or listener. Thus we might ask: If the transformative potential that literature holds primarily functions at the level of the individual, what is its value in terms of collective action and social change? Further, how does this pertain to the principle of conscious interconnectivity that I have placed at the center of this study, particularly as some might conceive of spirituality as a "personal" matter?

When we are emboldened to understand our mind, body, and spirit outside the limited parameters of rationalism, as mindbodyspirit, we can begin to break down and see through the illusions that fragment us. Further, when we experience literature as an encounter or confrontation that culminates in awareness (often a difficult awareness), we become more prepared and more obligated to participate in social action. In other words, the reflective experience of narrative can provide the foundation for the praxis, or embodied reflective action, necessary for social change. In this epilogue, I consider the works I have discussed in this book in the context of embodied spirituality, with consideration of how they might inform our understanding of contemporary social politics. For while each of these narratives is situated within its own historical specificity, both in terms of the time in which it was created and the time that it represents, the implications of all of them can be carried over into the present moment in vital and provocative ways.

Looking back at what Anzaldúa, Grise, and Mayorga were doing in their respective works—"Let us be the healing of the wound" and "Panza Brujería"—they used their narratives to directly and creatively critique the George W. Bush administration. More specifically, their critiques were a response to the experience of personal and political trauma that emerged from 9/11, the resultant War on Terror, the nationalist sentiments that arose in correlation with it, and perceived electoral corruption. The tone these works convey is not one of righteous indignation but one of spiritual exasperation paired with fierce determination. During the writing of this book, the 2016 presidential campaign took place, along with the inauguration and first year of the ensuing administration. The fracturing of society that has risen to the surface during this time has created comparisons to that earlier political period, causing these works to resonate in a new way.

These two works reveal the way in which an eroding sense of trust in the nation-state serves as a reminder that nationalism has never been a sufficient form of collectivity or identity. As Anzaldúa calls for a planetary-based consciousness that acknowledges global interconnectivity, Grise and Mayorga present a narrative that encourages us to heal our communities through the ancestral memory of our own embodied power. Indeed, through their mutual invocation of the ritual of limpia, these works call on readers to trust the ancestral spiritual knowledge that has been marginalized and cast off. The dire need to bring the mindbodyspirit back into harmony becomes a public project in these works, one that acknowledges the gaping ruptures and fissures laid bare by widespread dissonance. Not only do these works remind us now of the need to call our souls back into our bodies, but they also emphasize the importance of channeling the coraje (guts, anger, courage) we carry within us—not only our own, but that of those who came before—as a tool for collective healing. We are encouraged to feel its power within our bodies and to sense the body as capable of exceeding the bounds of our given social roles and prescribed subjection or malaise.

Turning to Viramontes's classic short story "The Moths," when we read this story today, it continues to remind us of the need to take stock of the persistent patriarchal structures we encounter at home as well as in the public domain. These structures are embedded in such a way as to be simultaneously obvious and hidden as they operate in our lives. Viramontes shows how patriarchy's violence turns us against each other (e.g., sister against sister), alienating us from even our most beloved (our own mothers, ourselves) until we become islands apart, our hands resigned to either helplessness or the shape of fists. In 2017, the active public discourse around the silencing and normalization of sexual assault, particularly in relation to men in powerful positions, has brought attention not only to the ways some misuse their power, but also to the reality that entire systems are set up to protect that power and to exploit and isolate those in positions of vulnerability. In the current moment of public witness to the destructiveness of those systems and the shadows cast in our private lives, scars and wounds are held up to the light.

In Viramontes's story, the narrator bears witness to the scars on her abuela's deceased body, which reveal the map of a life that had been secret, hidden; it is only through the washing of her grandmother's body that the girl comes to know that her own pain and isolation are shared. And through the loving ritual of honoring her abuela's body and life, she finds herself spiritually united with her mother, her grandmother, and all the women who preceded them. The moths that, at the story's end, escape from the body and flutter toward the light suggest how witness borne by others can release the soul-consuming experiences we hold inside, sometimes a whole life long. Further, the earlier scenes of the story suggest how we might provide spaces of growth, nurturing, and protection for each other where we ritually labor in reciprocity with each other, and also with the ground from which we grow our sustenance. The healing of the story continues to work when we ask ourselves, "How can I offer a healing space for others, bear witness to their wounds, and allow them to bear witness to mine?" This is a question we continue to grapple with, particularly amid the realization that patriarchy, at the base of our social structures, is designed to keep us apart.

Mourning our losses is central to the fables written by Cisneros and Anaya, *Have You Seen Marie?* and *The Old Man's Love Story*. Reading these very personal narratives of grief (over a mother, over a beloved partner), how can we as readers become more prepared to be agents of social change? As these narrators search for the missing bodies of their loved ones in the landscapes of their lives, they struggle with the experience of being uprooted from the axis of existence, disoriented so that they no longer feel the pull of their weight to earth. Through the theft they have been subject to, these narrators gradually come to experience their grief as a deep attention to their environment—sunsets, hummingbirds, trees and rivers, wind and stars. In this attention, they come to sense themselves as participants involved in the great, ineffable, and ongoing love story of the universe. Ultimately, rather than sensing themselves solely as victims of theft, they understand themselves as recipients who have been given much; further, they learn that it is possible to continue loving relationships even after death, a counterknowledge that resists the story of isolation told in Western culture. As readers, we step into the shared knowledge that even in our most visceral grief we are part of an ongoing flow of existence that connects us to all others who have ever lived, in every part of the world. These global, cosmic threads of existence urge us to defy the fictions of exceptionalism wrought on a daily basis in our individual lives as well as on the level of the nation. For every part of ourselves and society that we deem lost in the current whirlwind of racism, sexism, religious discrimination, and other forms of violence, we must confront the ways in which this story, our story, is part of a larger one. We must learn to pay deep attention to what is around us and in us, opening ourselves up to being changed by the process.

This attunement with our environments is modeled in Maya Christina Gonzalez's illustrated children's picture books *I Know the River Loves Me / Yo sé que el río me ama* and *Call Me Tree / Llámame árbol*. Gonzalez uses word and image to narratively describe a process of moving into conscious interrelationship with the natural world, a relationship in which our role as humans is not situated as superior or dominant. In the first work, she demonstrates the potentialities of the body flowing with nature, which allow us to view ourselves in loving relationship with nature, and beloved by it, until our respective bodies (e.g., human bodies and bodies of water) no longer exist as entirely independent entities. Readers can begin to understand environmental concerns not as a unidirectional flow in which the earth provides us resources or we protect the earth, but rather in terms of a reciprocal relationship that flows in both directions. Reflecting on the protests at Standing Rock against the Dakota Access Pipeline (DAPL) in 2016–17, we might recall signs declaring statements such as "We Are Water" and "Defend the Sacred." Gonzalez's stories prepare both children and adults to better understand these statements, which articulate relationships to the earth outside the logics of capitalism, erasing the binary split that enables possession and exploitation.

Taking this idea further in *Call Me Tree*, Gonzalez depicts the body as nature, a seed born from the earth and developing as part of a larger community of trees, diverse but connected by an underground root system. The brown, gender-free narrator in this story is able to know the self as natural, and know it in relationship to others who move and inhabit their tree-bodies differently yet remain a collective. This story removes "diversity" from a context of color-blind sameness that either flattens out or stigmatizes difference; further, the nature of the work as an origin story asks readers to remember our connections to the earth. Thus these short picture books prepare us to consider what is required of us amid the current government's removal of environmental protections despite ongoing evidence of climate change, and the targeted discrimination against transgender and genderqueer people. Further, these stories prepare us to perceive intersections between these issues and to trace the links of oppression that undercut our spiritual and embodied connections to one another.

Lastly, I examine the embodied states of dreaming in Luis Alberto Urrea's novels *The Hummingbird's Daughter* and *Queen of America*, which imagine the life of Teresa Urrea, "La Santa de Cabora," as a popular healer in Mexico eventually exiled to the United States because of the land-based epistemologies of her healing. As "Teresita" learns from her teacher, Huila, about the power of dream work, she learns to propel herself—and others—across space and time, experiencing her body both in and outside of the material state. In this way, she comes to know her soul as expansive, transcendent, and itself embodied. But further, as she encounters other souls and, most importantly, as her teacher returns to cross her over into the spirit world at her life's end, she learns that she is not as alone or isolated as she has often felt in her life. Works such as these may enable attentive readers to tap into spaces and forms of knowing (ourselves, our existence, and our relations) that have been delegitimized and even erased from our consciousness in contemporary life. To reclaim these terrains of consciousness is a transformative decolonial act because of the ways it can alter our felt, embodied experience, manifesting change in our perception of material circumstances.

Aside from the literal dreaming depicted in Urrea's novels, in a broader framework these texts more generally reflect the power of those who use their perceptive capabilities to see beyond the boundaries of "reality" and dare to envision their own movement through and across boundaries. Today, the term "dreamer" has its own important, though distinct, connotation that must be highlighted. Here I refer to DREAMers, young people who would benefit from the as-yet-unpassed DREAM Act (Development, Relief, and Education for Alien Minors) and presently confront the potential termination of DACA (Deferred Action for Childhood Arrivals), which is itself an insufficient solution to the need for comprehensive immigration reform. Amid the threat of deportation, whether their own or that of a loved one or valued community member, today's DREAMers continue to carry forward their own dreams and those of their families as epistemological resources. They embody the dreams they hold as they move through each day into the next, not knowing what the outcome will be; the political actions of DREAMers, and those who support them, model the expansiveness of a vision that refuses to be quelled, cast aside, or dissolved. While this context is quite distinct from the literal dreaming I analyze in Urrea's novels, both cases share the common premise that to recognize our dreams as sacred and embodied knowledge is to recognize our own connections to a larger story, as well as our role within it.

Throughout this book, I have considered the implications of a spirituality that not only connects us to others across space and time but also incites radical transformation in the ways we perceive and act in the world. When we place the reader's locus of perception in the body as it relates to mind and spirit (mindbodyspirit), we engage in decolonial work to disrupt the assumptions and logics of Western epistemologies that split and fragment us from ourselves, others, and the world at large. This is the political work (both epistemological and ontological) that must undergird our actions in our daily lives as we rethink our relationships and what it truly means to be in relation. As I have suggested, narrative and readerly practice can be an important starting place of reflection that changes the way we perceive and experience the world.

When I reflect on my own position as a reader, the works I have examined in this book shape my consciousness in that they acknowledge values of compassion, empathy, and a deep interconnectivity across time and space—concepts too rarely mediated in the messages and images of contemporary discourse. Most significantly, the intersubjectivity at hand in Chicanx narrative helps me become more attuned to my own mindbodyspirit and perceive my connection to a living ancestral knowledge that moves both within my body and beyond it. This perception dissolves the isolation that wounds, and brings life to the awareness that I am connected not only to those who live now, but also those who lived before and those who follow after. These stories remind me that the wisdom of my maternal grandmother, now passed, remains present in more than just abstracted memory; I learn to validate the felt sensation of her presence when she visits me in dreams that are more than dreams, and to carry it with me into waking consciousness. I learn to honor such encounters as a gift, not only because they bring us into spiritual communication but because they facilitate precious knowledge: that mine is a living body, which, like hers, will age and change and pass into another form of existence, but also that through the force of an attuned attention to the continuity of spirit, the chasms of death can be bridged in some sense. Such visceral forms of encounter are narrated over and over again in the works at the center of this book, and indeed it is my contention that narrative is a powerful way to deliver and receive this knowledge, so that we may learn to remember what we already know. For as these authors contemplate the relationship between the temporalities of embodied existence and an ongoing spirit, they bring to the fore a healing knowledge that we are part of the sacred. For my part, as mother to a child who grows and evolves more each day, I seek ways to reconcile the rupture and dissolution caused by life's impermanence. Narratives like these give me strength and information that I yearn to pass on. A believer in the power of story, I hope this knowledge takes root in my son as we share stories through the years; and as he becomes older and wiser, I hope that he will find and create his own stories, ones that will give him strength, and that he will pass on.

WORKS CITED

"About Patrisia Gonzales." *Mexican American Studies, College of Social & Behavioral Sciences.* University of Arizona, https://mas.arizona.edu/user/patrisia-gonzales. Accessed 18 November 2017.

Acosta, Grisel Y. "Environmentalism." *The Routledge Companion to Latino/a Literature,* edited by Suzanne Bost and Frances R. Aparicio, Routledge, 2015, pp. 195–203.

Ada, Alma Flor. "Foreword: Literature in the Lives of Latino Children." *Multicultural Literature for Latino Bilingual Children: Their Words, Their Worlds,* edited by Ellen Riojas Clark, Belinda Bustos Flores, Howard L. Smith, and Daniel Alejandro González, Rowman & Littlefield, 2016, pp. ix–xviii.

———. *A Magical Encounter: Latino Children's Literature in the Classroom.* 2nd ed., Pearson Education, Inc., 2003.

Ahmed, Sara. *The Cultural Politics of Emotion.* Routledge, 2012.

Alamillo, Laura A., and Rosie Arenas. "Chicano Children's Literature: Using Bilingual Children's Books to Promote Equity in the Classroom." *Multicultural Education,* vol. 19, no. 4, Summer 2012, pp. 53–62.

Alberto, Lourdes. "Nations, Nationalisms, and Indígenas: The 'Indian' in the Chicano Revolutionary Imaginary." *Critical Ethnic Studies,* vol. 2, no. 1, Spring 2016, pp. 107–27.

Alexander, M. Jacqui. *Pedagogies of Crossing: Meditations on Feminism, Sexual Politics, Memory, and the Sacred.* Duke University Press, 2005.

Anaya, Rudolfo. *The Old Man's Love Story.* University of Oklahoma Press, 2013.

———. "Shaman of Words." *The Essays,* University of Oklahoma Press, 2009, pp. 52–63.

Anzaldúa, Gloria. "Bearing Witness: Their Eyes Anticipate the Healing." *Ofrenda: Liliana Wilson's Art of Dissidence and Dreams,* edited by Norma E. Cantú, Texas A&M Press, 2015, pp. 31–33.

———. *Borderlands / La Frontera: The New Mestiza.* 3rd ed., Aunt Lute Books, 2007.

———. "Creativity and Switching Modes of Consciousness." *The Gloria Anzaldúa Reader*, edited by AnaLouise Keating, Duke University Press, 2009, pp. 103–10.

———. "Feminist Knowledge Through Spiritual and Culture." WWU Women's Studies, 29 January 1996. Presentation. Gloria Evangelina Anzaldúa Papers, box 162, tape 2, Benson Latin American Collection, University of Texas Libraries, University of Texas at Austin.

———. "Flights of the Imagination: Rereading/Rewriting Realities." *Light in the Dark / Luz en lo oscuro: Rewriting Identity, Spirituality, Reality*, edited by AnaLouise Keating, Duke University Press, 2015, pp. 23–46.

———. "Geographies of Selves—Reimagining Identity: Nos/Otras (Us/Other), las Nepantleras, and the New Tribalism." *Light in the Dark / Luz en lo oscuro: Rewriting Identity, Spirituality, Reality*, edited by AnaLouise Keating, Duke University Press, 2015, pp. 65–94.

———. "Gestures of the Body—Escribiendo para idear." *Light in the Dark / Luz en lo oscuro: Rewriting Identity, Spirituality, Reality*, edited by AnaLouise Keating, Duke University Press, 2015, pp. 1–8.

———. "Let us be the healing of the wound: The Coyolxauhqui imperative—la sombra y el sueño." *Light in the Dark / Luz en lo oscuro: Rewriting Identity, Spirituality, Reality*, edited by AnaLouise Keating, Duke University Press, 2015, pp. 9–22.

———. "Llorona Coyolxauhqui." *The Gloria Anzaldúa Reader*, edited by AnaLouise Keating, Duke University Press, 2009, pp. 295–97.

———. "Now Let Us Shift . . . Conocimiento . . . Inner Work, Public Acts." *Light in the Dark / Luz en lo oscuro*, edited by AnaLouise Keating, Duke University Press, 2015, pp. 117–59.

———. "Woman Falling 28 enero 89." Gloria Evangelina Anzaldúa Papers, box 149, file 3, Benson Latin American Collection, University of Texas Libraries, University of Texas at Austin.

Avila, Elena, with Joy Parker. *Woman Who Glows in the Dark: A Curandera Reveals Traditional Aztec Secrets of Physical and Spiritual Health*. Jeremy P. Tarcher / Putnam, 1999.

Avilés, Elena. "Reading Latinx and LGBTQ+ Perspectives: Maya Christina Gonzalez and Equity Minded Models at Play." *Bilingual Review / Revista Bilingüe*, vol. 33, no. 4, 2017, pp. 34–44.

Barbas-Rhoden, Laura. "Toward an Eco-Cosmopolitanism: Bilingual Children's Literature in the United States." *Interdisciplinary Studies in Literature and Environment*, vol. 18, no. 2, Spring 2011, pp. 359–76.

Barceló, Margarita T. "Tapestries of Space-Time: Urban and Institutional Spaces in Helena María Viramontes's Short Fiction." *Rebozos de Palabras: An Helena María Viramontes Critical Reader*, edited by Gabriella Gutiérrez y Muhs, University of Arizona Press, 2013, pp. 122–44.

Barnes, Linda L., and Inés Talamantez, editors. *Teaching Religion and Healing*. Oxford University Press, 2006.

Bennett, Jane. *The Enchantment of Modern Life: Attachments, Crossings, and Ethics.* Princeton University Press, 2001.

Bogzaran, Fariba, and Daniel Deslauriers. *Integral Dreaming: A Holistic Approach to Dreams.* State University of New York Press, 2012.

Bost, Suzanne. *Encarnación: Illness and Body Politics in Chicana Feminist Literature.* Fordham University Press, 2010.

Brady, Mary Pat. "Children's Literature." *The Routledge Companion to Latino/a Literature,* edited by Suzanne Bost and Frances R. Aparicio, Routledge, 2013, pp. 375–82.

Broyles-González, Yolanda. "Indianizing Catholicism: Chicana/India/Mexicana Indigenous Spiritual Practices in Our Image." *Chicana Traditions: Continuity and Change,* edited by Norma E. Cantú and Olga Nájera-Ramírez, University of Illinois Press, 2002, pp. 117–32.

Carrasco, Davíd. *Religions of Mesoamerica: Cosmovision and Ceremonial Centers.* Harper & Row, 1990.

Castillo, Ana. *Massacre of the Dreamers: Essays on Xicanisma.* 20th anniversary updated ed., University of New Mexico Press, 2014.

Cisneros, Sandra. *Have You Seen Marie?* Illustrated by Ester Hernández, Alfred A. Knopf, 2012.

———. *A House of My Own: Stories from My Life.* Alfred A. Knopf, 2015.

Contreras, Sheila Marie. *Blood Lines: Myth, Indigenism and Chicana/o Literature.* University of Texas Press, 2008.

Copeland, M. Shawn. *Enfleshing Freedom: Body, Race, and Being.* Fortress Press, 2010.

Cordova, Cary. "Portable Murals: Children's Book Press and the Circulation of Latino Art." *Visual Resources,* vol. 33, no. 3/4, 2017, pp. 332–62.

Cotera, María Eugenia, and María Josefina Saldaña-Portillo. "Indigenous but Not Indian? Chicana/os and the Politics of Indigeneity." *The Worlds of Indigenous North America,* edited by Robert Warrior, Routledge, 2015, pp. 549–68.

Crawford, Suzanne J. "Religion, Healing, and the Body." *Teaching Religion and Healing,* edited by Linda L. Barnes and Inés M. Talamantez, Oxford University Press, 2006, pp. 29–45.

Cruz, Cindy. "Toward an Epistemology of a Brown Body." *Chicana/Latina Education in Everyday Life: Feminista Perspectives on Pedagogy and Epistemology,* edited by Dolores Delgado Bernal, C. Alejandra Elenes, Francisca E. Godinez, and Sofia Villenas, State University of New York Press, 2006, pp. 59–75.

Cuevas, T. Jackie. "'Power to the Panza': Stomaching Oppression in Virginia Grise and Irma Mayorga's *The Panza Monologues.*" *Praxis: Gender and Cultural Critiques,* vol. 23, no. 1, Spring 2011, pp. 1–10.

Delgadillo, Theresa. "Spirituality." *The Routledge Companion to Latino/a Literature,* edited by Suzanne Bost and Frances R. Aparicio, Routledge, 2015, pp. 240–50.

———. *Spiritual Mestizaje: Religion, Gender, Race and Nation in Contemporary Chicana Narrative.* Duke University Press, 2011.

Delgado Bernal, Dolores. "Learning and Living Pedagogies of the Home: The Mestiza Consciousness of Chicana Students." *Chicana/Latina Education in Everyday Life:*

Feminista Perspectives on Pedagogy and Epistemology, edited by Dolores Delgado Bernal, C. Alejandra Elenes, Francisca E. Godinez, and Sofia Villenas, State University of New York Press, 2006, pp. 113–32.

Duran, Eduardo. *Healing the Soul Wound: Counseling with American Indians and Other Native Peoples.* Teachers College Press, 2006.

Eaton, Heather, and Lois Ann Lorentzen. "Introduction." *Ecofeminism & Globalization: Exploring Culture, Context, and Religion*, edited by Heather Eaton and Lois Ann Lorentzen, Rowman & Littlefield Publishers, 2003, pp. 1–7.

Espinosa, Gastón, and Mario T. García. "Introduction." *Mexican American Religions: Spirituality, Activism, and Culture*, edited by Gastón Espinosa and Mario T. García, Duke University Press, 2008.

Estés, Clarissa Pinkola. "Foreword." *Massacre of the Dreamers: Essays on Xicanisma*, by Ana Castillo, 20th anniversary updated ed., University of New Mexico Press, 2014, pp. xi–xviii.

———. "Introduction." *Woman Who Glows in the Dark: A Curandera Reveals Traditional Aztec Secrets of Physical and Spiritual Health*, by Elena Avila with Joy Parker, Jeremy P. Tarcher / Putnam, 1999, pp. 1–14.

———. *Untie the Strong Woman: Blessed Mother's Immaculate Love for the Wild Soul.* Sounds True, 2011.

———. *Women Who Run with the Wolves: Myths and Stories of the Wild Woman Archetype.* Ballantine Books, 1992.

Evers, Larry, and Felipe S. Molina. *Yaqui Deer Songs / Maso Bwikam: A Native American Poetry.* Sun Tracks / University of Arizona Press, 1987.

Facio, Elisa. "Spirit Journey: 'Home' as a Site for Healing and Transformation." *Fleshing the Spirit: Spirituality and Activism in Chicana, Latina, and Indigenous Women's Lives*, edited by Elisa Facio and Irene Lara, University of Arizona Press, 2014, pp. 59–72.

Facio, Elisa, and Irene Lara, editors. *Fleshing the Spirit: Spirituality and Activism in Chicana, Latina, and Indigenous Women's Lives.* University of Arizona Press, 2014.

Fernandes, Leela. *Transforming Feminist Practice: Non-Violence, Social Justice and the Possibilities of a Spiritualized Feminism.* Aunt Lute Books, 2003.

Folsom, Raphael Brewster. *The Yaquis and the Empire: Violence, Spanish Imperial Power, and Native Resilience in Colonial Mexico.* Yale University Press, 2014.

Franco, Jean. "Foreword." *In Other Words: Literature by Latinas of the United States*, edited by Roberta Fernández, Arte Público Press, 1994, pp. xiv–xx.

Freud, Sigmund. "Mourning and Melancholia." 1917. *The Standard Edition of the Complete Psychological Works of Sigmund Freud*, translated and edited by James Strachey, vol. 14, Hogarth Press and the Institute of Psycho-Analysis, 1957, pp. 243–58.

Furumoto, Rosa. "Chapter Four: Future Teachers and Families Explore Humanization Through Chicana/o/Latina/o Children's Literature." *Counterpoints*, vol. 321, 2008, pp. 79–95.

Garcia Lopez, Christina. "'This Land is Holy!': Intersections of Politics and Spirituality in Luis Alberto Urrea's *The Hummingbird's Daughter*." *Journal of Transnational American Studies*, vol. 7, no. 1, 2016.

Gauthier, Tim. *9/11 Fiction, Empathy, and Otherness*. Lexington Books, 2015.

Gonzales, Patrisia. *Red Medicine: Traditional Indigenous Rites of Birthing and Healing*. University of Arizona Press, 2012.

Gonzalez, Maya Christina. "Bio." *Maya Gonzalez: Fine Artist*, www.mayagonzalez.com /artist/bio. Accessed 2 August 2017.

———. *Call Me Tree / Llámame árbol*. Translated by Dana Goldberg, Children's Book Press, 2014.

———. "Call Me Tree Gender Free: A Note to My Readers." *Maya Gonzalez Blog*, 24 October 2014, http://www.mayagonzalez.com/blog/2014/10/gender-free-multi cultural-childrens-book/. Accessed 18 November 2017.

———. *I Know the River Loves Me / Yo sé que el río me ama*. Children's Book Press, 2009.

———. "The Rainbow Alphabet and the Girl in the Library: Finding Voice in a World of Silence." *Maya Gonzalez Blog*, 14 November 2016, http://www.mayagonzalez.com /blog/2016/11/rainbow-alphabet-girl-library/. Accessed 12 November 2017.

Grise, Virginia, and Irma Mayorga. *The Panza Monologues*. 2nd ed., foreword by Tiffany Ana López, University of Texas Press, 2014.

———. *The Panza Monologues*. DVD, Plaza de la Raza's Margo Albert Theatre, 2009.

Grosz, Elizabeth. *Volatile Bodies: Toward a Corporeal Feminism*. Indiana University Press, 1994.

Guilfoyle, Brooke Manross. "Colorblind Ideology Expressed Through Children's Picture Books: A Social Justice Issue." *Jesuit Higher Education: A Journal*, vol. 4, no. 2, 2015, pp. 37–56.

Gutiérrez, Ramón. *When Jesus Came, the Corn Mothers Went Away: Marriage, Sexuality, and Power in New Mexico, 1500–1846*. Stanford University Press, 1991.

Gutiérrez y Muhs, Gabriella. "Introduction." *Rebozos de Palabras: An Helena María Vira- montes Critical Reader*, edited by Gabriella Gutiérrez y Muhs, University of Arizona Press, 2013, pp. 1–23.

———, editor. *Rebozos de Palabras: An Helena María Viramontes Critical Reader*. Univer- sity of Arizona Press, 2013.

Harjo, Joy, and Tanaya Winder. "Becoming the Thing Itself." *Soul Talk, Song Language: Conversations with Joy Harjo*, Wesleyan University Press, 2011, pp. 3–26.

Hartley, George. "Curandera of Conquest." *Aztlán: A Journal of Chicano Studies*, vol. 35, no. 1, Spring 2010, pp. 135–61.

———. "Indigeneity." *The Routledge Companion to Latino/a Literature*, edited by Suzanne Bost and Frances R. Aparicio, Routledge, 2015, pp. 182–93.

Hernández-Ávila, Inés. "In the Presence of Spirit(s): A Meditation on the Politics of Solidarity and Transformation." *This Bridge We Call Home: Radical Visions for Trans- formation*, edited by Gloria E. Anzaldúa and AnaLouise Keating, Routledge, 2002.

Herrera-Sobek, María. "The Nature of Chicana Literature: Feminist Ecological Literary Criticism and Chicana Writers." *Revista Canaria de Estudios Ingleses*, no. 37, 1998, pp. 89–100.

Hillman, David, and Ulrika Maude, editors. *The Cambridge Companion to the Body in Literature*. Cambridge University Press, 2015.

Hogan, Linda. *Dwellings: A Spiritual History of the Living World*. W. W. Norton & Company, 1995.

———. *The Woman Who Watches Over the World: A Native Memoir*. W. W. Norton & Company, 2001.

Holden, William Curry. *Teresita*. Stemmer House Publishers, 1978.

Holland, Sharon Patricia. *Raising the Dead: Readings of Death and (Black) Subjectivity*. Duke University Press, 2000.

Holmes, Christina. *Ecological Borderlands: Body, Nature, and Spirit in Chicana Feminism*. University of Illinois Press, 2016.

Isasi-Díaz, Ada María, and Yolanda Tarango. *Hispanic Women, Prophetic Voice in the Church: Toward a Hispanic Women's Liberation Theology*. Harper & Row, 1988.

Jiménez García, Marilisa. "The Pura Belpré Medal: The Latino/a Child in America, the 'Need' for Diversity, and Name-Branding Latinidad." *Prizing Children's Literature: The Cultural Politics of Children's Book Awards*, edited by Kenneth B. Kidd and Joseph T. Thomas, Jr., Routledge, 2017, pp. 104–17.

Johnson, Mark. *The Meaning of the Body: Aesthetics of Human Understanding*. University of Chicago Press, 2007.

Keating, AnaLouise. "Appendix 5: Historical Notes on the Chapters' Development." *Light in the Dark / Luz en lo oscuro: Rewriting Identity, Spirituality, Reality*, by Gloria Anzaldúa, edited by AnaLouise Keating, Duke University Press, 2015, pp. 190–99.

———. "Editor's Introduction: Re-envisioning Coyolxauhqui, Decolonizing Reality: Anzaldúa's Twenty-First-Century Imperative." *Light in the Dark / Luz en lo oscuro: Rewriting Identity, Spirituality, Reality*, by Gloria Anzaldúa, edited by AnaLouise Keating, Duke University Press, 2015, pp. ix–xxxvii.

———. "Gallery of Images." *The Gloria Anzaldúa Reader*, by Gloria Anzaldúa, edited by AnaLouise Keating, Duke University Press, 2009, p. 217.

———. "Glossary." *The Gloria Anzaldúa Reader*, by Gloria Anzaldúa, edited by AnaLouise Keating, Duke University Press, 2009, pp. 319–23.

Kevane, Bridget. *Profane & Sacred: Latino/a American Writers Reveal the Interplay of the Secular and the Religious*. Rowman & Littlefield Publishers, 2008.

Kimmerer, Robin Wall. *Braiding Sweetgrass: Indigenous Wisdom, Scientific Knowledge, and the Teachings of Plants*. Milkweed Editions, 2013.

Kirk, Gwyn. "Ecofeminism and Chicano Environmental Struggles: Bridges Across Gender and Race." *Chicano Culture, Ecology, Politics: Subversive Kin*, edited by D. G. Peña, University of Arizona Press, 1998, pp. 177–200.

Krasner, James. "Doubtful Arms and Phantom Limbs: Literary Portrayals of Embodied Grief." *PMLA: Journal of the Modern Language Association of America*, vol. 119, no. 2, 2004, pp. 218–32.

Lara, Irene. "Bruja Positionalities: Toward a Chicana/Latina Spiritual Activism." *Chicana/Latina Studies*, vol. 4, no. 2, Spring 2005, pp. 10–45.

———. "Healing Sueños for Academia." *This Bridge We Call Home: Radical Visions for Transformation*, edited by Gloria E. Anzaldúa and AnaLouise Keating, Routledge, 2002, pp. 433–38.

Lara, Irene, and Elisa Facio. "Introduction: Fleshing the Spirit, Spiriting the Flesh." *Fleshing the Spirit: Spirituality and Activism in Chicana, Latina, and Indigenous Women's Lives*, edited by Elisa Facio and Irene Lara, University of Arizona Press, 2014.

León, Luis D. "Borderlands Bodies and Souls: Mexican Religious Healing Practices in East Los Angeles." *Mexican American Religions: Spirituality, Activism, and Culture*, edited by Gastón Espinosa and Mario T. García, Duke University Press, 2008, pp. 296–322.

———. *La Llorona's Children: Religion, Life, and Death in the U.S.-Mexican Borderlands.* University of California Press, 2004.

Levine, Marc N. "Reflections on Obsidian Studies in Mesoamerica: Past, Present, and Future." *Obsidian Reflections: Symbolic Dimensions of Obsidian in Mesoamerica*, edited by Marc N. Levine and David M. Carballo, University Press of Colorado, 2014, pp. 3–42.

López, Tiffany Ana. "Forward." *The Panza Monologues*, by Virginia Grise and Irma Mayorga, 2nd ed., University of Texas Press, 2014.

Luciano, Dana. *Arranging Grief: Sacred Time and the Body in Nineteenth-Century America.* New York University Press, 2007.

Mah y Busch, Juan D. "Lovingly: Ethics in Viramontes's Stories." *Rebozos de Palabras: An Helena María Viramontes Critical Reader*, edited by Gabriella Gutiérrez y Muhs, University of Arizona Press, 2013, pp. 147–66.

Martín, Desirée A. *Borderlands Saints: Secular Sanctity in Chicano/a and Mexican Culture.* Rutgers University Press, 2014.

Martínez, Demetria. *Confessions of a Berlitz-Tape Chicana.* University of Oklahoma Press, 2005.

McClure, Barbara J. "Divining the Sacred in the Modern World: Ritual and the Relational Embodiment of Spirit." *Pastoral Psychology*, vol. 62, 2013, pp. 727–42.

McGuire, Meredith. *Lived Religion: Faith and Practice in Everyday Life.* Oxford University Press, 2008.

———. "Religion and the Body: Rematerializing the Human Body in the Social Sciences of Religion." *Journal for the Scientific Study of Religion*, vol. 29, no. 3, 1990, pp. 283–96.

———. "Why Bodies Matter: A Sociological Reflection on Spirituality and Materiality." *Spiritus: A Journal of Christian Spirituality*, vol. 3, no. 1, 2003, pp. 1–18.

Medina, Lara. *Las Hermanas: Chicana/Latina Religious-Political Activism in the U.S. Catholic Church.* Temple University Press, 2004.

———. "Nepantla Spirituality: My Path to the Source(s) of Healing." *Fleshing the Spirit: Spirituality and Activism in Chicana, Latina, and Indigenous Women's Lives*, edited by Elisa Facio and Irene Lara, University of Arizona Press, 2014, pp. 167–85.

Mellor, Mary. "Gender and the Environment." *Ecofeminism & Globalization: Exploring Culture, Context, and Religion*, edited by Heather Eaton and Lois Ann Lorentzen, Rowman & Littlefield Publishers, 2003, pp. 11–22.

Mignolo, Walter. *The Darker Side of Western Modernity: Global Futures, Decolonial Options.* Duke University Press, 2011.

Mora, Pat. "Poet as Curandera." *Nepantla: Essays from the Land in the Middle*, University of New Mexico Press, 1993, pp. 124–31.

Moraga, Cherríe. "Epílogo: Xicana Mind, Beginner Mind." *A Xicana Codex of Changing Consciousness: Writings, 2000–2010.* Duke University Press, 2011, pp. 193–99.

———. "An Irrevocable Promise: Staging the Story Xicana." *A Xicana Codex of Changing Consciousness: Writings, 2000–2010.* Duke University Press, 2011, pp. 34–46.

Morales, Aurora Levins. *Medicine Stories: History, Culture and the Politics of Integrity.* South End Press, 1998.

Nichols, James Michael. "'Call Me Tree': A Children's Book with No Gender Specific Pronouns." *The Huffington Post,* 4 April 2015, https://www.huffingtonpost.com/2015/04/04/call-me-tree_n_6994138.html. Accessed 18 November 2017.

Otero, Solimar, and Toyin Falola. "Introduction: Introducing Yemoja." *Yemoja: Gender, Sexuality, and Creativity in the Latina/o and Afro-Atlantic Diasporas,* edited by Solimar Otero and Toyin Falola, State University of New York Press, 2013, pp. xvii–xxxii.

Pérez, Laura E. *Chicana Art: The Politics of Spiritual and Aesthetic Altarities.* Duke University Press, 2007.

———. "Spirit Glyphs: Reimagining Art and Artist in the Work of Chicana Tlamatinime." *MFS: Modern Fiction Studies,* vol. 44, no. 1, March 1998, pp. 36–76.

———. "Writing with Crooked Lines." *Fleshing the Spirit: Spirituality and Activism in Chicana, Latina, and Indigenous Women's Lives,* edited by Elisa Facio and Irene Lara, University of Arizona Press, 2014, pp. 23–33.

Pilar Aquino, María, Daisy L. Machado, and Jeanette Rodríguez, editors. *A Reader in Latina Feminist Theology: Religion and Justice.* University of Texas Press, 2002.

Prieto, Elvira. *An (Im)possible Life: Poesía y Testimonio in the Borderlands.* CreateSpace Independent Publishing Platform, 2015.

Rebolledo, Tey Diana. "Prietita y el Otro Lado: Gloria Anzaldúa's Literature for Children." *The History of the Book and the Idea of Literature,* special issue of *PMLA: Journal of the Modern Language Association of America,* vol. 121, no. 1, January 2006, pp. 279–84.

———. *Women Singing in the Snow: A Cultural Analysis of Chicana Literature.* University of Arizona Press, 1995.

Robinson, Amy. "From Private Healer to Public Threat: Teresa Urrea's Writings in *The Hummingbird's Daughter* and *Queen of America.*" *A Contracorriente: A Journal of Social History and Literature in Latin America,* vol. 13, no. 2, Winter 2016, pp. 240–63.

Rodríguez, Jeanette. *Our Lady of Guadalupe: Faith and Empowerment among Mexican-American Women.* University of Texas Press, 1994.

Román-Odio, Clara. *Sacred Iconographies in Chicana Cultural Production.* Palgrave, 2013.

Romo, David Dorado. *Ringside Seat to a Revolution: An Underground Cultural History of El Paso and Juárez: 1893–1923.* Cinco Puntos Press, 2005.

Rosaldo, Renato. *The Day of Shelly's Death: The Poetry and Ethnography of Grief.* Duke University Press, 2014.

Saldaña-Portillo, María Josefina. *Indian Given: Racial Geographies Across Mexico and the United States.* Duke University Press, 2016.

Saldívar-Hull, Sonia. *Feminism on the Border: Chicana Gender Politics and Literature.* University of California Press, 2000.

Santos, Boaventura de Sousa. "Public Sphere and Epistemologies of the South." *Africa Development*, vol. 37, no. 1, 2012, pp. 43–67.

Sellers, Allison P. "An Introduction to the Divine Mother and Water Goddess." *Yemoja: Gender, Sexuality, and Creativity in the Latina/o and Afro-Atlantic Diasporas*, edited by Solimar Otero and Toyin Falola, State University of New York Press, 2013, pp. 131–49.

Smith, Linda Tuhiwai. *Decolonizing Methodologies: Research and Indigenous Peoples*. 2nd ed., Zed Books, 2012.

Somé, Malidoma Patrice. *Ritual: Power, Healing and Community*. Swan / Raven & Company, 1993.

Stockton, Sharon. "Rereading the Maternal Body: Viramontes' *The Moths* and the Construction of the New Chicana." *Americas Review*, vol. 22, no. 1/2, 1994, pp. 212–29.

Stubblefield, Thomas. *9/11 and the Visual Culture of Disaster*. Indiana University Press, 2015.

Tai, Brena Yu-Chen. "The Permeable Body Paradigm: Exploring the Symbiotic Body in Gloria Anzaldúa's Work." El Mundo Zurdo Conference, May 2015, University of Texas, Austin, Tex. Conference Presentation.

Talukdar, Jaita. "Rituals and Embodiment: Class Differences in Religious Fasting Practices of Bengali Hindu Women." *Sociological Focus*, vol. 47, no. 3, 2014, pp. 141–62.

Tanner, Laura E. "Holding On to 9/11: The Shifting Grounds of Materiality." *PMLA: Journal of the Modern Language Association of America*, vol. 127, no. 1, January 2012, pp. 58–76.

———. *Lost Bodies: Inhabiting the Borders of Life and Death*. Cornell University Press, 2006.

Terrero, Nina. "Chicana Author Sandra Cisneros Reveals Pain and Suffering Were Inspiration for Latest Book." *NBC Latino*, 1 Oct 2012, http://nbclatino.com/2012/10/01/chicana-author-sandra-cisneros-reveals-pain-and-suffering-was-the-inspiration-for-her-latest-book/. Accessed 3 March 2017.

Torres, Eliseo "Cheo." *Healing with Herbs and Rituals: A Mexican Tradition*. Edited by Timothy L. Sawyer, Jr., University of New Mexico Press, 2006.

Torres, Eliseo "Cheo," with Timothy L. Sawyer, Jr. *Curandero: A Life in Mexican Folk Healing*. University of New Mexico Press, 2005.

Turner, Kay. *Beautiful Necessity: The Art and Meaning of Women's Altars*. Thames & Hudson, 1999.

Urrea, Luis Alberto. *The Hummingbird's Daughter*. Little, Brown and Company, 2005.

———. *Queen of America*. Little, Brown and Company, 2011.

van der Kolk, Bessel. *The Body Keeps the Score: Brain, Mind, and Body in the Healing of Trauma*. Penguin Books, 2014.

Vanderwood, Paul J. *The Power of God Against the Guns of Government: Religious Upheaval in Mexico at the Turn of the Nineteenth Century*. Stanford University Press, 1998.

Viramontes, Helena María. "Faith in the Imagination: An Interview with Helena María Viramontes." Interview with José Antonio Rodríguez. *Rebozos de Palabras: An Helena María Viramontes Critical Reader*, edited by Gabriella Gutiérrez y Muhs, University of Arizona Press, 2013, pp. 251–63.

———. *The Moths and Other Stories*. Arte Público Press, 1995.

Williams, Patricia J. "On Being the Object of Property." *Signs*, vol. 14, no. 1, 1988, pp. 5–24.

Windt, Jennifer M. *Dreaming: A Conceptual Framework for Philosophy of Mind and Empirical Research*. MIT Press, 2015.

Wohlleben, Peter. *The Hidden Life of Trees: What They Feel, How They Communicate; Discoveries from a Secret World*. Translated by Jane Billinghurst, foreword by Tim Flannery, Greystone Books, 2016.

Woodward, Kathleen. *Aging and Its Discontents: Freud and Other Fictions*. Indiana University Press, 1991.

Ybarra, Priscilla Solis. *Writing the Goodlife: Mexican American Literature and the Environment*. University of Arizona Press, 2016.

INDEX

Note: Page numbers in *italic* type refer to illustrative matter.